Americanization in the States

Working in the Americas

UNIVERSITY PRESS OF FLORIDA
Florida A&M University, Tallahassee
Florida Atlantic University, Boca Raton
Florida Gulf Coast University, Ft. Myers
Florida International University, Miami
Florida State University, Tallahassee
New College of Florida, Sarasota
University of Central Florida, Orlando
University of Florida, Gainesville
University of North Florida, Jacksonville
University of South Florida, Tampa
University of West Florida, Pensacola

Working in the Americas is devoted to publishing important works in labor history and working-class studies in the Americas. This series seeks work that uses traditional as well as innovative, interdisciplinary, or transnational approaches. Its focus is the Americas and the lives of its workers.

Florida's Working-Class Past: Current Perspectives on Labor, Race, and Gender from Spanish Florida to the New Immigration, edited by Robert Cassanello and Melanie Shell-Weiss (2008)

The New Economy and the Modern South, by Michael Dennis (2008)

Film Noir, American Workers, and Postwar Hollywood, by Dennis Broe (2009)

Americanization in the States: Immigrant Social Welfare Policy, Citizenship, and National Identity in the United States, 1908–1929, by Christina A. Ziegler-McPherson (2009)

Black Labor Migration in Caribbean Guatemala, 1882-1923, by Frederick Douglass Opie (2009)

Migration and the Transformation of the Modern South since 1945, by Robert Cassanello and Colin J. Davis (2010)

AMERICANIZATION IN THE STATES
IMMIGRANT SOCIAL WELFARE POLICY, CITIZENSHIP, & NATIONAL IDENTITY IN THE UNITED STATES, 1908–1929

Christina A. Ziegler-McPherson

Foreword by Richard Greenwald & Timothy J. Minchin, *Series Editors*

University Press of Florida

Gainesville · Tallahassee · Tampa · Boca Raton · Pensacola · Orlando · Miami · Jacksonville · Ft. Myers · Sarasota

Copyright 2009 by Christina A. Ziegler-McPherson
Printed in the United States of America
All rights reserved
First cloth printing, 2009
First paperback printing, 2010

Library of Congress Cataloging-in-Publication Data
Ziegler-McPherson, Christina A.
Americanization in the states: immigrant social welfare policy, citizenship, and national identity in the United States, 1908–1929 / Christina A. Ziegler-McPherson; foreword by Richard Greenwald and Timothy Minchin, series editors.
p. cm.—(Working in the Americas)
Includes bibliographical references and index.
ISBN 978-0-8130-3361-7 (alk. paper)
ISBN 978-0-8130-3550-5 (pbk.)
1. United States—Emigration and immigration—Government policy. 2. United States—Emigration and immigration—History—20th century. 3. Immigrants—United States—States—Social conditions. 4. Citizenship—United States. 5. National characteristics, American. 6. United States—History—20th century. I. Title.
JV6483.Z54 2009
325.7309'0419-dc22   2009004172

The University Press of Florida is the scholarly publishing agency for the State University System of Florida, comprising Florida A&M University, Florida Atlantic University, Florida Gulf Coast University, Florida International University, Florida State University, New College of Florida, University of Central Florida, University of Florida, University of North Florida, University of South Florida, and University of West Florida.

University Press of Florida
15 Northwest 15th Street
Gainesville, FL 32611–2079
http://www.upf.com

For my father and Scott

CONTENTS

Figures   ix

Foreword   xi

Preface   xiii

Introduction   1

1 **The Start of a Movement**:
  The New York Bureau of Industries and Immigration, 1908–1914   20

2 **The California Plan**:
  The Commission of Immigration and Housing, 1913–1917   39

3 **An Unhealthy Relationship**:
  Eugenics and Americanization in New York, 1914–1917   54

4 **Americanizing the Home**:
  Housing Reform and the California Home Teacher Act of 1915   66

5 **Wartime Americanization in the States**:
  New York, California, and Massachusetts, 1917–1918   84

6 **Cosmopolitanism Cut Short**:
  The Illinois Immigrants Commission, 1919–1921   105

7 **Schooling the Immigrant**:
  Americanization and Adult Education, 1919–1929   122

8 **Americanization versus Restriction**:
  Immigrant Social Welfare Policy in New York, California, and Massachusetts, 1919–1929   144

Conclusion   164

Notes   175

Bibliography   211

Index   229

FIGURES

Figures follow page 102.

Figure 1. Immigrants at the Battery: cart men, immigrant passengers and baggage, circa 1901

Figure 2. Tent or shelter, in the hop pickers' camp on the Durst ranch near Wheatland in the season of 1913

Figure 3. Immigrants outside Chicago's Immigrants' Protective League

Figure 4. Italian men in a classroom, 1914

FOREWORD

Christina A. Ziegler-McPherson's *Americanization in the States: Immigrant Social Welfare Policy, Citizenship, and National Identity in the United States, 1908–1929* offers us a fresh reappraisal of the relationship between national identity, immigration, and citizenship in the early twentieth century, which should have great influence on today's debates about immigrant policy. She moves us beyond immigrant communities and squarely into the realm of policy and the meaning of Americanism. Labor historians and working-class-studies scholars are reminded here that immigrant workers in the early twentieth century navigated complex political waters. Those progressive reformers might offer assistance, but that previous assistance often came with a steep price.

Current debates about immigration too often make reference to the successful history of previous immigrant groups. Here we have a detailed and important study of the early twentieth century immigration debate. By 1920 the federal and state governments were taking an aggressive and activist stance to "Americanize" and assimilate immigrants, believing passive wait-and-see attitudes were dangerous for America's future. These efforts and policies have had a lasting legacy on how we view American identity today and form the backdrop for present debates about the place of aliens in American culture. *Americanization in the States* explores its subject through a richly detailed set of case studies that allow us to understand the important local issues of a national debate. Through a careful examination of New York, California, Massachusetts, and Illinois, Ziegler-McPherson illuminates not just the debates surrounding policies but, more important, the social welfare policies that were implemented to "Americanize" the foreign-born population. Her book is good intellectual history as well as solid political history. Its guiding question is what motivated political activists who took the lead in these debates and how did they translate ideas into policies.

Ziegler-McPherson's greatest contribution is in the area of providing a deeper understanding of the policies and programs connected to the Americanization effort. By rooting her study in political and policy history, Ziegler-

McPherson connects these efforts to other efforts underway in the Progressive Era, as well as the growing and important literature on state-building.

Labor historians should pay particular attention to this book because at its center is an understanding that Americanization is all about class relationships: Immigrants are mostly workers after all. What did it mean that social welfare policies were aimed at immigrants as immigrants and not as immigrant workers? How did this affect their view of themselves and that of others as workers? Smartly, Ziegler-McPherson also roots her book in the ongoing debate about racial identity and whiteness, through the lens of Americanization and citizenship. By connecting identity to policy, and looking at policy differences from location to location, we are able to see just how complex an issue identity is. In offering us four discrete case studies, we see differences, but also the similarities in ideology that united these four state efforts into a national movement that set a public agenda for years to come.

Americanization in the States is an example of the vibrant labor history that is being done in policy history. By reconnecting class and politics in as a serious way, through a study of immigration, Ziegler-McPherson has moved the field of labor history forward.

Richard Greenwald, Drew University
Timothy J. Minchin, LaTrobe University

PREFACE

Although my name alone is on the cover, I—like all writers—recognize that this book is not the work of one individual. I began this project in the spring of 2004 while my husband attended business school at the University of Virginia. It was at UVA's Miller Center for Public Affairs that I met former Miller Fellow Alethia Jones, now at the State University of New York–Albany, who provided me with valuable feedback on early drafts. My perspective on politics, public policy, social knowledge construction, and state building has been deepened by the time I spent at the Miller Center, and I thank directors Brian Balogh and Sidney Milkis for being so welcoming and generous with their time.

Even more important to me than the Miller Center are the history faculty and students at the University of California–Santa Barbara. Classes and conversations with W. Elliot Brownlee, Randolph E. Bergstrom, Laura Kalman, Mary O. Furner, and Alice O'Connor set me on my original course in studying Americanization as public policy, and to them I owe intellectual and personal debts that can never be repaid. I have also benefited greatly from conversations with classmates Beth Nelson, Benjamin C. Zulueta, and John Baranski over the past several years.

I must also acknowledge Dr. John C. Burnham of Ohio State University for the idea of using values as a tool of analysis for class relations. Discussions with Robert D. Johnston of the University of Illinois–Chicago also helped me sharpen my thinking about class relations. And I enjoyed a series of charming conversations with Dr. William J. Maxwell, distinguished service professor at New Jersey City University, about his research into the life of Frances A. Kellor.

Like all researchers, I could not have done this project without the help of many librarians and archivists. I especially appreciate the assistance of the staff at the Bancroft Library at the University of California–Berkeley; the University of Illinois–Chicago Daley Library Special Collections and Archives Department (especially librarian Patricia Bakunas); and the University of Chicago Regenstein Library Special Collections Research Center (particularly librarians Kathleen Feeney, Julia Gardner, and David Pavelich). Barbara Addison of the Peace Collection at Swarthmore College provided useful tips in researching the Emily Greene Balch papers, and staff at the Library of Congress and the New York Public Library taught me how to navigate the nation's largest library systems. Charles Greifenstein and Earle E. Spamer of the American Philosophical Society archives in Philadelphia helped me find valuable correspondence in the Charles B. Davenport Papers when I belatedly discovered a connection between New York's Americanization policy and eugenics.

I would also like to thank series coeditor Richard Greenwald, who taught me several useful tricks in doing research in New York City. I express gratitude to University Press of Florida director Meredith Morris-Babb and acquisitions editor Eli Bortz for teaching me the ins and outs of publishing. UPF staff members Jen Graham and Heather Romans Turci also provided valuable assistance.

Finally, this book would not have been possible without the moral and financial support of my husband, Scott M. McPherson, who endured, without complaint, five years of living on one paycheck, vacations planned around research trips, and quite a lot of complaining about progressivism, assimilation, and the challenges of writing. His patience, constructive criticism, great editing skills, and the admonition: "Just write, damn it!" confirmed once again that he is truly the only partner this historian needs.

Introduction

Along with territorial sovereignty and national security, citizenship is a fundamental concern of government, and the question of who belongs to a national community—and who does not—is closely intertwined with the issues of security and stability. Citizenship can be defined narrowly, in terms of which individuals belong to a particular nation-state and thus derive various benefits (e.g., the right to leave and enter unhindered) and owe certain obligations (e.g., voting, military service). Citizenship can also be defined broadly, as in the case of individuals whose loyalty to the nation is not questioned, who feel they belong to one national community and to no other, and who are recognized by other citizens as belonging to the nation.

While creating American citizens can be as simple as giving birth on U.S. soil, there is also a formal process, naturalization, by which non-citizen residents change their legal status to become U.S. citizens. The role the state plays in this process is passive; the U.S. Congress establishes the legal criteria for naturalization, and as of 2009, the Department of Homeland Security's Bureau of Citizenship and Immigration Services (BCIS) determines whether resident aliens met these criteria when they petition for citizenship on the basis of birth, parentage, or completion of the naturalization process. The federal government does not approach non-citizens to recruit them to become citizens, nor does it require that all U.S. residents be American citizens. The burden is upon the alien to begin the naturalization process by approaching the federal government and declaring his or her desire to become a citizen.

But what happens when the state ceases to be passive in the citizenship process, and instead actively lobbies aliens to naturalize, and then works to mold them to meet its definition of citizen? This is what happened in the first two decades of the twentieth century, when the federal and state governments debated broad conceptions of American citizenship and sought to more clearly shape American national identity by aggressively lobbying aliens to naturalize and assimilate into a culture pre-defined by the country's British heritage. The ideas and policies generated during this Americanization movement of the 1910s and 1920s had a lasting impact on American social welfare policy and perceptions of American national identity and citizenship.

It is necessary here to distinguish between Americanization and assimilation. Assimilation is the process by which a society becomes more homogeneous through such means as socioeconomic interaction, intermarriage, and shared identity and values.[1] While the term "Americanization" is often used to describe both the United States' annexation of California and the Southwest from Mexico in 1848 and the assimilation of immigrants into American society, in this case, the term "Americanization" is used to identify a U.S. social and political movement that promoted American citizenship among immigrants in the early twentieth century.

As immigration to the United States has reached a level comparable to entrance figures achieved before 1920, scholars have, in turn, devoted their attention to the relationship between federal immigration policy and national identity.[2] Questions about the role of the state, interest groups, and racial prejudice in determining the character of American society by controlling who is allowed to enter the country are important. But this emphasis on immigration policy misses an equally important question: What about immigrants already living in the United States?

This book examines a group of Americans who attempted to answer that question one hundred years ago. It looks at how four states with large immigrant populations—New York, California, Massachusetts, and Illinois—purposefully sought to "Americanize" their foreign-born residents, the social welfare policies they developed between 1908 and 1929 to do so, and the theories of citizenship and national identity used to justify these policies. The connection of citizenship and assimilation to social welfare shaped the policies that these states developed and determined the survival of Americanization programs in the face of changing political contexts.

Yet when state governments established commissions, bureaus, and divisions dedicated to immigrant social welfare, cultural adjustment, and assimilation, what exactly did this mean? How did political activists' visions of "Americanism" translate into public policy? How did these agents of state power define the problem of Americanization and attempt to implement the monumental task of immigrant assimilation? Who was targeted by these new social welfare programs and who was left out, and why? Why was social welfare and protective legislation defined in terms of citizenship and national identity? These are the central questions of this study.

Just as the Americanization movement has only recently received recognition as an important component of American immigration history, so has the role of public policy within the Americanization movement been largely ignored.[3] Only a handful of historians have considered the policy aspects of Americanization, but they focus almost exclusively on the national campaign between 1915 and 1920, during the intense years of World War I, and the immediate aftermath of the Red Scare.[4] This literature rightly scrutinizes the xenophobic and oppressive elements in Americanization but misses the ideological and methodological complexity of the movement as well as the diversity of its participants.

Ethnic studies scholars, meanwhile, are interested in group formation, structure, and identity. Questions about the structure and nature of American society, the interrelationship of groups, and the degree to which American society is assimilationist or pluralistic dominate this literature.[5] The role of the state in these sociological processes is often minimized or is seen as strictly an instrument of oppression.[6] Yet a closer examination of the "disciplinary state" supposedly needed to enforce a coercive Americanization regime reveals poorly funded programs, inadequate enforcement of compulsory laws, and very low participation rates by immigrants. Clearly, the state was not so strong nor was Americanization so coercive. Rather, immigrant social welfare programs represented a weak state's efforts at social control through persuasion, as befitting a movement within progressivism.

But Americanization was more than a social movement: It was also public policy. In analyzing policy, it is necessary to examine the definition of the problem, the development of the policy response to this problem, and the implementation of that policy. Other key themes to be studied include the goals and motivations of those who define, develop, and implement the policy; the role of outside forces, such as resources and events; and the responses of those who are the target of the policy.[7] Furthermore, this study analyzes Americanization policy from the perspective that the state is not "captured" by economic or political interest groups but has its own interests in promoting a national identity shared by its citizens.[8]

This study examines Americanization policies in four states with large immigrant populations: New York, California, Massachusetts, and Illinois. But why these four states? New Jersey and Rhode Island also created immigration commissions between 1908 and 1920, and the Pennsylvania legislature assigned responsibilities for immigrant social welfare to its Department of Labor and Industry and eventually created a Division of Immigration within its Bureau of Employment.

The Americanization policies of New York, California, Massachusetts, and

Illinois are worthy of study because each of these states had distinctive immigrant social welfare policies that reflect significant aspects of the movement to assimilate immigrants in the United States. These states' Americanization policies explicitly and often exclusively targeted immigrants as their core constituency. Other states provided social welfare to immigrants—but as workers, the unemployed, women, etc. This study focuses on states that purposefully designed social welfare policies for immigrants as immigrants.

Furthermore, although many different organizations participated in the Americanization movement of the 1910s and 1920s, the focus on public policy requires an emphasis on representatives of the state. Private organizations that influenced public Americanization policy will be discussed, but they are not the main characters of this story.

In 1910 New York, California, Massachusetts, and Illinois had populations that represented approximately 22 percent of the 91,641,195 people living in the United States. Furthermore, these four states were also home to 5,623,000 immigrants, 40 percent of the nearly 14 million foreign-born residents counted in the census of 1910.[9] And these figures do not include native-born residents with one or two foreign-born parents.

In 1910 New York was the most populous state in the Union, with 9,113,614 residents. Of these, 2,729,272 were foreign-born, 2,241,837 were native-born with foreign-born parents, and 765,411 were native-born with one foreign-born parent. Thus, 5,736,520 people, more than half of New Yorkers, had some close family connection to the immigrant experience.[10] Furthermore, of the 1,041,570 immigrants who entered the United States in 1910, one-third arrived through Ellis Island in New York Harbor, the nation's busiest immigration station in the nation's largest port.

In 1910 New York's progressive Republican governor Charles Evans Hughes created the Bureau of Industries and Immigration (NYBII), the first Americanization agency of its kind in the country, to provide social welfare services to the hundreds of thousands of immigrants who arrived in New York each year. New York educators, meanwhile, implemented their own program of immigrant education totally separate from the policy initiated by the NYBII. New York's Americanization policy was marked by political battles, bureaucratic reorganizations, and responsibilities divided amongst competing agencies. Yet New York warrants careful examination simply by being the largest immigrant state and having the first immigrant social welfare program in the country. It is also the great size and the massive scale of immigration to New York that demands that New York not be considered alone as representative of U.S. Americanization policy.

California also had an extensive Americanization policy and a rapidly growing immigrant population. In 1910 the Golden State had 2,377,549 residents, 517,250 of them foreign-born, 403,364 native-born with foreign-born parents, and 232,525 native-born with one foreign-born parent. Demographically, California's population was still predominantly northern European: Britons, English Canadians, Irish, Germans, and Scandinavians comprised more than 60 percent of the state's population. Mexicans were less than 5 percent, but would comprise nearly 13 percent of the state's growing population in 1920. Asian immigrants, particularly Chinese and Japanese, made up less than 2 percent of the state's total population in 1910 (36,000 Chinese and 41,000 Japanese, respectively), but were highly visible and had long been a source of bitter conflict over the nature of immigration to the United States and to California.[11]

Inspired by the New York Bureau of Industries and Immigration, California created the nation's second Americanization agency, the California Commission of Immigration and Housing (CCIH) in 1913. But once established, the CCIH paved a different policy path from those of its eastern counterparts, reflecting the state's economy and demography, as well as progressives' control of the state government for most of the 1910s and 1920s.

Another high immigration state in the East, Massachusetts, also developed an Americanization policy in the late 1910s and early 1920s. Massachusetts had 3,366,416 residents in 1910, according to the thirteenth U.S. census: 1,051,050 foreign-born, 846,820 native-born to immigrant parents, and 323,627 native-born with one foreign-born parent.[12]

Massachusetts' immigrant social welfare policy developed with fits and starts. The state appointed a temporary Immigration Commission in 1913 but did not act on the recommendation that a permanent agency be created until the initial hysteria of World War I in 1917. It was only after the war that Massachusetts' Americanization policy achieved some degree of stability in time to confront the challenge of providing social welfare benefits to immigrants at a time when anti-immigration sentiment was at its peak. With the passage of a series of quota laws restricting immigration in the 1920s, the Massachusetts Division of Immigration and Americanization (MDIA) spent most of its time addressing the consequences of restriction, not immigration as its founders had intended. In addition, educational work among immigrants in the 1920s was provided by the Division of University Extension. Thus, Americanization in Massachusetts was divided between two agencies, which sometimes competed within the Department of Education.

Meanwhile, the one state where one might assume a strong Americanization program, due to the presence of nationally recognized immigrant advocates, ultimately had no lasting public policy for immigrant social welfare. Illinois had 5,638,591 residents in 1910, making it the third largest state in the country (after New York and Pennsylvania). Of these, only about a quarter, 1,202,560, were foreign-born, yet another 1,232,155 were native-born with foreign-born parents and 491,692 had one immigrant parent.[13]

Despite having a large immigrant population and being home to some of the nation's leading immigrant organizations, Illinois did not establish an Americanization policy until after World War I. The Illinois Immigrants Commission (IIC) was formed in 1919, largely due to pressure from the Immigrants' Protective League (IPL), whose director, Grace Abbott, had directed the 1913 Massachusetts Immigration Commission. But the new commission soon fell victim to machine politics, and Illinois quickly abandoned public Americanization. The story of the Illinois Americanization policy thus is one of the blending of private organization and public agency so common during the progressive period.

State Americanization policies differed, sometimes significantly; but the immigrant welfare programs in New York, California, Massachusetts, and Illinois were products of that amorphous impetus for reform called progressivism. The meanings of progressivism—and how reformers and politicians used its rhetoric and theories of change—framed the ambitions and actions of Americanization activists at the state level.

For more than two generations, scholars have debated how to interpret the decades between the end of Reconstruction in 1877 and the beginning of the New Deal in 1933. There is still little consensus about what progressivism was; whether there was a "progressive movement"; when the "Progressive Era" began or ended; or how to identify who the progressives were, what motivated them, or how to evaluate their actions.[14]

Elements that most scholars agree upon, however, were the abandonment of nineteenth-century liberal economic theory; the rejection of the primacy of individualism; the belief in the transformative power of the social environment; the malleability of the individual; and a new emphasis on government as an acceptable and even proper vehicle for changing the economy and society.[15]

Progressivism was a collection of sometimes conflicting values that motivated middle-class Americans to respond to the forces of modernism in the late nineteenth and early twentieth centuries. Progressives were middle-class Americans who shared these values and formed political coalitions to pursue a series of institutional and policy responses to the inequity, inefficiency, environmental and social destruction, and general socioeconomic disorder caused by industrial capitalism and the accompanying phenomena of immigration, urbanization, and internal migration. Progressives emphasized community rights over individual rights, the interdependence of people, and the dynamism of society.

"Middle class" is primarily defined here in terms of cultural values and personal identity, not income, property ownership, or occupation, although there is a close and complex relationship between socioeconomic status and values, behavior, and identity.[16] This definition recognizes the importance of how a person lived, the life choices he made, and the values and belief system that caused him to choose one economic or social option over another. The more income or property one had, the more socioeconomic choices were available. But one's cultural values and personal identity both reflected and determined the actual decisions and choices made. As important as income and occupation were in determining middle-class status, an individual's attitudes toward work, wealth, property, education, family, sex, recreation, and even clothes and household decoration were all rooted in cultural values.[17]

Using values and identity as tools to define class avoids the arbitrariness of choosing income levels and occupations dictated by Marxian theories for inclusion or exclusion in a definition of "middle class." Using values and identity as lenses into class relations also allows historical actors to define themselves, and reflects the fact that while income and occupation can suddenly be lost or gained, personal identity and values evolve more slowly.

For the white American middle class, values of self-control, hard work, sobriety, stability, politeness, piety, family privacy, respect for private property, and the willingness to postpone immediate gratification for long-term goals were vehicles for socioeconomic improvement for most of the nineteenth century. Regardless of religious affiliation, the individuals who held these values subscribed to the norms of Anglo-Saxon Protestantism.[18]

Yet these values only served those with enough resources and stability to make use of them. The poor—both native- and foreign-born—often found it next to impossible to save enough wealth to plan ahead and make long-term investments in education, apprenticeships, or real property (such as land and tools), the material things that publicly announced middle-class status in nineteenth-century America. Many immigrants, particularly those arriving in the late nineteenth and early twentieth centuries, postponed immediate gratification to save large sums of money; but these funds were used to bring more family from Europe or Asia to America or were nest eggs for investment back in the Old Country.[19] Immigrants who adopted the values of the Anglo-Saxon Protestant middle class were often derided by their working-class neighbors as selfish, "uppity," or "lace curtain" for their rejection of working-class values of mutualism and socialism.[20]

By the late nineteenth century, however, new social and economic forces prompted some middle-class Americans to question traditional values of liberty, individualism, and equality of opportunity. The complexity of industrial capitalism and the growing impersonality of society due to urbanization, immigration, and internal migration made it difficult for many people to succeed on their own merits without assistance from others. As communities began to experience the social, economic, and environmental consequences of industrial capitalism, some middle-class Americans began to try to balance the nineteenth-century values of individualism and personal responsibility with equally old values of community and social service. Although not all Americans became progressives, those who did organized themselves into professional, social, civic, and ultimately political organizations to reform American politics, the economy, and society in order to both preserve and adapt nineteenth-century, middle-class values to the new twentieth century.[21]

As the first generation born after the Civil War, progressives placed a premium on national unity; after the turbulent 1870s, 1880s, and 1890s, they also sought social stability. But progressives wanted this stability to develop self-consciously, through the internalization of middle-class values by an increasingly foreign working class. The alternatives to this social control, progressives feared, were a continuation of laissez-faire, which was economically unjust and socially and politically destructive, or external control, which government had used repeatedly in the 1890s to protect private property rights during labor disputes.[22] Such continued use of the state's police power threatened civil liberties and was ultimately self-defeating, progressives had come to believe by the early twentieth century.

Americans who called themselves "Progressive" found it far easier to identity what they were against than what they were for or how to achieve their goals of national unity and social stability. Progressives objected to uncontrolled industrial capitalism, messy urbanization, and political corruption, but they disagreed about how society should address these newly identified problems and of the role of the state in this effort. Some progressives advocated government tolerance or even encouragement of corporate self-regulation and organization, as in trusts or pools; others advocated providing businesses with information about markets; while a third group lobbied for government to create a "level playing field" through anti-monopoly policies. Other progressives sought new kinds of government regulation, ranging from restrictions ("Thou Shall Not" laws) to mandates ("Thou Shall" type commands). Political progressives were primarily interested in altering the structure and functions of government to both professionalize and democratize the state, while social progressives worried more about the socioeconomic experiences of disadvantaged groups. But the philosophical choices were not between, say, Theodore Roosevelt's New Nationalism and Woodrow Wilson's New Freedom, with one representing the opposite, competing alternative to the other.[23] Instead, progressives existed within an ever-expanding, ever-contracting spectrum of debate about the appropriate use of government power in relation to the economy, society, and the individual. The position of an individual or a group on that spectrum depended on the issue, the target, and the tactic to be used.

Despite their political and philosophical differences, progressives shared a common methodology of reform based upon new social science values of expertise and scientific rationalism. Fundamental to progressive activism was the collection of social knowledge (information about social and economic conditions), and the development of specialized institutions—particularly universities, investigative commissions, national magazines, and social settlements—to gather such data and use it to shape public policy. The use of the social survey, the investigative article, the commission, the lobbyist, and the interest group reflected progressives' fascination with social investigation, their belief in the need for professionalism and expertise in government, and their desire to circumvent existing institutions, particularly political parties.[24]

Another commonality progressives shared was an obsession with citizenship, both literally, in the sense of legal status, and figuratively, in the sense of behavior. Inseparable from progressives' worries about urbanization and industrialization was doubt about the character of the millions of immigrants who were populating America's rapidly growing cities. Progressives might have talked about workers, women, and consumers; but never far from their minds was the fact that the vast majority of these individuals were newcomers to the United States, and their values, allegiances, ability, and willingness to be productive citizens were in question. It is not coincidental that the decades which historians have deemed the Progressive Era (1890–1930) were also the years when the United States experienced its highest rates of immigration until the turn of the twenty-first century.

Conservative Americans were also concerned about citizenship, but they defined citizenship in terms of measurable demonstrations of loyalty to an already perfect nation-state, exceptional and unique in the world. Conservatives rejected progressives' argument that citizenship and democracy were tools to reform the polity and economy to reflect the complexity, diversity, and interconnectedness of American society. Instead, conservatives viewed liberty, democracy, and republican government as static political values to be revered and defended against foreign ideas of pluralism and collectivism.

Several important conservative organizations—including the Sons and Daughters of the American Revolution, the National Security League, and the American Legion—did work actively with government at all levels to prepare immigrant men for American citizenship. But these citizenship classes taught English literacy, the mechanics of American government, patriotic rituals, and a reverential, unquestioning view of American history. Naturalized immigrants were not encouraged to use their new American citizenship to try to change American society. Skeptical of the ability of immigrants from feudal and autocratic societies to become good American citizens, even conservatives involved in immigrant education often favored immigration restriction and more stringent naturalization requirements as ways of protecting the polity and society against dangerous foreign influences.[25]

Most progressives opposed immigration restriction because they believed it was discriminatory and unnecessary. Instead, progressives reacted to the surge in immigration before World War I with the Americanization movement, just as they responded to the industrialization and urbanization fueled by migration with new ideas about political economy, social organization, and citizenship.

Progressivism and Americanization were fundamentally about class relations. Labor unions, immigrant churches, immigrant societies, and foreign-language newspapers played essential roles in introducing American cultural practices, political processes, and work habits to new arrivals. But Americanization as a social and policy movement was envisioned and directed primarily by political activists from a variety of religious and national backgrounds who shared a common set of middle-class values. Americanization was the means by which middle-class progressives sought to assimilate working-class immigrants into a culture of middle-class values and behaviors, with the hope that socioeconomic status would eventually follow. In addition, progressive Americanizers sought to amend traditional nineteenth-century middle-class values to be more accommodating of progressive theories of cooperation, expertise, and consumption. In short, progressives defined their values and lifestyle as the standards to which other classes and groups should conform. If immigrants assimilated and adopted these new progressive, middle-class values and behaviors, then society would become more stable, harmonious, and democratic.²⁶

Conservatives agreed with progressives that the working class and immigrants should adapt, but they strongly resisted the progressive suggestion that native-born Americans had any responsibility to alter their behavior or attitudes as well. They rejected the progressive idea that American society was a "melting pot," in which foreign- and native-born cultures and people intermingled, creating a new identity and nationality called "American." Conservatives believed assimilation followed an Anglo-conformist model: Immigrants abandoned their traditional cultural practices and adopted Anglo-American ways of living. Not only did immigrants have nothing of cultural value to contribute to American society, but the continued existence of foreign cultures threatened to contaminate America. Heritage societies, such as the DAR, which restricted membership based on genealogy, were particularly resistant to the progressive suggestion that immigrants could be equal citizens to themselves.²⁷

The class and cultural components of Americanization were strong and often overt. Americanizers fretted that immigrants were following the bad examples of native-born Americans and earlier immigrants and adopting the wrong values and practices. The foreign-born labor contractor, employer, landlord, or shopkeeper who ill-treated his employees, tenants, or customers to make a larger profit; girls who disobeyed their parents, were sexually active, or who spent their money on clothes and city entertainment instead of saving for education or marriage, or contributing to family needs; men and boys who spent their leisure time in saloons or brothels instead of with their families; the prevalence of child and female labor, often within the home; the taking in of boarders and lodgers; disdain for the law and American political values—all indicated that immigrant assimilation needed to be directed away from working-class values and toward an Anglo-Saxon Protestant middle-class lifestyle. Americanizers and their foreign-born clients routinely clashed over such basic life issues as food preparation, child rearing, and household economics.

Americanizers' program of class and cultural assimilation had strong racial tones as well. Although all male European immigrants were eligible for legal citizenship, not everyone who conformed to the middle-class ideal was accepted as full Americans in the nineteenth century. Americans of northern European, particularly British, heritage dominated the United States politically, economically, and socially, and viewed African Americans, Asian Americans, American Indians, Jews, and Catholics as foreign, regardless of place of birth or length of time in the country.²⁸

Virtually all progressives unconsciously defined being "American" as being "white." (Conservatives were usually explicit about this.) This form of racial nationalism, to use Gary Gerstle's term, existed within Americanization, particularly in regards to Americans of African descent.[29] White progressives included black Americans in their statistics and social mapping, but did not target them in their social welfare programs except in the rare instances of being confronted with immigrants from the Caribbean, who, because of racial interpretations of the Fourteenth Amendment, were eligible for citizenship because they were considered black.

The primary justification for not including African Americans in Americanization was that they were not proper candidates for assimilation because they were American citizens. Yet, while black Americans spoke English and grew up within the larger context of American society and culture, generations of segregation and discrimination had resulted in a unique Afro-American culture, distinct in cultural and class aspects. Americanization activist Frances A. Kellor, who had begun her early sociological work researching African Americans, was well aware of the conditions under which black Americans lived and worked. But Kellor did not target black Americans for Americanization, nor did Americanization activists anywhere else in the country.[30]

The few progressives who did include African Americans into their vision of the American community, such as University of Southern California sociologist Emory S. Bogardus, still could not envision true equality between blacks and whites, and full assimilation of blacks could only come through "miscegenation," which was socially undesirable and illegal in most states.[31] Asian immigrants were included in some Americanization programs in California, but on a limited scale and not with the purpose of challenging Asians' exclusion from legal citizenship. Americanization for American Indians was its own unique policy, initiated and implemented by individuals separate from the efforts to integrate European immigrants into white American society.

The Americanization movement has been faulted for not including African Americans, but this suggestion fails to recognize the fine line between possessing and exercising citizenship.[32] Black Americans were American citizens according to the Fourteenth Amendment; they did not need to gain American citizenship or learn the workings of American government or society. They needed the liberty to exercise their citizenship, both legally and socially, and an end to racial segregation. Only when Americanization is conflated with assimilation does it make sense to decry the failure of white Americans to share full citizenship with black Americans. When progressives spoke of the need to "Americanize" the native-born, they were highlighting the political and socioeconomic power white Americans possessed over immigrants and non-whites. Being relatively powerless and often in economic competition with immigrants, African Americans were not in the position to improve the conditions under which European immigrants—and they—lived and worked.

The theoretical underpinnings of Americanization policies were further complicated by the fact that the definitions of such critical concepts as "race," "white," and "assimilation" were contested in the early twentieth century.[33] Until the 1930s, most Americans believed in the multiplicity of races, the immutability of cultures, and the biological determinism of hereditary. Culture was thought to be the outward expression of inherited genetic characteristics of racially distinct groups of people. These groups were hierarchically ranked, with Anglo-Saxons at the top and darker people progressively lower according to skin color. The fact that northern Europeans had colonized non-white peoples was explained in terms of racial supremacy, not superiority of technology, military power, or economy.

What people now call "ethnic groups" were thought to be distinct races, biologically predisposed to certain cultural behaviors and values that could be described by what we now consider to be stereotypes. Thus, Italians were biologically versus culturally predisposed toward crimes of passion; Germans had a "natural" love of music; Jews were cunning and avaricious, etc. A few scholars, such as Julius Drachsler and Robert Park, were beginning to explore the concepts of assimilation and ethnicity in relation to intermarriage and personal identity, but these were in the minority in the 1920s. Eugenicists' ideas about race and hereditary held more sway with the general public and many social scientists. Philosophers Randolph Bourne's and Horace Kallen's theories of cultural pluralism would be largely ignored until the 1950s.[34]

This weakness of social theory meant that the Americanization movement had the capacity to hold within it both assimilationists and eugenicists, pro-immigrationists and restrictionists, immigrant leaders and cultural pluralists. Most Americanizers fell somewhere in the middle of this wide and fluid range, shifting back and forth between insisting upon conformity to middle-class Anglo-Saxon Protestant values and behaviors and celebrating cultural diversity, depending on the context and the group they were addressing.

Separate from but intimately related to the biological and sociological theories of race and assimilation was the legal relationship between race and citizenship in America. Since 1790, American citizenship had been limited to (male) "free white persons," but neither the courts nor the founders clearly defined what this meant or specified who was a "white person." The presence of Slavic, Semitic, Middle Eastern, Mediterranean, and Asian immigrants arriving in the late nineteenth to early twentieth centuries forced redefinitions of "white" as the legal basis of U.S. citizenship.[35] But while the legal meanings of "white" and "non-white" were being debated within the legal system, U.S. law limiting citizenship to "free white persons" and, after 1868, "persons of African nativity, or African descent" was not changed until the 1940s and 1950s, when proscriptions against Asian immigration, naturalization, and citizenship were finally lifted. Whether or not Americanization activists accepted Chinese, Japanese, and other Asian immigrants as worthy targets of social welfare, Asians were excluded from becoming American citizens and so could never be full Americans, in either a legal or a social sense. Americanization policies in the 1910s and 1920s were designed for European immigrants, both because they made up the vast majority of migrants to the United States (primarily due to racially exclusionary immigration policies) and because they were deemed to be more desirable future citizens by white Americanizers.

Americanization activists also had different understandings of the role the social environment played in assimilation. Progressive Americanizers believed that the assimilation was inevitable and desirable; they often spoke of "making a new American race" through social and cultural interaction that would lead, eventually, to intermarriage. The social environment played a powerful role in assimilation and in molding people's values and behaviors for good or ill. Progressive Americanizers believed that they could influence immigrants' assimilation by changing the social environment. But a major point of confusion for these progressive Americanizers was how active a role the foreign-born played in their own assimilation: Did immigrants assimilate, were they assimilated, or was assimilation a process of mutual cultural exchange between foreign- and native-born?

Progressives were also confused about whether this "new American race" resulted primarily through intermarriage, forming a "community of descent," in which Americans shared a common racial background, or was a "community of consent" based on ideology.[36] Forming a "new race" certainly suggested amalgamation, but such integration immediately butted up against social prejudices, legal prohibitions, and religious proscriptions against such mixings. There was little agreement about the workings of these processes, and few progressives gave deep thought to these questions.

Conservative Americanizers placed their faith in biology and eugenics rather than government or social institutions. While eugenicists shared environmentalists' advocacy of social engineering, they rejected their faith in the power of the social environment. Instead, eugenicists believed that they had to circumvent the social environment by selecting individuals on the basis of genetic desirability.[37] These Americanizers favored immigration restriction as the first step toward creating a healthier nation; only those immigrants who could contribute positively to the national gene pool would be allowed to enter and eventually assimilate into American society.

Eugenicists were ideological wolves in progressive sheep's clothing; their denial of the power of the social environment to transform individuals rejected a core premise of Americanization that even immigration restrictionists accepted: that immigrants could assimilate and become American. Restrictionists simply believed that assimilation could only happen in an environment isolated from constant cultural infusions from immigrants' homelands. While eugenicists supported restriction, not all restriction advocates believed in eugenics. Eugenicists viewed the United States as a community of descent in which Americans of full citizenship shared a common heritage of biology, not ideology.[38]

The national leaders of the progressive Americanization movement were white, native-born, middle-class Protestant women of British heritage. Frances A. Kellor, Grace and Edith Abbott, and Sophonisba Breckinridge, just to name a few, were all university-educated, native-born Americans from the Midwest, and, as such, they gravitated initially to Chicago, where many of them stayed.

Yet the portrait of the progressive immigrant advocate as "WASP" and female is undermined when one looks just below the leadership of the national organizations. Many important progressive Americanizers active at the state level were either immigrants themselves or first-generation Americans. Simon J. Lubin; Edward Joseph Hanna; Paul Scharrenberg; Joseph Mayper; Bernard J. Rothwell, and Lillian D. Wald were all either immigrants or the children of immigrants, and several were Jewish or Catholic and represented the "New Immigration" from southern and eastern Europe. Marian K. Clark, a conservative Americanizer, was the daughter of Irish immigrants.

This national and religious diversity among state Americanization leaders frequently resulted in social welfare policies that showed greater sympathy and tolerance for immigrant cultures and traditions than those promoted at the national level. While English fluency was the primary goal in Americanization, most state-level Americanizers realized that communication with immigrants could best be achieved through bilingualism. American citizenship was deemed essential, but could not be achieved by denigrating immigrant cultures. There was more discussion at the state level of the cultural contributions immigrants could and should make to American society than was heard from national Americanization leaders.

Furthermore, although these state-based Americanizers promoted values rooted in the country's British heritage, they did not believe that these values were the property of one national group or that such values reinforced WASP hegemony. To the Catholic archbishop of San Francisco, the Rt. Rev. Edward Joseph Hanna, and the devout Jew Simon J. Lubin, American civic values were universal and did not conflict with non-Anglo-Saxon cultures or religions. A Polish Jew or an Irish Catholic had just as much claim on the title "American" as a member of the Mayflower Society. American freedom of religion, in particular, made the United States exceptional in its tolerance of pluralism, and built pluralism into the very political structure of the nation.

Americanization was a mass movement by the time the United States entered World War I, yet only a handful of states initiated formal immigrant social welfare policies. This fact reflected the unwillingness of many state political leaders to extend social welfare benefits to non-citizens, who were perceived as undeserving. Progressive Americanizers struggled to justify the need for immigrant social welfare and found their definitions of citizenship and national identity challenged by conservatives, who had their own ideas about immigrants' ability to assimilate into American society and the best ways to facilitate that assimilation.

Comparing Americanization policies in New York, California, Massachusetts, and Illinois reveals differences in policy design and implementation, but similarities in ideology, reflecting the fact that many Americanization activists were part of a larger progressive network. Each of the four states assigned responsibility for immigrant social welfare to different agencies with different structures, powers, and locations in each state's bureaucracy, resulting in a wide variety of programs. The personalities of the individuals responsible for these policies influenced the method and aggressiveness of policy implementation, while external factors—funding, politics, riot, the economy, and war—determined the degree of success or failure of Americanization programs in each of the four states.

Yet the Americanization activists in these four states shared similar ideas about immigration, immigrants, and social welfare. These Americanizers had four broadly defined goals: to improve relations between native-born Americans and immigrants; to support immigrant families by helping parents maintain filial control over their rapidly assimilating children; to incorporate the cultural strengths or "immigrant gifts" of immigrant groups into American culture; and, most importantly, to integrate immigrants socially and economically into American society with minimum disruption to existing political, economic, and social institutions and systems.

First and foremost, Americanizers in New York, California, Massachusetts, and Illinois defined Americanization as immigrant social welfare, usually couched in terms of education, job services, legal aid, and the regulation of labor and housing conditions. Despite several generations of immigration evidence to the contrary, these progressives believed that while assimilation could occur without governmental social engineering, such unsupervised assimilation would be more likely to produce the wrong kind of Americans.

Progressive Americanizers rejected the traditional American value of equality of opportunity because they believed this rhetoric denied the reality of immigrants' socioeconomic status in American society. These reformers argued that immigrants deserved special assistance and protection because the foreign-born suffered from unique disadvantages that stemmed from their status as immigrants, not simply poor or working class. But these disadvantages did not result from immigrants' legal status as non-citizens. Rather, progressives viewed the disadvantages of the foreign-born through cultural lenses: Immigrants arrived in the United States often speaking a foreign language (Americanizers almost totally ignored English-speaking immigrants), were inexperienced with urban industrial life, and were unfamiliar with American institutions, social customs, and the U.S. political system. Given these disadvantages, Americanizers believed that immigrants needed friendly, nonsectarian, nonpartisan information and assistance to successfully adjust to urban industrial life in the United States.

Also, in contrast to conservatives, progressive Americanizers argued that assimilation should be mutual, affecting both the foreign- and native-born. While conservative Americanizers focused on changing immigrants, primarily through education, progressive activists believed that Americanization was as much about adjusting the cultural, social, economic, and political attitudes and practices of native-born Americans as it was about encouraging the foreign-born to adopt "American" ways. Americanization, according to the progressive model, was a two-staged process that first required the "Americanization" of the native-born. Only after native-born Americans had created a more progressive political economy and society could the foreign-born be expected to assimilate.

This theory of Americanization as having two components resulted from the fact that progressive Americanizers perceived immigrants to be too socially and politically disorganized to direct the course of their own lives and influence the larger native-born American society. This view was paternalistic but often accurate. Progressives recognized that as employers, landlords, teachers, and (most importantly) voting citizens, native-born Americans had the power, and thus the moral obligation to improve the country's social environment in order to make American society a desirable place into which immigrants would want to assimilate. Thus, Americanization held the promise of creating a new and better society in which both native- and foreign-born would value each other's unique talents and contributions in the creation of a new nationality called "American."

Thus, Americanization as implemented by progressive activists used two distinct, yet often combined, methods: environmental and educational. Environmental Americanization policies tried to reform the social environment in which immigrants lived and worked, with the hope that the improved environment would then change the immigrant. Educational Americanization programs alternately sought to change some aspect of the immigrant's culture or lifestyle. Conservatives participated in educational Americanization programs but rejected most environmental Americanization policies as socialistic and thus "un-American."

Most important for state Americanization activists was the idea that immigrant assimilation needed to be publicly directed and state-supervised. Time was too slow and unpredictable, and the dominant American society was either too hostile or too slow (or both) to effectively absorb the large numbers of immigrants entering the country each year. Most of the Americanizers in New York, California, Massachusetts, and Illinois had some connection to the settlement house movement; yet by 1910, they had come to believe that immigrant social welfare could no longer be left to the private sectors of charities and churches. By the middle of the 1910s, many progressives working with immigrants believed that Americanization should be supervised, if not directly handled, by government, preferably state government with national coordination, or municipal government under state guidance at the minimum. Government management of Americanization was seen as necessary because labor markets employing immigrants failed to operate efficiently, industry pursued profits at the exclusion of social needs, and private organizations working with the foreign-born were overwhelmed, underfunded, and often worked at cross-purposes.

Thus, examining the immigrant social welfare policies of New York, California, Massachusetts, and Illinois reminds one of the public nature of the Americanization movement. Americanizers used public monies, public resources, and public power to craft policies designed to encourage the assimilation of the foreign-born into American society. In doing so, they promoted their particular visions and understandings of American society and American citizenship in the collective name of the community of citizens. Immigrant assistance conducted by settlement houses, churches, and civic and immigrant organizations reflected visions of citizenship held by their members and was done in their name alone. Americanization by local, state, and federal governments was done in the name of all Americans, native- and foreign-born, citizen and alien.

As a branch of progressive reform, Americanization helped lay the foundations of liberal social welfare, particularly in the areas of adult education and the regulation of labor and housing conditions. But in the short term, Americanization was a policy failure. By focusing on one group in society— immigrants— Americanization programs were vulnerable to shifting political winds, particularly since the targeted population was comprised of non-citizens who could not vote and therefore had limited options in the political arena. Americans have been traditionally cautious in granting social welfare benefits to distinct groups unless they are perceived by the larger society to be particularly vulnerable or deserving, such as widows, orphans, and war veterans.[39] "Immigrant" has been judged to be too broad a category, including both genders, many nationalities, and those not clearly deserving. The Americanization movement of the 1910s and 1920s is the only period in American history when immigrant assimilation and citizenship have been so aggressively promoted and publicly debated. Today, in 2009, Americans vigorously debate immigration policy while ignoring the needs and interests of millions of immigrants already in the country.

Once immigration restriction was instituted in the 1920s, the justification for Americanization was nominally removed. In the minds of many Americans, fewer immigrants meant less need for resources to assist them. Social welfare for the poor or the working class, however, included many more people, citizen and non-citizen, and so had a greater chance of political survival. Citizenship and social welfare began to be delinked, and Americanization as a social movement and public policy faded from public consciousness. Before that happened, though, Americanization transformed American understandings of national identity and the rights and obligations of citizenship.

1 ✷ The Start of a Movement

The New York Bureau of Industries and Immigration, 1908–1914

More than 19 million immigrants entered the United States in 1900–1930, one-third of them at the nation's largest city and busiest port, New York. The challenges these new arrivals faced began at the federal immigration station on Ellis Island and followed them, literally and figuratively, as they moved through New York City in search of housing and work—or on their way west.

Immigration to New York was nothing new in the early twentieth century, but what was new was the idea that the state should know something—and perhaps even do something—about the experiences of the hundreds of thousands of immigrants who passed through the Port of New York every year.

After experiencing the arrival of more than one million immigrants each year in 1905, 1906, and 1907, New York launched in 1908 a social welfare policy for immigrants that it called "Americanization." This new policy was initiated and implemented by social progressives who were from New York City settlement houses and who believed that their foreign-born status and newness to America put immigrants at an inherent disadvantage in finding jobs and housing and defending their rights and property. These activists advocated state intervention to protect immigrants from labor exploitation, housing discrimination, and urban crime. Americanization in New York was just one part of progressives' larger effort to reform the state's political economy and establish a modern social welfare system. As such, Americanization in New York was oriented almost entirely toward changing the social environment in which all New Yorkers lived and worked. Immigrant social welfare was to be the means by which a more compassionate, just, and progressive society would be created, one into which immigrants would want to assimilate by adopting the values and lifestyle of middle-class progressives.

Yet the agency initially responsible for this new policy, the New York Bureau of Industries and Immigration (NYBII), found itself hindered by a lack of resources and political support, and overwhelmed by the sheer number of immigrants in New York. The organization of the bureau, its powers and resources, and the individuals responsible for implementing its programs significantly impacted the agency's degree of success in achieving its vague and ambitious goal of immigrant assimilation. Outside forces—state and national politics and immigrants themselves—also influenced New York's Americanization policy in 1908–1914. The combination of limited funds and a high demand for services in New York City resulted in a policy that focused primarily on the lower portion of the state and was heavily dependent on assistance from private organizations and cooperation from federal immigration authorities and other state and municipal agencies. These limitations of New York's Americanization policy reflected the tensions between progressives and conservatives about definitions of citizenship, equality, and political economy.

Americanization was just one aspect of a larger reform agenda that New York began implementing after progressive Republican Charles Evans Hughes was elected governor in November 1906. Despite the fact that conservative Democrats affiliated with Tammany Hall controlled the state legislature, under Hughes' leadership New Yorkers saw the passage of a wide range of policies long agitated for by social progressives: worker compensation, industrial accident insurance, child and female labor regulation, mothers' pensions, and public sanitation regulations.[1]

In May 1908 Hughes responded to pressure from the Woman's Municipal League, the Inter-Municipal Committee on Research, and several New York City settlement houses and appointed a temporary Commission of Immigration to study issues of immigrant adjustment, exploitation, educational opportunities, and naturalization rates in New York.[2]

After nearly one year of hearings and field research, the New York Commission of Immigration proposed legislation to regulate private bankers, steamship ticket agents, and notaries public, and to create a permanent department of immigration.[3] This new agency, the Bureau of Industries and Immigration, located within the New York Department of Labor, was finally established in October 1910. Hughes appointed temporary commissioner Frances A. Kellor to be the bureau's chief investigator. Almost thirty-seven-years old, she was the first woman to run a state agency in New York and one of the youngest heads of an executive department in the state.[4]

The most common adjectives used to describe Kellor are "authoritarian," "imperious," and "an aggressive personal style."[5] While the descriptions are accurate, the pejorative connotations are unfair; Kellor's desire for order, efficiency, and "social control" marked her as the quintessential progressive.[6]

What was distinctive about Kellor as compared to other immigration activists, such as Jane Addams or Grace Abbott, was her obvious ambition: Kellor had high expectations for herself and progressive reform. Not content with local settlement house activism, her scope was national; and she aggressively sought to influence public policy—at first at the state level and then the federal level.

Born October 20, 1873, in Columbus, Ohio, and raised in Coldwater (Branch County), Michigan, Frances Alice Kellor challenged the typical profile of the progressive. Although she was a native-born Anglo-Saxon Protestant, she grew up poor in a small town. Despite her initial disadvantages, Kellor absorbed the values of Coldwater's middle class; and with the assistance of a few prominent local families, she took advantage of new educational opportunities becoming available to women in the 1880s and 1890s. She earned a law degree from Cornell University and then entered the recently opened University of Chicago in 1898 to study sociology.[7]

Kellor's education under sociologist Albion Small and criminologist Charles Henderson and her graduate research into the experiences of African-American female prison and workhouse inmates led her to reject moral, racial, and biological explanations for crime and social deviancy. Instead, she emphasized the role of the social environment in determining human behavior. In an era when many intellectuals embraced eugenics and biological determinism, Kellor remained a consistent environmentalist. She also held unusually liberal racial attitudes for the time.[8] Kellor believed that just as she had transformed herself into a middle-class social scientist, so could immigrants—with government assistance—reinvent themselves as middle-class Americans.

In 1902 Kellor moved to New York City to attend the Summer School of Philanthropy. Having lived at Hull-House while a student in Chicago, she quickly gravitated to the New York College Settlement House at 95 Rivington Street on the Lower East Side. It was through the Summer School and the Rivington Settlement House that Kellor met Margaret and Mary E. Dreier, the daughters of wealthy German immigrants. The Dreier sisters were active in the Women' Trade Union League, the Woman's Municipal League, and Lillian D. Wald's Henry Street Settlement.[9] These friendships immediately linked Kellor to dynamic women doing pioneering social science research and grassroots political activism and their wealthy patrons, particularly New York's German-Jewish elite, such as Louis B. Marshall, Solomon Loeb, Jacob Schiff, and Felix Warburg.

Kellor's ongoing research into the working conditions of black and immigrant women quickly brought her to the attention of President Theodore Roosevelt and newly-elected governor Hughes.[10] With access to two of the most prominent progressive politicians in the country, Kellor was in a unique position to lobby for an institutional response to immigration and its socio-economic consequences.

By late 1910 Kellor had succeeded in getting the Bureau of Industries and Immigration created. She now confronted the realities of translating untested theories of social adjustment and assimilation into public policy despite few resources, internal structural limitations, and external political forces beyond her control.

As chief investigator of the NYBII, Kellor reported to labor commissioner John Williams, but she had a great deal of autonomy in making policy decisions and managing staff. Legally, the bureau was a coordinating versus regulating agency, responsible for reporting "exploitation, fraud or prevailing evil" to other, more powerful departments that had the authority to enforce laws and regulations.[11]

The stated policy goals of the bureau were to:

- Resolve complaints brought by immigrants against those who would exploit them, and to act as a mediator between aggrieved parties.
- Seek the enforcement of existing laws and to gain the passage of additional laws, if and when necessary.
- Investigate the conditions under which New York's foreign-born residents lived and lobby for improvements.
- Publish and distribute information that would "facilitate assimilation."[12]

State resources for this project were slim. Governor Hughes may have been liberal in political or administrative reform, but he was not in the area of finances. While the legislature granted the bureau $41,000 for 1910–1911, Hughes slashed that amount to $9,700, which paid for a staff of eight: six investigators (including Kellor), one legal counsel, and one stenographer. Refusing to accept a budget of less than $10,000, Kellor and fellow investigator Carola Woerishoffer contributed $9,695 of their own money to supplement the bureau's meager appropriation.[13]

The Americanization policy Kellor crafted reflected her enormous faith in social science expertise, state power, and the transforming power of the social environment.[14] Kellor described Americanization in three ways: as equality, efficiency, and most of all, citizenship. Kellor's emphasis on citizenship (defined in social terms) reflected her opinion that New Yorkers had failed in their duties as citizens; that they were, in effect, bad Americans because they chose economic opportunity and individual self-interest over civic virtue. Kellor and other progressives believed that a good citizen should not pursue his or her self-interest; but, rather, be disinterested, placing community welfare over personal gain.[15] Kellor's solution to the perceived problem of New Yorkers' poor citizenship was a stronger state to control those unvirtuous citizens who took advantage of aliens.

This environmental approach to Americanization was also based upon Kellor's belief that immigrants were vulnerable newcomers, preyed upon by native-born Americans and more experienced immigrants, and abandoned by American society and government to sink or swim in an unregulated capitalistic marketplace. The state expected obedience to its laws, and society to its customs, yet neither provided immigrants easy means by which to learn those laws and customs.

Kellor assumed that if immigrants were treated well by Americans, they would become loyal citizens in turn. She also did not distinguish among the many nationalities arriving in New York; as far as Kellor was concerned, all had the capacity to become good Americans if given an example of good citizenship. Greater social justice, true equality of opportunity, and cultural tolerance would create a more humane social environment into which immigrants would want to assimilate by adopting the values of the middle-class progressives who had reformed that environment. Correspondingly, exploitation, discrimination, and prejudice by provincial native-born Americans were creating a potentially dangerous working class comprised of embittered, unassimilated aliens who would learn to exploit later arrivals.

Problems of immigrant criminality, poverty, and civic apathy reflected the malleability of foreigners' characters, not personal moral failings or defects of foreign cultures. The type of citizen an alien became was determined largely by the Americans he or she encountered. Therefore, a significant share of the burden of Americanization fell upon the native-born, Kellor believed.[16]

Progressives working with immigrants frequently discounted the resourcefulness of new arrivals who had often traveled half way around the world, arriving with surprisingly up-to-date information about their economic prospects in America, courtesy of letters from friends and relatives.[17] Kellor was no different; she and her staff viewed their clientele as helpless and lost in the Big City. Having "lived the narrow, static domestic life of peasants," immigrants arrived in New York "homeless, unemployed, migratory, and to a considerable degree unattached to families—conditions which make them as easy prey to exploitation," Kellor argued.[18]

Perceiving immigrants as unable to defend themselves against exploitation by the native-born and other immigrants who had "incorrectly" adjusted to American labor practices and social prejudices, the bureau staff believed government supervision of Americanization was necessary. Kellor insisted that immigrant protection work had to be done by the state, not private charity, immigrant societies, churches, or foreign consuls. And because the federal government refused to protect or assist immigrants, the state government would have to because it experienced the consequences of federal policy.

Kellor believed that true equality of opportunity was only possible with government assistance; liberty through laissez faire was a myth that masked unfair advantages held by the native-born. Only with special government help could the foreign-born compete equally with the native-born and participate fully in American society. Once immigrants had more experience in the United States, they would no longer need special assistance, only the general protection a progressive social welfare state provided to all of its citizens.

Kellor also looked to state government because of progressives' past frustrations in dealing with New York City's Democratic Tammany Hall.[19] Not only did progressives now have a foothold in state government (thanks to Hughes), but state authority was also broader and theoretically more powerful than that of municipalities.

The NYBII was charged with "the making of new races into Americans." Yet how this sociological, cultural, and demographic process was to occur was unknown in 1910. Like most university-trained progressives, Kellor had great faith in the power of social science. The first step she and her staff took in developing their Americanization policy was to gather information, using the standard methodology of progressive social reform. Information was gathered and classified in systematic forms; patterns were investigated and analyzed; and judgments were reached using data as evidence to support conclusions. Photographs, statistics, charts, and social mapping were key tools in supporting conclusions and recommendations. Investigations were conducted largely "in the field" by simply going to a place and observing conditions. Sometimes bureau investigators pretended to be immigrants, going "under cover," while at other times they interjected themselves into situations as agents of the state.[20]

The bureau's small appropriation meant that the staff had to collaborate with other public agencies and private organizations. The NYBII worked closely with the Henry Street, College, and Greenwich settlement houses; New York's Charity Organization Society; the state's Farm Labor Bureau; foreign consuls; and the federal Bureau of Immigration and Naturalization to develop and implement its programs.[21]

The bureau's closest partnership in its first three years was with the North American Civic League for Immigrants (NACL), a group of pro-immigration businessmen in Boston with whom Kellor had partnered to lobby for the creation of the NYBII. Although progressives regularly attacked political parties and politicians for their supposed biases and conflicted interests and worshipped the ideal of "nonpartisan" and "apolitical," Kellor saw no conflict in being both the NYBII's chief investigator and continuing to be the salaried secretary of the NACL's New York–New Jersey Committee.[22] In this respect, Kellor represented progressives' willingness to blur the lines between public and private when it suited them. In 1910 Kellor found that maintaining her affiliation with the NACL gave her access to private funds, staff, office space, and other resources necessary to supplement the bureau's small appropriation, a blending of public and private moneys that was legal at the time.

The NACL's private status also allowed Kellor to transcend the jurisdictional limitations of the NYBII, particularly in regards to immigration to and from New York through New Jersey. Six steamship lines and five railroads had terminals in Hoboken and Jersey City, and many New York-bound travelers initially docked in New Jersey on the western side of the Hudson River, and then took ferries to Manhattan.[23]

The NYBII's view of its target clientele as passive and socially disoriented meant that Kellor and her staff did not—could not—expect immigrants to come uninvited to the bureau for help. Therefore, the bureau widely advertised its services, submitting notices to 962 foreign language newspapers across the country, noting the opening of the bureau, its locations, and the services available. Within a few years, the bureau developed a network of fifty New York-based foreign-language newspapers to disseminate information about popular scams targeting immigrants in the city and new federal and state immigration and citizenship laws and regulations.[24]

A key source of data for the bureau was the hundreds of complaints that disgruntled immigrants brought to the agency's offices. Between September 1910 and September 1911 the NYBII received 515 complaints; gave 551 pieces of information or advice; conducted 749 investigations into complaints; and held 81 hearings. By fall 1913 the bureau had received more than 3,700 complaints. Bureau staff investigated each complaint to determine the facts of the case and to see if there was a violation of the law. Conflicts not covered by law were resolved by the bureau when possible, while legal violations were referred to the agency with jurisdiction. When the bureau was unable to provide remedy because no law had been broken, investigators directed aggrieved immigrants to private organizations, such as settlement houses, charities, or consulates for assistance the bureau could not give. Despite having staff counsel, the NYBII did not take legal action on its own on behalf of complaining immigrants; instead, it referred aliens to the New York Legal Aid Society. The bureau also referred cases to the city or state district attorneys for prosecution.[25]

It was through the investigation of complaints that the bureau learned what problems immigrants faced and which issues they considered important. This information—combined with the staff's previous experiences with immigrants through settlement houses and immigrant societies and first-hand observations of immigrant neighborhoods, Ellis Island, and the Port of New York—caused the NYBII to focus its attention on five aspects of immigrant life: labor distribution and transportation; living and working conditions; finances; legal affairs, and education. In all of these areas, Kellor sought to interject the power of the state to mediate, regulate, and control the interactions of native- and foreign-born New Yorkers.

Bringing order to the free market chaos of New York's transportation system was the first challenge for the bureau. Every day, steamships filled with thousands of passengers arrived in New York Harbor. During the busy spring-fall sailing season, as many as twenty ships per day could dock at the Port of New York.

An unregulated market for goods, services, and labor operated in New York City, and newcomers unfamiliar with American society, customs, and laws were seen as legitimate prey by many Americans and more experienced immigrants seeking to profit off of the "greenhorns," as new immigrants were called. Pickpockets, confidence men, and other unsavory types frequented the Battery and New York's ferry, ship, and railroad terminals; and crime and fraud were common.

At all points during a trip through New York City, rail and steamship ticket agents, luggage porters, cab drivers, city guides, and hotel owners found ways of charging special fees, usually at higher "immigrant rates," to anyone who resembled a non-English-speaking foreigner. These fees were extracted by both independent contractors and by railroad, steamship, and hotel employees trying to make a few extra dollars on the side by charging whatever the market would bear.[26]

The majority of people traveling through New York City were foreigners, so entrepreneurs opened "immigrant hotels," also called lodging or transfer houses. These hotels catered to immigrants and provided a variety of services beyond simply a bed for the night: food and drink, including box lunches for long train trips; luggage storage and transport to the rail or steamship terminal; steamship and train ticket sales; currency exchange and other banking services; even the sale of American-style clothing to "green aliens desiring to acquire an American appearance."[27]

Although there was nominal city licensing of the non-rail transportation trades, decentralization in New York City administration had resulted in a dual licensing system whereby cab drivers, teamsters, and luggage porters were licensed by the City Licensing Bureau, while city guides were licensed by the police department. Only citizens could get a license from the police. Hotel runners (recruiters) worked on commission for one or more hotels and were not required to be licensed. Two individuals performing basically the same job could be licensed by different departments. However, given the absence of enforcement by either city office, few cabbies, teamsters, porters, or runners were licensed at all.[28]

Finally, there was outright fraud, in which individuals posed as employees of the railroads, steamship companies, or hotels in order to charge fees for services not rendered or illegally sold tickets for steamship and railroad companies.

Kellor viewed the conditions of immigrant transit through Manhattan as a prime example of market failure in need of government correction. "There is something radically wrong with a business system which loses money for passengers; enables them to be misguided, robbed and detained; makes them pay special rates for baggage, and even bonuses as high as $5 to have their tickets stamped on the docks in times of rush; and fifty cents for having their trunks labeled," she declared.[29] New Yorkers who sought to profit off of immigrants' inexperience and unfamiliarity with the local economy through fraud and other unsavory behavior had failed the progressive test of good citizenship.

But New York City officials did not share progressives' enthusiasm for government regulation. The granting of licenses was a source of revenue; regulation of license holders and increased policing of the Battery and the rail and ferry terminals were administrative costs of time and labor. Furthermore, many people traveling through Manhattan were aliens and did not intend to stay, so city officials had no political incentive to interfere with the business activities of local citizens. In the eyes of many New York City politicians, the activities of runners, porters, cabbies, and others indicated a market need being met by entrepreneurs pursuing their interests in a free market, not crime that needed to be prevented. This disagreement about the very definition of the problem reflected the differing visions of political economy of progressives and conservatives who subscribed to nineteenth-century ideas about liberty, individualism, and political economy.

Unwilling to wait for city officials to embrace progressive ideas of political economy and good citizenship behavior, Kellor tackled the problems affecting immigrant travel through New York City by successfully lobbying for a state law that required that only authorized steamship and railroad agents to be allowed to sell ship and train tickets, and that such agents be licensed. The bureau also shepherded through the legislature a bill that prohibited hotel runners from soliciting transportation tickets from passengers, a practice that frequently caused travelers to miss their ships or trains.[30]

Not content with regulating the relationship between hotels and steamship agents, Kellor successfully sought state licensing of immigrant lodging places themselves. Although New York already had an (unenforced) law governing immigrant hotels or transfer houses, the bureau successfully lobbied for a law in 1911 that required immigrant hotel owners to apply to the bureau for a license to operate. The license application required such information as business location, capacity, rates, charges for services, names and addresses of employees and their compensation, as well as "other business connections, etc., together with satisfactory proof of the good moral character of the applicant." The bureau would inspect the facility for sanitary conditions (and any evidence of prostitution). Furthermore, licensees were required to present a bond with the state, against which a complainant could bring action and have the business's license revoked.[31] Hotels that did not cater to alien travelers were not included in the Immigrant Lodging Places bill, thus ensuring that establishments with upper-class foreign, or American customers would not become politically mobilized to fight the new law.

By regulating immigrant lodging houses Kellor hoped to achieve a greater equality of condition between foreign- and native-born. Foreign hotel guests, with their different standards of service quality and price, would receive a minimum standard of service guaranteed by the state. The bureau produced pamphlets in various languages explaining the new law to the business owners and the foreign customers, and even paid for the printing of foreign-language rate cards "in order to insure a uniform standard and make it possible for the alien to know the terms and conditions under which the hotel has agreed to lodge him."[32]

As challenging as traveling through New York City could be, it was the final stage in a long journey from Europe or Asia to America. Most immigrants to the United States came for economic reasons, and finding work was the first goal of all new arrivals. New York City was the nation's largest labor market and had long operated according to the principle that the labor contract negotiated between two free individuals was sacrosanct.

In Kellor's opinion, a major problem affecting the immigrant labor market was a maldistribution of population. In 1910 half of New York state's nearly ten million residents lived in New York City, which also included Brooklyn. The rest of New York was rural, with a handful of cities—Albany, Rochester, and Syracuse—having more than 100,000 residents. Buffalo, with more than 400,000 residents, was the only large upstate city.[33] From the progressive perspective, southern New York was congested and suffered from poor housing conditions and expensive rents, both the result of high demand caused by overcrowding, while upstate New York had labor shortages and millions of acres waiting to be developed and farmed. Besides the perceived economic and health benefits of country life, distribution of immigrants to upstate rural areas would facilitate assimilation by separating immigrants from their urban neighborhoods and exposing them to American lifestyles and agricultural practices. Progressives assumed that European peasants, many of whom had been landless farm laborers, would return to agricultural work if given the chance.[34]

Realizing that immigrants would not leave New York City without accurate, timely information about opportunities elsewhere, the NYBII partnered with the NACL to disseminate information about upstate farm conditions in Polish and Italian at Ellis Island and in labor camps and foreign colonies in western New York.[35]

But few newly arrived immigrants had the capital necessary to start farms, and so the best that most of them could hope for was seasonal farm labor, which often resulted in the migrant laborer moving to the nearest big city for winter work or charitable relief. While the bureau was aware of the challenges facing would-be immigrant farmers, it was more concerned with labor distribution issues and the problems of real estate fraud than it was with devising means by which the state could assist potential new farmers through subsidies or loans. The NYBII did not concern itself with migratory farm labor, nor did it receive many complaints from agricultural workers.[36]

Many immigrants found work through employment agencies and labor contractors, both of which progressives viewed with great suspicion. Despite the conviction that private agencies were economically inefficient and morally dangerous, Kellor recognized that private agencies were more popular among foreign-born workers than public offices, and they did fulfill a need in the economy.[37]

Yet, like most progressives, Kellor still strongly advocated state regulation of private employment agencies, a power she was able to gain for the NYBII. In 1910 the legislature amended the powers of the Department of Labor, requiring its commissioner to create a registry of all employment agencies in

New York, regardless of whether they charged a fee for services. The new law also required that all employment agencies charging a fee be licensed by the state, following an inspection of their records and business practices (enforcement of this regulation in New York City was left to municipal authorities).[38]

These new labor regulations were designed to impact all employment service businesses operating in New York, not simply large ones, and represented a significant new intrusion of the state into private business activities. The registration law allowed the state government greater opportunity to know not simply who was operating an employment business, but also extensive detail about clients and the employers who hired them, including the locations and nature of the businesses, wages to be paid, nationality of alien clients, and their length of time in the country. Kellor and other progressives believed that with more efficient and accurate data collection, the state could more effectively facilitate the private market's distribution of labor, theoretically reducing unemployment, low wages, the mismatch of workers' skills to job requirements, and even urban congestion.

Labor camps in New York fell into three loose categories: public works (roads, canals and aqueducts, and public buildings); private industries (usually mines and quarries, brickyards, fertilizer plants, and canneries); and railroads. In 1910 the state's regulation of labor camps was limited to hours on public works, the time of payment of wages, and the establishment of company stores.[39] Lacking the authority to do anything more than inspect camp conditions, Kellor used the progressive tactic of investigation and publicity in the hopes of shaming both private businesses and public authorities into improving camp sanitation, housing conditions, and workplace safety.

Since the bureau did not have the budget for an extensive field survey of labor camps, Kellor first determined the number and location of camps in the state, and then had her investigators inspect a sample of them. In 1910–1913 the bureau investigated 689 labor camps, most of them permanent facilities, making observations of industrial and living conditions, health and sanitation, and facilities for education, recreation, and religion.[40]

Americanization, as the NYBII defined it, required the exposure of the immigrant to American culture and an "American" standard of living. Not surprisingly, the bureau staff deemed most labor camps a poor influence on immigrant workers. Many camps were remote, often temporary, and had no educational, recreational, or religious facilities; culture typically consisted of drinking and gambling. Even more upsetting to Kellor, the bureau's investigators found stark differences in conditions experienced by native-born workers versus immigrants in New York's public works camps: Native-born workers lived in permanent housing, while foreign-born laborers were often housed in shacks, stables, and abandoned boxcars.

Bureau investigators also discovered that American-born workers on public works projects dealt directly with the contractor for wages, food, and housing, while foreign-born laborers were required to go through a subcontractor, or *padrone*, who was responsible for supplying, housing, feeding, and paying the recruited workers. To Kellor this was an offense worse than the oft-unsanitary conditions her investigators found. Like most progressives, Kellor perceived the *padrone* system of contract labor to be the chief evil of New York's labor market, and she vigorously lobbied state and company officials to assume direct responsibility for their workforces.[41]

In labor camps run by private industries, the bureau found similar unsanitary conditions as those in public works camps, but not as much discrimination between foreign- and native-born workers. For mines and quarries, most labor camps were permanent sites, operating as company towns; while in the brickmaking industry, immigrant workers tended to live in foreign neighborhoods or colonies on the outskirts of nearby communities. The canning industry also provided permanent housing where workers could live with their families, but here, child labor was prevalent.[42]

Eliminating double standards and discrimination against immigrants was at the core of the bureau's Americanization policy. Attacking what she considered to be the bad citizenship behavior of native-born employers, Kellor argued: "It has been said that the laborers are used to these conditions and that camp life is on the whole wholesome. The answer to this is that this State is responsible for maintaining an American, not a foreign, standard of living, and, once admitted to this country, equal protection and opportunities are guaranteed to all."[43]

To address the problem of poor living conditions, particularly in remote camps, the bureau made a two-pronged attack. It first sought to pressure corporations by threatening to expose the unsanitary living conditions in their labor camps. The bureau frequently enlisted local reform groups, especially women's and health organizations, to lobby companies to improve conditions. Second, Kellor included permanent labor camps and foreign colonies in the Immigrant Lodging Places licensing bill, thus giving the bureau inspection authority over those places.[44]

But the licensing of immigrant lodging houses posed great challenges for the bureau because investigation and enforcement required staff to travel outside of New York City, which cost both time and money. Immigrant lodging places ranged from immigrant transfer stations—hotel-like businesses located near the port and rail areas of cities—to boarding houses and private homes in rural labor camps. Simply determining the number of such lodging places and then locating them was difficult. The bureau also quickly discovered that language difficulties hindered many foreign-born lodging house operators from filling out the license application, and Kellor insisted that the bureau inspect each applicant's facility before granting the license. The bureau's limited resources, insistence on personal inspection, and refusal to delegate to another agency hindered the regulatory effort; after one month, the NYBII had licensed only twenty-four lodging houses among 140 applicants.[45]

The practice of taking in boarders was one area where the bureau staff's middle-class values most clearly clashed with those of working-class immigrants. The immediate family—living in privacy in a single-family home—was the cornerstone of the American middle class. Although Kellor knew that few immigrant families could afford to live without the rent contributions of boarders, she still considered the presence of unrelated men or young unattached women in the home to be harmful to immigrant family life and an impediment to the adoption of American middle-class family organization.[46]

Equal protection under the law was another core middle-class value Kellor hoped to transmit to immigrants. Unlike in the labor camp inspection program, where she had promoted equality of condition, here she emphasized equality of opportunity. Many of the complaints the NYBII received centered around real estate fraud; legal representation, particularly for injury claims; notaries public; and banking. Many immigrants had difficulty seeking redress in these areas because of language barriers, cost of legal representation, and lack of familiarity with the American justice system.

Kellor considered the problem of illegal and unscrupulous business dealings threats to immigrants' Americanization because they had the potential to warp the foreign-born's perception of the sanctity of American law and hinder his ascendancy into the middle class through property ownership.[47]

Kellor and other progressives also measured assimilation by the degree to which immigrants relied upon native-born professionals versus foreign-born entrepreneurs. But American professionals had to be trustworthy and deserving of immigrants' business.

The solution to this problem of fraud on the part of professionals was twofold: Immigrants needed special assistance (particularly foreign-language-speaking court interpreters and free legal aid) to ensure equality before the law in fact as well as in theory, and foreign- and native-born doctors, lawyers, notaries, and bankers required state supervision to ensure ethical behavior.

The NYBII encountered its greatest challenge in trying to regulate immigrant banks. Much of this work overlapped with the bureau's efforts to supervise steamship ticket sales because many immigrant bankers sold train and steamship tickets, as well as handling deposits, loans, currency exchange, and transferring money overseas. Many immigrant bankers worked as employment agents as well, which also earned them progressives' disapproval. Progressives objected to immigrant banks because failures were common, and informal banking kept immigrants from participating in the formal, American banking system.[48] Participation in the mainstream economy, which was dominated by native-born Americans, was a key indicator of assimilation for progressives.

But immigrants used informal banks run by their countrymen because they felt (and were) unwelcome in American banks, which were typically located outside of immigrant neighborhoods and did not provide the wider range of services available at the immigrant bank, including foreign-language-speaking staff. Also, unlike European countries, most of which had strong central banks, America's banking system was notoriously unstable, and many immigrants believed that their money was safer in the corner grocer's safe than in the downtown bank.[49]

After the Panic of 1907, in which hundreds of banks failed, New York began to more closely regulate financial institutions. In 1910 and 1911 the state passed laws requiring the licensing of private banks and the auditing of the books belonging to applicants for private banking licenses. To avoid offending powerful foreign banks, which had had branches in New York City for many years, the 1911 revisions applied only to banks that had opened for business after 1892 (this was later amended to 1885). Another law prohibited corporations other than telegraph and express companies with railroad contracts from running money transmission businesses. This new regulation quickly forced many immigrant bankers to drop their non-banking services or quit the banking business altogether.

With these new laws, Kellor partnered with the state comptroller and Department of Banking to continue the investigations she had begun in 1909 for the New York Commission of Immigration. By October 1911 the bureau had examined the operations of 495 private banks: Forty-nine were licensed under the 1911 law, and only twelve were able to file the $100,000 bond to remain in the banking business. The rest either had left banking entirely or had gone to work for the steamship and express companies, which did brisk business in transferring money overseas.[50]

In tackling the banking industry, the bureau found itself dealing with powerful economic and politically connected actors. Immigrant bankers challenged each attempt by the state to regulate their businesses, first rejecting the assertion that their activities constituted banking, and then denying the state's right to regulate their businesses. While the state's position was ultimately upheld by the courts, the bureau experienced much more resistance to its efforts to regulate this arena of economic life than in other areas. There were hundreds of private banks in New York, and some found ways of getting around the 1911 banking laws by seeking various exemptions allowed under the law or by re-incorporating themselves as express companies, which were allowed to transmit money abroad.[51]

Investigating and lobbying for the regulation of hotels, lodging houses, employment agencies, labor camps, intercity transportation, and immigrant banks left the bureau little time or resources to promote immigrant education. In this area, the bureau was charged with collecting the names of newly arrived school-aged children and distributing them to education officials to help them enforce state truancy laws.

This project was largely unsuccessful because of a lack of clerical staff and the inability to locate many immigrants after they entered New York. The bureau experienced frequent delays in getting children's names from federal immigration officials, and then found that few school districts had the resources to follow up. Furthermore, many immigrants coming to the United States in part to escape European government surveillance provided incorrect or false information about where they intended to live.[52]

Although the Bureau of Industries and Immigration was designed to investigate conditions and provide information and recommendations to other governmental agencies, Kellor used her legal education to write and lobby for legislation when the bureau's investigations revealed what she considered to be a need for governmental intervention. Of the eleven bills Kellor and her staff prepared, only one was withdrawn and two were vetoed. The other bills—covering the sale and advertisement of steamship tickets; lodging house licensing; real estate fraud; and corporate and private banking—all passed and were signed into law by Hughes' successor Democrat John A. Dix. The bureau also endorsed bills and lobbied against legislation it believed to be harmful; in all these instances, it was successful. It even engaged in lobbying of legislation outside of New York, particularly in neighboring New Jersey and Pennsylvania, in an effort to prevent businessmen it considered unethical from relocating their activities outside of New York but still within range of New York's immigrant communities.[53]

Progressives' initial forays into immigrant social welfare and protection did not go unnoticed. Even before the bureau began its work, it encountered more powerful offices that resisted encroachment on their political turf. This was initially a problem in New York City, where Kellor frequently left enforcement of state laws to municipal officials as part of a campaign to improve relations between state and city authorities. Although most of New York's problems of immigrant exploitation were found in Manhattan, Kellor was not about to step on the toes of New York City officials. Other cities, particularly Buffalo and Rochester, also occasionally asserted their autonomy from state authority, particularly in the area of regulating employment agencies.[54]

Kellor was also careful to avoid any appearance of interference with federal immigration policy, and she stressed that the bureau's work concerned itself only with the conditions immigrants faced after leaving federal authority at Ellis Island. But this did not prevent her from being at the forefront of the lobbying effort to persuade Congress to create a Bureau of Distribution in the Department of Labor, and she also regularly urged the federal government to address the interstate nature of immigrant labor.[55]

Some businessmen and property owners, particularly immigrant bankers and lodging house owners, objected to the state's efforts to interfere with their businesses and the management of their property; and they challenged the bureau's authority in court.[56] The bureau's position was upheld, but the time spent litigating about the definition of the term "temporary sleeping quarters" took away from the enormous tasks of inspecting labor camps and licensing lodging houses.

By early 1913, when Kellor made her second report for September 1911–September 1912, the bureau had gained more credibility within New York's progressive community and state administration. As a result, the bureau was granted a larger appropriation of $14,800 to hire new investigative and clerical staff, increasing the total number of employees to fourteen in 1912. (Kellor continued to use her own funds to employ additional clerical help.) The bureau also gained the right to subpoena witnesses and interview them, and to adjust differences between private parties.[57]

Even with more resources, the years 1912–1914 were a period of evaluation and withdrawal from areas in which the bureau lacked the resources—particularly the staff—to implement Kellor's ambitious program of immigrant social welfare. In the area of labor camp inspection, the NYBII abandoned its goal of inspecting all work camps and focused instead on permanent facilities. Inspecting and licensing immigrant lodging houses remained a priority, but by the spring of 1912 the bureau realized that it had overreached and persuaded the legislature to amend the law to make the previously required filing of a bond now discretionary to encourage family lodging house owners to comply with the law. The bureau also quietly turned its educational work over to the New York Department of Education, which also had little interest or capacity to enforce school attendance laws.[58]

More problematic, the bureau continued to encounter interference from New York City officials in its efforts to enforce new state laws in the city. For instance, the NYBII had the power to inspect employment agency files, and agencies were required to keep such records on all of their clients and employees. But the municipal authorities of the communities where the businesses operated were responsible for licensing employment agents and enforcing the new state laws. In New York City, municipal officials, not wishing to increase their workload, often told employment agencies that they did not have to maintain records.[59]

Despite these setbacks and limitations, the Bureau of Industries and Immigration did impact the lives of some immigrants in New York. One indication that the bureau was having an effect was the increase in the number of complaints registered with the agency. In 1911–1913 the number of complaints the bureau received grew dramatically as immigrants learned through foreign-language newspapers and word of mouth about the services available at the bureau. The number of complaints registered with the bureau jumped from 515 in 1911 to 1,112 in 1912 and doubled again to 2,121 in 1913.[60]

But in a state as large as New York, with thousands of immigrants arriving every day, the bureau's efforts were a drop in the proverbial bucket. More active enforcement of the law by other agencies, particularly municipal law enforcement, would be required to significantly improve immigrants' early experiences in the United States.

Most studies of Americanization emphasize the intense scrutiny that progressives subjected immigrants' cultural practices in trying to measure assimilation.[61] But for progressives such as Frances Kellor, Americanization required equal, if not more, concern for the behavior of native-born Americans. If good American citizenship was to be determined by behavior, then state monitoring of citizens would be required. This the Bureau of Industries and Immigration did through its programs to rationalize New York City's transportation and hotel industries and to improve housing conditions in labor camps and immigrant lodging houses. The NYBII also worked to protect immigrants against crime by helping them to defend their rights and resolve their grievances with Americans and other immigrants.

In August 1912 Kellor returned to Chicago to attend the Progressive Party convention and to help Jane Addams of Chicago's Hull-House and Emily Greene Balch of Wellesley College to write the immigration plank of the new party's platform. While in Chicago she almost certainly renewed her acquaintance with Grace Abbott, a Hull House resident and the director of the Immigrants' Protective League.[62] Kellor also possibly met a Californian, Simon J. Lubin, who was in Chicago with California governor Hiram W. Johnson, who was nominated to be Theodore Roosevelt's vice presidential running mate.

Increasingly drawn into national progressive politics, Kellor left the Bureau of Industries and Immigration in January 1913 to work for the Progressive Party's Progressive Service.[63] She also broke with the North American Civic League after the Boston leadership responded to the 1912 Lawrence, Massachusetts, textile strike with industrial espionage and strikebreaking activities. Still pro-organized labor, Kellor persuaded the New York–New Jersey Committee to separate from the league and become the Committee for Immigrants in America in early 1914. The Committee for Immigrants in America and its sister organization, the National Americanization (Day) Committee, formed in the spring of 1915, soon became the leaders in the emerging national Americanization movement. Investigator Joseph Mayper served as acting chief investigator of the NYBII until social worker Marian K. Clark was hired as chief investigator in 1914. He left to work with Kellor at the Committee for Immigrants in America.[64]

In its first three years, the New York Bureau of Industries and Immigration developed programs and helped write and pass laws designed to create healthy social conditions in which immigrants would be able to successfully adjust to American society. The bureau's pioneering work in immigrant protection and advocacy in the name of making immigrants better Americans inspired the creation of similar agencies and commissions in New Jersey, Massachusetts, Illinois, Pennsylvania, and California. It was in California that progressives would pursue their most ambitious Americanization program.

2 ✠ The California Plan

The Commission of Immigration
and Housing, 1913–1917

The immigrant welfare activities of the New York Bureau of Industries and Immigration inspired progressives in other parts of the country to develop similar programs to address their states' immigration issues. California, already under the leadership of progressive Governor Hiram W. Johnson, followed New York's lead, and in 1912–1913 established first a temporary immigration commission and then a permanent agency, the California Commission of Immigration and Housing (CCIH).

The CCIH shared the New York bureau's progressive philosophy of Americanization through social environmental reform, but focused its energies on improving living and working conditions in California's agricultural labor camps. California progressives believed that an unsanitary and dangerous social environment fostered social unrest and threatened the health of the larger society, and so they sought to interject the state into farmers' businesses to ensure greater social stability and social justice.

But there were limits to progressive Americanization in California: Radicals who rejected state social welfare and market regulation were to be excluded from the new "American" community that progressives were working to create. The driving force behind California progressives' concerns about migratory labor, seasonal unemployment, and agricultural working conditions was a desire to undermine the Industrial Workers of the World (IWW). Seeing itself in competition with the IWW for the loyalty of California's poorest workers, the Commission of Immigration and Housing worked to improve both foreign- and native-born Californians' standard of living through progressive reform.

The CCIH was one of three commissions Johnson created in 1913 (the others were the Industrial Accident Commission and the Industrial Welfare Commission) to institutionalize the progressive belief that it was the responsibility of the state to assist individuals when the private sector failed to provide adequately for their social welfare. Between 1911 and 1915, California instituted several components of the national progressive agenda: women's suffrage; mothers' pensions; workers' compensation; and a ban on child labor. By 1913 the state had the structural political reforms of initiative, referendum, recall, nonpartisan local elections, and cross filing; a stronger Railroad Commission to check the powerful Southern Pacific "Octopus"; and a Board of Control to supervise state finances to ensure more honest and efficient government accounting. Working with Johnson was a coalition of progressive Republicans and pro-labor Democrats who dominated the state legislature.[1] Thus, as in New York, Americanization was simply one component of a larger progressive reform effort.

The first and longest serving members of the CCIH were: Simon J. Lubin, president from 1913 to 1923; the Archbishop of San Francisco, the Rt. Reverend Edward Joseph Hanna, vice president from 1913 to 1923 and president from 1923 to 1927; Paul Scharrenberg, secretary from 1913 to 1923; Mary Simons Gibson, from 1913 to 1922; and Dr. James Harvey McBride, from 1915 to 1927. These five individuals served at the pleasure of the governor and were uncompensated except for travel expenses to attend meetings. An executive director (first University of California–Berkeley economist Carleton H. Parker and then commission counsel George L. Bell) was responsible for implementing the policy decisions of the commissioners, running its San Francisco office and managing a staff of twelve to twenty-five employees.[2] Unlike in New York, the California legislature was fiscally generous, appropriating $50,000 for the new agency for 1913–1915.[3]

Among the rules governing the operations of the commission, the most important were the bar against employing aliens (which assured that all the CCIH's interactions with immigrants would be within the hierarchical relationship of citizen versus non-citizen) and the prohibition against lobbying for or against immigration.[4] This was a concession to the California Federation of Labor (CFL), which had opposed the commission's creation out of fear that the agency would be used by business groups to increase immigration and import strikebreakers. This enforced neutrality effectively shielded the commission from the heated national debate about immigration restriction. The fact that some members favored some types of restriction also meant that the requirement of neutrality on questions of federal immigration policy allowed the commissioners to maintain a consensus on domestic policy issues that was essential to their ability to work together harmoniously for several years.⁵

As was common with Progressive Era commissions, the CCIH was given several investigative powers to accomplish its charge of "expediting the distribution and assimilation of immigrants."⁶ It was to gather information and publish the results of its work; cooperate and coordinate with all levels of government to help immigrants become citizens; and inspect labor camps, tenements, lodging houses, employment agencies, immigrant banks, charitable aid societies, ports, and other immigrant receiving stations. The commission was also to determine whether state laws regarding wages, conditions, and child and female labor were being upheld, and to report to the proper authorities any illegal activities it discovered in its investigations. Ultimately, the CCIH was given the power to hold hearings and administer oaths, enter tenements and similar dwellings, and demand from all governmental officials any information it required to fulfill its mandated duties.⁷

The commissioners divided their work into four areas—complaints, labor camp sanitation, housing, and immigrant education—with each member responsible for a department. For the first ten years of the commission, Scharrenberg was responsible for camp sanitation; Gibson for immigrant education; McBride for housing; Hanna for the complaints bureau; and Lubin for legislation and lobbying.⁸

Simon Julius Lubin was the guiding force behind the Immigration and Housing Commission, and he largely defined its ideology and policies for its first ten years.⁹ Born in Sacramento in 1876, Lubin was the son of David Lubin and the nephew of Harris Weinstock, prominent Russian Jewish immigrants who owned the successful retail and wholesale dry goods store, Weinstock, Lubin & Co. Simon Lubin studied economics, philosophy, and sociology at Harvard University, graduating in 1903. While at Harvard, he did research on immigration for the university's Sociological Museum; and in 1902 he toured southern and eastern Europe. Wanting to become a social worker, Lubin pursued a master's degree in sociology and did settlement work at Boston's South End House and on New York's Lower East Side between 1904 and 1906. But in 1906 David Lubin became ill, and Simon was called home to run the family business. Although David Lubin recovered, he and Weinstock retired from business and devoted themselves to philanthropy and state service. Simon Lubin continued the family tradition of political activism, helping to found the Lincoln-Roosevelt League to elect Hiram Johnson in 1910 and joining the California Progressive Party in 1912.¹⁰

Lubin believed in using the power of government to mitigate and prevent the excesses of industrial capitalism, but he did not believe radical structural changes in American political economy were necessary or desirable. Lubin viewed radicalism and radicals, such as members of the IWW (popularly known as Wobblies), with a mixture of sympathy and disgust, but he did not consider them a serious social threat, unlike many Californians who were prone to hysteria about the IWW. As a political moderate, Lubin feared both radicals who sought drastic socioeconomic change and conservatives who were willing to undermine civil liberties in the name of combating radicalism.

Lubin also had unusually liberal racial views for the time, perhaps the result of being an observant Jew in a period of growing anti-Semitism. He opposed anti-Asian legislation and the exploitation of Mexican labor, and he supported the integration of African Americans while a student at Harvard. At his store, Lubin developed retirement plans and credit unions for employees, and experimented with a cooperative whereby customers would share in the business' profits. A supporter of mainstream unionization, he opposed the use of militias in resolving labor strikes, and favored arbitration.[11] He was a member of the California Conference of Social Workers, and he joined Frances Kellor's Committee for Immigrants in America in 1915. Although he worked full-time managing the store, Lubin's real love was social reform.

By 1913, after nearly a decade of work with settlements and Jewish organizations, Lubin had come to advocate immigrant social welfare managed by the state because he believed that private immigrant societies encouraged the segregation and isolation of minority groups. Lubin sided with those in the Jewish-American community who believed that minorities, especially Jews, should integrate themselves into American society rather than devoting their efforts to building national or religious homelands, either within or outside the United States.[12]

Mary S. Gibson represented California's well-organized women's movement. A native of San Jose, the fifty-eight-year-old Gibson was a leader in the California Federation of Women's Clubs (CFWC), a suffrage activist, and a Progressive Republican. A teacher before her marriage, Gibson and her husband, banker Frank Gibson, had been active in the kindergarten movement in Los Angeles and helped found that city's first Protestant orphanage. After Frank Gibson's death in 1902, his widow and her son, Hugh, spent four years living in Europe while Hugh studied at France's L'Ecoles des Sciences Politiques to become a diplomat. (He would become the U.S. ambassador to Belgium during World War I.) Upon returning to Los Angeles, Mary Gibson threw herself into civic activism and progressive politics. In 1910–1913 she campaigned vigorously for Johnson's gubernatorial election, California women's suffrage, and the Progressive Party ticket of Theodore Roosevelt and Hiram Johnson.¹³ Her appointment to the CCIH reflected Johnson's awareness of the political debt he owed Gibson and California's "organized womanhood."

The other Southern California representative, James H. McBride, was a sixty-four-year-old medical doctor from Pasadena who was interested in the relationship between sanitation and health. A Progressive Republican like Lubin and Gibson, McBride also worked extensively in the developing field of mental health, and was connected to California's eugenics program of sterilizing the mentally ill.¹⁴ Before settling in California, he had worked at New York City's Charity Hospital on Blackwell's Island, the Northern Hospital for the Insane in Oshkosh, Wisconsin, and the Hospital for the Insane in Milwaukee.¹⁵

The Rt. Rev. Edward J. Hanna was the liberal Catholic auxiliary bishop of San Francisco (archbishop after 1915), a Democrat, and a strong supporter of organized labor. A relative newcomer to California—the fifty-three-year-old priest arrived in San Francisco from his hometown of Rochester, New York, in February 1913—he quickly became one of the most respected church leaders in the state. Hanna's parents had immigrated from County Ulster, Ireland, to Rochester in 1837. The senior Hanna was a cooper and successful enough to send his eldest son to parochial school and then to seminary to become a priest. Hanna studied in Italy for eight years, earning a doctorate in sacred theology from the Urban College de Propaganda Fide in Rome. He returned to Rochester in 1887 to teach at St. Andrew's Seminary, where his fluency in Italian endeared him to his Italian parishioners. Unlike many Irish-American church leaders, Hanna greatly respected Italians, and he believed they had much to contribute to American culture. While in New York, Hanna had been a member of the North American Civic League for Immigrants, connecting the commission to important East Coast Americanization activists, such as Kellor.¹⁶

One member who stood out from his fellow commissioners was Paul Scharrenberg of San Francisco. A Democrat and one of the most powerful labor leaders in California, Scharrenberg was the secretary of the California Federation of Labor and editor of the *Seamen's Journal*, the newspaper of the Sailor's Union of the Pacific, then the largest union in the state. Along with virtually all western labor leaders, Scharrenberg opposed Asian immigration, believing that Asian immigrants undercut the wages of white workers and could not culturally integrate into European-American society.¹⁷ Not surprisingly, he advocated unionization as the solution to most labor problems. But Scharrenberg did not object to the state improving working and living conditions in areas where labor organization was weak or nonexistent, such as in agriculture.[18]

Scharrenberg's life most clearly reinforced his and the other commissioners' faith in the ability of immigrants to succeed in America through hard work, political participation, and cultural assimilation. Born in Hamburg in 1877, Scharrenberg went to sea at the age of twelve when his middle-class family suffered economic disaster upon the death of his father. He arrived in San Francisco in 1898 after his ship wrecked in Monterey Bay. Joining the Sailor's Union of the Pacific, Scharrenberg took classes in English, shorthand, and typing at the Young Men's Christian Association to help him in his new career, that of newspaper editor. By 1913 the thirty-six-year-old Scharrenberg was a "white shirt sailor," in contrast to the "dungaree sailors" who worked dangerous and dirty maritime jobs. He was a member of the Elks and the Commonwealth clubs of San Francisco, and his family was active in a local Masonic temple. The Scharrenbergs owned their own home, attended Trinity Lutheran Church, and lived a German-American, middle-class lifestyle.[19]

The California commissioners and the staff of the New York Bureau of Industries and Immigration shared many assumptions about immigrants, assimilation, and the methods of Americanization. The California commissioners believed that immigrants were at a cultural disadvantage in American society, but they would willingly embrace an American way of life if they were welcomed into the national community and treated as equals by the native-born. Once the social environment was improved or "Americanized," immigrants could overcome their cultural deficiencies through education provided by public schools and unions, and improve their lives through participation in American political culture. Anticipating criticism that its programs provided special privileges for undeserving non-citizens, the CCIH followed Kellor's line of argument, asserting the progressive theory of positive liberty: The only way immigrants could become equals of American citizens was through special assistance, preferably provided by government. With state action removing the barriers to assimilation, working-class immigrants would adopt middle-class values, such as upward mobility, self-control, hard work, dependability, and respect for private property. The adoption of these values would enable immigrants to move up into the American middle class, as Scharrenberg's, Lubin's, and Hanna's parents had done.

The commissioners had all been active in various private organizations and institutions prior to joining the CCIH, but they had all come to advocate a public approach to immigrant social welfare. Immigrants should be Americanized by the state and the local community, and those two levels of government were responsible for providing public education and sanitary living and working conditions in both urban and rural areas for all residents—citizens and aliens alike.

As Americanizers (or Americanists, as they called themselves), the commissioners believed assimilation to be natural, inevitable, and desirable; and they considered immigrants to be culturally flexible enough to integrate into American society. They also believed that American culture was dynamic and evolving, receiving contributions from many groups. Lubin argued: "If we take away those elements borrowed from the foreigner—the ideas of law from the ancient Roman, the conceptions of art and philosophy from the Greek, the doctrines and precepts of religion from the Hebrew, the teachings of science from the German and the French I am not quite sure whether there would be anything left of our American civilization."[20]

This was the settlement house theory of "immigrant gifts" to which the commissioners subscribed. This idea argued that immigrants contributed significantly to American culture and society, and therefore, advocates of Americanization should not seek to strip away immigrants' cultural heritages. Maintaining immigrants' cultural traditions also meant preserving their native languages, and, most importantly, not interfering in their religion. Lubin, in particular, objected to missionaries posing as Americanizers or the introduction of religion into Americanization work.[21]

But as much as the commissioners believed that immigrants' cultural traditions should be maintained, they also believed that immigrants' lifestyles could and should be changed, i.e., Americanized. When the members spoke of "immigrant gifts," they were not talking about the peasant traditions of Sicily or the Russian Jewish Pale, but of high European culture and history. Initially, the commission described immigrants assimilating into an already defined Anglo-American culture, rather than contributing their "immigrant gifts" to a country in the active process of developing a sense of nationhood.

The ability and desirability of Asian immigrants to assimilate was less clear. The same year that Johnson created the CCIH to protect and facilitate the settlement and adjustment of European immigrants, he signed the Alien Land Act, which prohibited "aliens ineligible for citizenship" (code language for Asian immigrants) from owning land.[22] The commission did not publicly oppose anti-Asian policies, but it also did not exclude Asians, Mexicans, or other immigrants of questionable whiteness from participating in its Americanization programs. Even though the commissioners were unwilling to challenge the denial of citizenship to Asians and the de facto segregation of African Americans, Mexicans, and American Indians, they frequently spoke out against discrimination and "race prejudice" against any group. The members were able to envision a type of social citizenship that included nonwhites within the limits of social convention. In interactions with non-Europeans, socioeconomic class counted more than color: Westernized Asians and upper-class Mexicans were in less need of Americanization than their working-class countrymen.

Despite the similarities in philosophy between the NYBII and the CCIH, there were important differences. Kellor and her staff viewed immigrants primarily as victims of American society and capitalism; the California commissioners were sympathetic to the foreign-born, but a sense of defensiveness underlay the commission's talk of immigrant gifts and its paternalistic social welfare policies. Unassimilated immigrants were both a cultural threat to American society in terms of unclear loyalties and different values and customs and the source of a potential for violent misunderstandings that could disturb America's social and economic order.[23] This fear was soon to be realized, even before the members of the commission were appointed.

In late July 1913 Ralph and Jonathan Durst, owners of the world's largest independent hop ranch, recruited approximately 2,800 men, women, and children to pick hops on their 609–acre ranch outside of Wheatland (Yuba County), north of Sacramento.[24] Half of the pickers were immigrants, representing twenty-seven nationalities, including Syrian, Mexican, Spanish, Japanese, Lithuanian, Italian, Greek, Polish, Cuban, Puerto Rican, "Hindoo" (Punjabi Sikhs), and Swedish. About 700–800 pickers were white American "hoboes," and the rest were local families "of the better middle class. . .in the habit of using the hop and fruit seasons to get their 'country vacations.'"[25]

To attract such a workforce, the Dursts advertised plentiful water, free firewood, and tents for rent at 75 cents per week. What the would-be pickers found at Wheatland were nonexistent camping facilities; low and fluctuating wages of 90 cents per 100 pounds of hops picked; an unusually high standard for picking and cleaning the hops; and a camp store that only accepted the growers' scrip. Within days, dysentery, diarrhea, malaria, and even typhoid appeared at the ranch because of the lack of garbage cleanup and poor sanitation. Angered by the conditions, thirty workers formed a loose chapter of the IWW and began agitating for a walkout. Fearful of the workers' sudden assertiveness, the Dursts called the authorities; and in a shootout at a workers' meeting, two pickers, a deputy sheriff, and the Yuba County district attorney were killed, and several people were wounded. The sheriff's posse fled, as did most of the workers; and the next morning the state militia was called to bring order to a deserted hop ranch.[26]

The Wheatland hop fields riot of August 3, 1913, has been interpreted as either a spontaneous protest against intolerable conditions or the work of opportunistic radicals looking for a fight.[27] The violence at Wheatland was the result of several unusual factors, but unsanitary conditions was not one of them. When the CCIH began investigating labor camps after the riot, it discovered working conditions as bad as or worse than Wheatland throughout the state's agricultural industry. The chief difference between Wheatland in 1913 and previous years was that when the Dursts attempted to squeeze their labor supply by cutting wages, labor suddenly and unexpectedly snapped back. The presence of the IWW in California farm labor was behind this new assertiveness.

The violence at Wheatland sharply redirected the attention of the CCIH from immigration via the soon-to-be-opened Panama Canal to the harsh conditions under which thousands of migrant laborers worked. The presence of the IWW at Wheatland also introduced limits to the commission's progressive approach to Americanization and its vision of a diverse yet harmonious society.

Faced with a national public outcry about the violence, and unwilling to turn to the state's Bureau of Labor Statistics for help, Johnson asked the newly appointed Immigration and Housing commissioners to investigate labor conditions, especially in agriculture, and to advise him on California's growing problem of seasonal unemployment, a phenomenon also tied to large-scale farming.[28]

By the time of the Wheatland riot, California agriculture was defined by a firmly established system of large farms and ranches owned by corporate interests growing diverse and specialized crops and employing migrant field workers for seasons of sometimes only a few weeks.[29] Logging operations in coastal Northern California and the eastern mountains also employed large numbers of unskilled workers who labored in dangerous and unhealthy conditions. In 1913 California agriculture was a mosaic of crops: citrus and other orchards in the south and inland valleys; truck farming of fruits and vegetables along the coast; and large tracts of grains and ranching in the central valleys. Diversity, specialization, and commercialization defined California agriculture after the turn of the twentieth century.

But what remained constant in California's "factories in the fields" was their dependence upon migratory hired labor, unlike most states in which the majority of agricultural landowners farmed their land with family help and the occasional assistance of non-landowning workers.[30] California's migrant workers traveled from spring to fall and from south to north picking crops. In the winter, they found seasonal work in canneries, mills, and other factories, or they were unemployed and sought charitable relief. Most migrant workers were men, but women and children also worked in the fields; and laborers were of all nationalities.

Like most agricultural states, California had devoted what little bureaucratic infrastructure the state had to the promotion and protection of its agricultural products, not the regulation of farm labor.[31] The Bureau of Labor Statistics gathered information and opposed state involvement in most labor issues. The California Board of Health devoted itself to combating infectious diseases, not monitoring the health of migrant workers and the diseases they carried with them. Existing state law established no standards for health or safety for labor camps.[32]

Suddenly Johnson's go-to agency for social research, the Commission of Immigration and Housing, conducted thirty-five studies between the fall of 1914 and January 1915, when it submitted its first annual report. Eight of these reports examined migratory labor and the IWW, and ten were housing surveys. The commission also conducted two studies of seasonal unemployment in the winter of 1913–1914 (a period of recession nationally) and the spring of 1915; investigated the causes of the Wheatland riot for the state and the federal commissions on industrial relations; established a program to inspect and clean up labor camps; and created a complaints bureau to mediate and resolve disputes.[33]

In the midst of all this research, in the spring of 1914 Lubin proposed to the governor and the state legislature that the CCIH, Bureau of Labor Statistics, or a reorganized California Board of Health, enforce the state's weak 1913 Labor Camps Sanitation Act to improve working conditions in California agriculture. The health and labor boards were unwilling, so the commission took over from the Board of Health the responsibility of inspecting labor camps. Enforcement of the law remained with state health officials until the CCIH gained this power in 1915.[34]

The commissioners knew that resistance or interference from the employers of farm labor would make their sanitation campaign far more difficult, if not impossible, to achieve.[35] The members also realized that they had to do more than simply reveal to the general public the existence of unsanitary conditions in California's labor camps; they had to persuade farmers and camp operators to run their businesses in a better, more "American" fashion. This was defined primarily in terms of sanitation: baths and showers; trash cans and incinerators; fly-proof toilets and kitchens; and vermin-free eating and sleeping areas.

The commission did not have the power to enforce the 1913 Labor Camps Sanitation Act when it began its inspection program in the spring of 1914, so the CCIH relied heavily upon persuasion to influence growers and camp operators to improve conditions. Adopting a conciliatory tone, the CCIH argued that camp operators simply did not know how to improve conditions, and thus did not intentionally seek to avoid or violate the law. The commission commented: "Our contact with the employers of labor made it clear to us that the undesirable sanitation was not the result of intentional carelessness but rather a relic of early California days when our people were good naturedly willing to put up with almost any housing conditions."[36]

In the commission's report on the causes of the Wheatland riot, executive director Carlton Parker promised that the CCIH would "condemn all dangerously unsanitary camps, and will, if necessary, prosecute the employers to the full extent of the law, which imposes both a heavy fine and imprisonment."[37] This tough talk was now noticeably absent from the commission's rhetoric, nor was there any hint of the critical attitudes held privately by Parker or the commissioners.[38]

To persuade—rather than force—employers to improve conditions, the CCIH worked with the California Board of Health to produce "An Advisory Pamphlet on Camp Sanitation and Housing," which was distributed widely to labor camp operators and farmers. The primary purpose of the camp sanitation pamphlet was to provide employers with ways to avoid diseases, which were a threat to workers, employers' profits (a sick laborer was an unproductive laborer), and the larger community. The pamphlet gave the operator of a would-be model camp recommendations on where to locate the facility; the services and supplies needed; the necessary maintenance to keep a camp sanitary; and blueprints, diagrams, instructions, and other technical data, such as cost estimates for materials. Unlike in New York, where the Bureau of Industries and Immigration inspected facilities and lobbied for improvements, the California Commission conducted inspections but also sent staff to assist with actual construction of model camps when needed.

In the advisory pamphlet—and the operative word was "advisory"—the commission appealed to employers' desire for greater productivity, arguing that improved sanitation would increase the efficiency of farmworkers, which would in turn justify the expense of improving conditions. Improving camp conditions would allow employers to fulfill their moral and legal obligations while simultaneously increasing their profits. Cleaner camps would also help address the problems of high unemployment and turnover, the commission believed, as men would be more willing to work longer at cleaner facilities.[39]

The advisory camp sanitation pamphlet was the CCIH's first public foray into agricultural labor issues, and was popular with farmers. However, the advisory nature of the booklet set the tone for the commission's dealings with large employers of farm labor. Lacking strong enforcement power and frequently unwilling to use the authority it did have, the CCIH depended on the goodwill of employers to do its bidding. The growers determined the conditions in their labor camps—not the commission—and the growers and the commissioners knew it.

Even so, the CCIH was not a pliant tool of welfare capitalists seeking to avoid state interference in their business operations.[40] The state, not growers, initiated the cleanup of labor camps after the Wheatland riot. The CCIH was conscious of and realistic about its capacity and the limits of its power; its goal was steady improvement of working conditions while respecting the rights of property owners.

Despite the unequal power dynamics, between 1914 and 1916 the commission developed an efficient system of camp inspection and re-inspection, collecting extensive statistics and notes on each facility and working closely with operators to build sanitary camps. The commission's inspection program was modern for its time, with inspectors using automobiles to reach isolated camps, taking photographs (and sometimes moving pictures) to document conditions, and recommending the latest technology for incinerators, waste disposal, and plumbing. The CCIH inspected ranches and camps in the following industries: hops; berries and orchard fruit; beets; grapes; construction; roads and highways; lumber; mines and quarries; oil; and railroads. The commission employed a minimum of three camp inspectors and as many as ten at one time between 1914 and 1916.[41]

However, the commission's camp sanitation program operated under severe limitations. Simply locating the thousands of camps in existence each summer was challenging, particularly because most were located in isolated rural areas. Automobiles were a necessity because train transportation did not allow the investigators to reach all of the camps in a season.[42]

Another hindrance to the CCIH's work, at least in the eyes of the commissioners, was farmworkers themselves. According to the commission's inspectors, many migrant laborers appeared indifferent or apathetic to conditions. Instead of complaining when a camp's sanitation was bad, they simply quit and searched for other work. The CCIH believed it needed to correct the attitude of camp operators and camp workers to improve conditions.[43] Through extensive propaganda posted in camps, the commission tried to teach working-class laborers middle-class standards of living: regular bathing, no spitting or outdoor urination, dependability, etc. Gradually, after much effort and outreach, farmworkers began to file complaints with the commission; although by 1917 these reports numbered fewer than 200 per month, far fewer than the number of nonfarm work-related grievances filed with the CCIH's Complaints Bureau.[44]

Despite these problems, the commission persisted. A significant motivation was the knowledge that the IWW was trying to organize migrant farmworkers along industrial (versus craft) lines. The CCIH hoped to persuade migrants to rely upon the state for assistance in dealing with employers rather than joining the Wobblies.

The CCIH supported labor organization, but only along craft lines. The commissioners doubted that unskilled laborers, particularly in agriculture, could be organized into AFL/CFL-style unions, and feared that the one union of farmworkers, the Fresno-based Agricultural Workers Organization, Local No. 400, was affiliated with the IWW.[45]

It was in large part because of Scharrenberg's membership in the California Federation of Labor that the commission accepted craft unionism as a critical tool to incorporate the foreign-born into American society. The CCIH believed that the California Federation of Labor's willingness to work within the industrial and political systems was the proper method of dealing with the negative consequences of industrial capitalism. Radicals such as the Wobblies, with their rejection of craft organization, the wage system, and even capitalism, were unacceptable to the CCIH. The IWW and similar organizations were dangerous to the craft union's dual function as counterweight to the power of capital and assimilator of immigrants into an American culture that was constantly being infused with new arrivals.

The CCIH established a labor policy based on the idea that the environmental conditions surrounding California's labor system needed to be changed, not the wage-labor system itself. To counter the influence of radicals among California's most exploited workers, the CCIH sought to improve the physical conditions that it believed drove people to radical organizations such as the IWW.

Although the CCIH did not consider the IWW to be a revolutionary threat, it was highly conscious of the union's role as a catalyst for violence, as at Wheatland. Rejecting conservatives' calls for violent repression of the IWW as illegal and self-defeating, the commissioners were concerned about the Wobblies' efforts to organize migrant workers. With this in mind, executive officer Parker and legal counsel Bell began monitoring the IWW in the summer of 1914, when the commission was in the middle of its first season of camp inspections. In addition to collecting newspaper clippings on "the IWW & terrorism," and on "incendiary fires & fires of unknown of suspicious origin," Parker proposed "that we send [camp inspector Fred C.] Mills into the Wheatland district to work and bum in it till hop picking begins around Aug 1st and that if necessary add [camp inspector R. Gordon] Wagenet to the district as a hobo."[46] This investigation of the Wobblies, which had Scharrenberg's full support, ultimately involved most of the commission's camp inspection staff, who reported on any IWW activity in the areas where they were working.[47]

The commission's surveillance of the IWW indicates the boundaries of its definition of social citizenship and its willingness to use social knowledge as a tool to repress civil rights. As a progressive agency, the Immigration and Housing Commission viewed the systematic collection of information as the first step toward developing sound public policy. In their investigations of the Wobblies, Lubin and Parker saw the use of social knowledge as essential to both effectively eliminate the IWW as a force in California labor relations and to justify its elimination. Carefully gathered "accurate" information was critical to the CCIH's efforts to de-legitimate intolerable ideas and behaviors.

The commissioners defined membership in the American national community in terms of ideology, not nationality. Any alien could become an American by changing his behavior and embracing American civic values, such as representative democracy, political equality, and capitalism. Individuals who rejected those values—such as the Wobblies—could not be considered good Americans.

Although the commissioners accepted ordinary labor organization and opposed the violent repression of unions, they did not treat the IWW as they did other legitimate "American" organizations, such as the American Federation of Labor, because the IWW did not respect the nation's legal or capitalist economic systems. The AFL was acceptable to the CCIH because it accepted the existence of private property, wage labor, and capitalism; the IWW rejected all of these things, and so violating Wobblies' civil rights was not seen as a problem.

By 1917 the CCIH had developed an effective program of inspecting agricultural labor camps, collecting and resolving immigrants' complaints, and monitoring IWW activity. The commission's labor camp inspection and complaints resolution work was similar to that of the New York Bureau of Industries and Immigration, but the Californians' concern about labor radicalism was distinctive and reflected the unique conditions of California's unskilled labor market. The interrelationship among immigration, migratory labor, and radicalism did not exist in New York, where Americanizers' focus continued to be on the experiences of immigrants in urban areas.

3 ❋ An Unhealthy Relationship

Eugenics and Americanization
in New York, 1914–1917

Americanization gained momentum as both a social movement and public policy in 1913–1915. In 1913 California created its Commission of Immigration and Housing, Massachusetts appointed a temporary Commission of Immigration, and Pennsylvania added a Division of Immigration and Unemployment to its new Department of Labor and Industry. Rhode Island created a temporary immigration commission in 1914.[1] Frances A. Kellor, the former chief investigator for the New York Bureau of Industries and Immigration, was working to build a national movement through the Committee for Immigrants in America while her successor, Marian K. Clark, was making her own mark on the NYBII.[2]

Clark maintained Kellor's programs, but she changed the underlying ideology of the bureau's Americanization policy. Unlike Kellor, Clark was a eugenicist who advocated immigration restriction as the best way to shape American culture and society. According to Clark, the genetically unfit had to be excluded from entering American society so the American "melting pot" could have the right kind of human ingredients to forge a new and stronger race of Americans.

The new chief investigator's attempt to graft eugenics onto Americanization weakened the bureau politically. As conservatives attacked the NYBII for interfering with businesses' labor practices, New York progressives were unwilling to defend the bureau because of Clark's advocacy of a eugenics-based immigration policy. Politicians who represented New York's many immigrant neighborhoods were also less inclined to support the bureau because of Clark's anti-immigrant language. As Americanization gained more attention nationally, the NYBII—the nation's first immigrant social welfare agency—should have been at the forefront of this new movement. Instead, Clark had to fight just to keep the bureau politically and fiscally alive. In 1915

New York's education officials initiated their own Americanization program, separate and independent of the NYBII, which focused on adult education.

The introduction of eugenics into New York's immigrant social welfare policy reveals the ideological elasticity of both prewar Americanization and eugenics.[3] On the surface, these two movements had much in common: Both relied heavily upon state power for social engineering. Both placed a premium upon expertise (especially eugenics, with its pretensions of science). And although eugenics was concerned with the genetic makeup of individuals and Americanization with personal identity, both emphasized observable behavior.[4] Most importantly, the slippery language and weak theoretical bases of eugenics and Americanization allowed both movements to be all things to all people.[5]

Although eugenics and Americanization were part of the larger progressive movement, the two were, nonetheless, incompatible. Americanization sought the transformation of the immigrant from foreigner into American, and this transformation was to occur by means of an improved social environment. Even the educational approach to Americanization was based upon the assumption that the immigrant could assimilate himself through instruction. But the Mendelian form of eugenics dominant in the United States rejected the power of the social environment and depended entirely upon biology; a genetically damaged individual was dangerous regardless of the type of environment he or she was in. The only solution was to segregate and exclude the "defective" from the rest of the population.[6]

Clark's conservative vision of Americanization challenged progressive assumptions about the role of the social environment in fostering assimilation. Some progressives advocated immigration restriction as a way of facilitating assimilation by cutting off continuously replenishing sources of foreign cultures. Assimilation was possible, but only in a more culturally stable, Anglo-American-dominated environment.[7]

But eugenicists denied that assimilation of the foreign-born was biologically possible under any conditions. Cultural traits were hereditary, and disease-carrying genes could never be eliminated—only made recessive. Descendents of genetically healthy immigrants could potentially assimilate, provided that they intermarried with eugenically correct native-born Americans, but the foreign-born could not change their culture any more than they could change their genetic composition or their ancestry.

Clark supported immigration restriction because she deemed most immigrants to be socially undesirable and culturally and biologically inferior. What distinguished Clark from other "racial nationalists" was that she did not single out particular immigrant groups, such as the Chinese or Jews, for exclusion or removal. Instead she reserved her ire for aliens who had been deemed defective by state medical, prison, or charity authorities.[8]

Clark maintained all of the bureau's policies started by Kellor and even improved the operations of several programs, but the philosophical differences between the two chief investigators nonetheless influenced the bureau's approach to Americanization after 1914. Kellor and Clark disagreed about virtually every major social question related to immigration and the methods of Americanization: restriction, employment, language, and relations with other agencies and organizations.

Kellor used increasingly harsh tones in advocating social change in the mid-1910s, but she retained her belief in environmental Americanization. In her 1916 book *Straight America* (which argued that Americanization was essential to military preparedness for war), Kellor demanded that immigrants assimilate by adopting "American standards" or be deported. But she still placed equal, if not more, responsibility on the native-born to improve working and living conditions for immigrants and to eliminate prejudice. Immigrant assimilation could not occur without native-born participation in the process; Americanization, according to Kellor, was still a two-way street.[9]

Clark, on the other hand, made such frequent and strong statements in favor of exclusion that as early as 1915 she was forced to "correct an erroneous impression" that the bureau had jurisdiction over admissions when it did not. She ignored the fact that the NYBII was legally barred from involving itself in issues of immigration exclusion and restriction, and frequently editorialized on the need for federal officials at Ellis Island to be stricter in their scrutiny of entering aliens.[10]

Kellor considered disorganized, unrationalized labor markets and the failure of government to stabilize them to be the chief causes of unemployment and economic inefficiency, and she rejected arguments that immigration restriction would strengthen the economy or stabilize society. Instead she favored government regulation of private employment agencies and the establishment of public employment offices and labor exchanges to help immigrants find productive work.[11]

For Clark, unemployment was not caused by international events, such as war, or internal policies, such as tariffs and antitrust measures, or even the size or composition of the labor market. Rather, unemployment was the result of the large number of the "unemployable," who were unemployable because of their genes. "The diagnosis [of unemployment] must reach before and beyond into the realms of the heredity of the bulk of our population and particularly of our foreign population," Clark argued.[12]

Kellor rejected the English-only branch of the Americanization movement as ineffective and a sure way to discourage immigrants from learning English and adopting Anglo-American cultural practices.[13] Always practically minded, Kellor believed that the foreign-language press, interpreters and translators, and multilingual state employees all played useful roles in interpreting American society for non-English speaking immigrants until they learned English.

Clark shared Kellor's enthusiasm for "eliminating the hyphen," and she agreed that Americanization was necessary for military preparedness; but the new chief investigator was skeptical of the value of multilingual communication with immigrants. In addition, Clark believed that non-English-speaking immigrants retarded the assimilation of their children, who were being educated in New York's public schools.[14]

Most critically to the bureau's initial success, Kellor had actively worked to develop close partnerships with Ellis Island commissioners William Williams and Robert Watchorn. Clark, however, routinely railed against the new immigration commissioner, Frederic C. Howe, for what she called the dumping of "defective" aliens upon the taxpayers of New York.[15] The number of aliens excluded or deported for "mental and physical defects" was no more than a few hundred to one thousand (out of hundreds of thousands admitted) each year before 1921, but Clark complained vociferously that the federal government was lax in its screening procedures.

After the European empires escalated into World War I in the summer of 1914, the U.S. Bureau of Immigration began releasing excludable aliens to family or friends upon the payment of a bond and the promise that the aliens would present themselves for deportation once the war was over.[16] Clark was incensed that the federal government did not detain these inadmissible individuals. Convinced that immigration authorities at Ellis Island did nothing to track bonded aliens after they had been released from federal custody, Clark tried, unsuccessfully, to enlist the aid of eugenics leader Charles B. Davenport and his patroness, Mrs. A. E. Harriman, to "develop a plan whereby the state might be relieved of the burden of not only deportable insane aliens, but also alien criminals, and other dependants."[17]

Clark also demanded that the federal government reimburse the New York legislature for the costs the state bore in supporting sick, mentally ill, poor, and criminal aliens in its public hospitals, poor houses, and prisons. She proposed that New York be granted most, if not all, of the head tax revenue the federal government collected from immigrants entering at Ellis Island.[18]

Clark's definition of Americanization incorporated exclusion as an essential component of shaping the nation's character, yet she could not decide whether a new "American type" was in the process of being created or being overwhelmed. Nor did she give deep thought to which national elements should be used and which rejected. "It is a necessity and a duty for the state to assist in the process of the amalgamation of its alien population and to thus accelerate the development of an American type," Clark argued. But "if the United States expects to move until it develops an American type, then exclusion should be enforced as long as the accession of the alien born exceeds the native born, otherwise we are clearly moving away from an American type and increasing the national problems of a heterogeneous population."[19]

This fear of a heterogeneous population was the crucial distinction between Kellor and Clark. Kellor did not object to the criteria the federal government used to determine entry into the country prior to 1921, but she opposed further state involvement in the international labor market through quotas or a literacy test. She had no fears about the religious, national, or racial nature of immigration to the United States, and she believed that the "New Immigrants" from southern and eastern Europe could successfully assimilate and contribute much to American society.

"What is an American?" Kellor asked in 1916. "Is he an Anglo-Saxon racial type, and if so, by what law? *Do we desire him to be this*? I do not despise the conclusion of ethnologists, but they seem to have so few conclusions and so many theories. And the root of them seems to be, not experience, but apprehension." She added, "Meanwhile, I see all around me valiant Americans, Southern European by birth and tradition, Americans now in spirit and loyalty and *tendency*."[20] Thus, Kellor rejected restrictionists' arguments as being determined by fear, not reason or experience.

Clark, on the other hand, wanted the federal government to play a much more active role in predetermining who was allowed to enter, and thus, have the opportunity to become a U.S. citizen and mix with the native-born population. By excluding undesirable immigrants, and sterilizing "defective" aliens and citizens, the United States would develop a healthy citizenry and a stable society.[21]

It was this strong belief in government's power to re-engineer society that motivated Clark in her immigrant protection work for the bureau, not any faith that the environment influenced individual behavior. She defined Americanization more in terms of naturalization than with the adoption of "American" social customs or values (which Kellor increasingly emphasized).[22]

Yet Clark's strong advocacy for a eugenics-based immigration policy effectively divorced the bureau's protective social work from the progressive foundation Kellor had established. Under Clark's supervision, the Bureau of Industries and Immigration would continue to collect complaints, monitor the Battery, inspect labor camps, and license immigrant hotels and lodging houses, but the ideological purpose of these efforts was gone. New York's chief Americanization agency had become, in effect, hostile and disdainful of the constituency it was supposed to serve. Clark would implement progressive policies while articulating an anti-progressive, conservative ideology.

Despite the ideological confusion Clark introduced into New York's Americanization policy, the NYBII's services improved under her direction. By 1914 the bureau's staff had stabilized to approximately twenty, about ten of whom were investigators, which allowed Clark to systematize inspection work. Sharpening their focus on lower and midtown Manhattan, bureau staff observed conditions at New York City's rail terminals and piers daily, with particular attention paid to the arrival and departure of large steamships.[23]

Despite this monitoring, transportation problems through Manhattan persisted. The NYBII continued to pressure steamship and railroad companies to change their business practices, take more responsibility for their customers, and more tightly control their employees. The NYBII really wanted more state supervision (beyond its own efforts) but after five years of publicity about the problems at the piers and rail terminals, bureau staff knew that neither the state nor the city governments were interested in devoting significant police resources to this issue.[24]

Furthermore, while Kellor had been very successful in getting measures passed by the state legislature, Clark had less luck with the New York City Board of Aldermen.[25]

Clark did have a few notable successes, however, and she built upon Kellor's work with other state and city agencies to try to resolve some of the ongoing problems the bureau encountered, particularly at the Port of New York.

For instance, railroad and steamship agents had long overcharged second-class ship passengers for the cost of upgrading train tickets to first-class. Steamship agents did a brisk business selling second-class ship passengers train tickets to their final destination; however, these tickets were for specially designated immigrant trains, which passengers caught at Ellis Island. (Passengers met there and were ferried to New York or New Jersey rail terminals.) Since second-class ship passengers did not enter the United States at Ellis Island, but rather at the piers of New York Harbor, Hoboken, and Jersey City, they had to pay for the ferry trip to Ellis Island to catch the crowded immigrant trains, a cost of time and money that most second-class passengers were unwilling to pay. However, the charge to upgrade the second-class passengers' train tickets to those that allowed them to travel directly from one of New York's train stations raised their total travel costs to more than the cost of the first-class train ticket, behavior that was illegal under the Interstate Commerce Act.[26]

By 1915 Clark had successfully persuaded the steamship companies to discontinue the sale of prepaid train tickets to second-class steamship passengers. She was also able to persuade the New York City commissioner of licenses to ban baggage checkers from charging for services already included in the cost of the steamship ticket, and to require that luggage checking be paid for at a central office at the pier, thus discouraging the charging of "special fees."[27] In addition, Clark persuaded the city commissioner of licenses, the municipal police department, and the surveyor of the port to more strictly control the granting of runner, porter, cab, and hack licenses, and to enforce the rules that governed these permit holders to operate in the city.

However, this partnership created more work for the bureau. In 1915 Clark negotiated to have her staff temporarily investigate the character of all applicants for licenses from the port surveyor, the police department, and the commissioner of licenses until the passage of a city ordinance that would consolidate the granting of all city permits in the hands of the licenses commissioner. (Enforcement of the rules of these licenses would continue to be shared by all of the agencies having authority to operate at the Port of New York.)[28] This proposed ordinance was not adopted, however, and licensing remained divided between the commissioner of licenses and the New York City police.[29]

But Clark's work with the licenses commissioner was not totally in vain. She was able to persuade the commissioner to inspect New York City and Buffalo employment agencies and report any violations to the NYBII for further investigation. This collaboration resulted in greater compliance with state employment law; prior to this agreement, New York City officials actively obstructed the bureau's efforts to regulate employment agents.[30]

NYBII and license commission inspectors ensured that employment agents posted the state's employment law and labor contracts in both English and the predominant language spoken by the agency's clients. Bureau of Industries and Immigration inspectors also investigated complaints against employment agents. Employment agencies and other organizations involved in the distribution of immigrants outside of New York City were now visited monthly by NYBII staff, and these businesses were required to submit their books for inspection each month as well." Immigrant lodging places were also inspected monthly, instead of annually, as had been the case under Kellor.[32]

The inspection of labor camps also increased under Clark's management, and she systematized the process of investigating labor conditions outside of New York City, sharing information with the state departments of health and education. Although the new sanitary code of 1913 gave the Health Department the authority to inspect labor camps, the Bureau of Industries and Immigration continued to do the actual work of inspection, in large part because the responsibility for sanitary code enforcement fell upon local health officers, whom Clark considered to be incompetent.[33]

In 1915 the Public Health Council established a statewide sanitary code for all labor camps, mandating that the operator of a new camp notify local health officials of the existence of the facility, and requiring a successful inspection to get a permit to operate if the camp was to have more than ten people for more than six days. The new regulations, built upon the industrial code established in 1914 for cannery housing, detailed specifications for water sanitation, bathing, toilets, and garbage facilities, location of camps and animal stables, and general cleanliness.[34]

In New York the most significant housing problems in labor camps existed in the canning and brick making industries. Clark was able to pressure the canning industry into adopting the state sanitary code as the basis of the industry standard for health and sanitation, but she had little luck with the brickyards, which employed large numbers of African Americans as well as immigrants. Besides grossly poor living conditions, bureau inspectors found widespread employment of youth and very long working hours that violated labor laws governing the employment of minors. As in California, where the Commission of Immigration and Housing encountered many native-born farmworkers, the Bureau of Industries and Immigration had no hesitation in trying to improve conditions in brickyards, although many of the workers were native-born black Americans.[35]

A series of complaints in 1915 brought the new issue of medical fraud to the attention of the bureau. In many instances, the crimes committed were traditional frauds in which thieves posing as doctors "diagnosed" immigrants with life-threatening diseases and then charged high fees for bogus cures. The bureau encountered the problem of unlicensed doctors much less frequently.

But the justification for the bureau's involvement—that most of the patients were immigrants—was flimsy, especially since New York had county medical societies that regulated medical practitioners. Furthermore, the most flagrant violators of the law often moved from state to state, making the issue one for the American Medical Association and/or federal law enforcement.

Yet, the bureau persisted in investigating the problem, using investigators posing as immigrants to try to entrap unlicensed and malpracticing doctors. In 1915 Clark and an assistant, Samuel Auerbach, worked with the New York County Medical Society to investigate forty New York City doctors who were later arrested and prosecuted for unethical behavior. After these investigations, the bureau was finally able to persuade the medical society to crack down on medical frauds.[36]

In 1915 the NYBII partnered with the New York County Lawyer's Association to implement another sting operation, this one of "bogus attorneys," most of whom were operating as notaries public without being licensed as either notaries or attorneys. Working with bureau counsel Miles O'Brien, investigator Auerbach spent a year posing as an immigrant needing legal assistance; and in October 1915 sixteen individuals were arrested and prosecuted by the city for practicing law without a license.[37]

The bureau also saw an increase in the number of complaints about immigrant banks. Under Kellor's management, the bureau had backed off its investigations of immigrant banks after initially pressuring the state to more closely regulate private financial institutions. But as war conditions in Europe disrupted the transmission of money between the United States and European banks, more problems with immigrant banks emerged. The NYBII began to receive a growing number of complaints about immigrant bankers and steamship agents collecting money to be sent abroad but not delivering the funds. Clark proposed that the bureau play the role of a centralized office that would oversee the transmission of funds abroad, but state banking officials rejected the idea.[38]

The end of Clark's first year as chief investigator saw the resurgence of conservatives in New York politics, which, combined with progressives' dismay at Clark's advocacy of eugenics and restriction, hurt the NYBII politically. Progressive reform of all kinds became more vulnerable in 1914, as conservatives blamed a sharp downturn in the economy on progressives' criticism of Big Business, their interjection of the state into labor markets, and the cost of progressive regulations. In November 1914 conservative upstate Republicans regained control of the New York legislature and began rolling back progressive policies and defunding social welfare programs.[39]

In 1915 Democratic Governor Martin H. Glynn signed legislation that reorganized the Department of Labor over the strong objections of social progressives and organized labor, who feared that protective labor laws would be weakened. The Bureau of Industries and Immigration survived the reorganization and even saw its budget increase slightly to $34,540.[40] But Clark had alienated important allies in the state legislature.

During the mid-1910s, there were enough naturalized foreign-born voters and their American-born children, particularly in New York City, to elect pro-immigrant representatives, a few of whom were foreign-born themselves.[41] These mainly Democratic representatives and their constituents objected to Clark's continued advocacy of eugenics and immigration restriction. On the other side of the political aisle, conservative Republicans were unhappy with the bureau's camp sanitation program and its interference in the labor market. Clark and the bureau were thus caught politically between a conservative rock and a liberal/progressive hard place.

In 1916 the bureau's appropriation was almost eliminated; only after vigorous lobbying by Clark and her allies was funding restored.[42] Even then, the appropriation was cut down to $25,494, almost all of which was needed to run the New York City office. With fewer personnel, the bureau did fewer investigations and did not inspect labor camps at all between July and September in 1916.[43] At the same time that Kellor was raising money from New York's wealthiest residents for her Committee for Immigrants in America, Clark had to fight for every dollar in the bureau's budget.

Clark's advocacy for immigration restriction and eugenics ultimately caused the bureau to lose the leadership of New York's Americanization movement, as state education officials began to develop their own program to match the direction that Americanization was moving nationally. Educational Americanization offered more possibilities for success, particularly with children, who were already required to attend school. And few could argue that providing English literacy and civics education was not useful to the foreign-born men who wanted to naturalize. In addition, educational Americanization eliminated the possibility of conflicts with employers, landlords, labor contractors, and other entrepreneurs whom the Bureau of Industries and Immigration inspectors sought to regulate.

The Americanization program of the New York Department of Education was dedicated to improving and expanding adult education programs. English literacy was a major component of this new policy, and state education officials clearly linked English literacy and fluency with assimilation; to be a good American was to speak, read, and write in the English language. Illiterates were a "menace" to their communities and society at large.[44]

This new focus on education narrowed the definition of citizenship to mean legal citizenship and the rudimentary civics knowledge required for naturalization. This emphasis on naturalization meant that the primary constituents of New York's educational Americanization policy would be men, since alien women could not naturalize on their own. Women derived their citizenship through their husbands and fathers until 1922, and New York did not grant women suffrage until 1917.

Preparation for naturalization increasingly became a significant part of educational Americanization in 1915 after the federal Bureau of Naturalization reported that more than 85,000 aliens had failed to complete the naturalization process since 1906 because they did not meet the educational requirements.[45]

In response to this newly discovered problem, cities began creating programs to help immigrant men study for their naturalization interviews. In New York City, the Board of Education started to tailor classes to students' level and need; students who were enrolled in evening schools and who had petitioned for naturalization received specialized instruction in civics and U.S. history; and teachers were trained to assist men in applying for citizenship. New York City also opened evening "naturalization bureaus" in September 1915 to make it easier for working men to file papers of intent to naturalize.[46] In Buffalo in the spring of 1916, the county court extended its hours by one day per week; while in Rochester the naturalization court clerk began offering a citizenship class to ensure that men who applied for their second papers were successful in completing the naturalization process.[47]

As useful as these programs were for their students, they lacked clear philosophical goals in relation to assimilation, and there was no coordination with the Bureau of Industries and Immigration or any other New York state office that worked with the foreign-born. Americanization, as defined by the Department of Education, was primarily the adoption of the English language in public life, and the rudimentary civics knowledge required for naturalization. How these things might contribute to assimilation and a new conception of what it meant to be an American citizen were not considered.

By 1915 Americanization had become a national movement, as progressives interested in immigration had established a nationwide network through such journals as *The Survey Graphic* and *Immigrants in America Review* and national and regional conferences. But New York was quickly losing its position as pioneer and leader of this new movement, as the Bureau of Industries and Immigration became distracted with Clark's efforts to graft eugenics onto

Americanization, and the New York Department of Education pursued its own theories of how to best encourage assimilation.

In 1915 Kellor, now in charge of the Committee for Immigrants in America, reported in the *Immigrants in America Review* that "California, through the broad policies adopted by its Commission on Immigration and Housing, is rapidly overcoming New York's original lead, in a large understanding of the immigrant's need."[48] A key aspect of that policy in California emphasized adult education, which was soon to become the cornerstone of Americanization. The CCIH's other program—housing reform—would not be embraced by the larger Americanization movement.

4 ✣ Americanizing the Home

Housing Reform and the California Home Teacher Act of 1915

In California, Americanization initially centered on interventions in the labor market through the Commission of Immigration and Housing's regulation of agricultural labor camps. However, the CCIH developed two other important programs, housing and education, that were like two sides of the same coin, reflecting progressive understandings of the home. This view of the home was both traditional—preserving the middle-class value of privacy—and progressive—asserting the state's right to intervene in the home and regulate private property to protect the community against disease and disorder. While the commission's housing program sought to clean up the exterior appearance of immigrants' homes and neighborhoods, the education program tried to inculcate foreign-born women with new, Anglo-American values that would inspire immigrant families to transform their homes from within. Both programs were concerned with demonstrations of good citizenship through pride in and care for the home. However, the CCIH experienced far greater resistance to its efforts to change California's housing laws than it did to its ideas about education for foreign-born adults.

Believing that the social environment shaped individuals' behavior and values, the commissioners defined clean and safe housing conditions as a crucial tool in assimilating the foreign-born into American society. Since immigrants frequently congregated (and were segregated) in poor neighborhoods, housing needed to be included in the commission's Americanization work, both to improve immigrants' standard of living and to better distribute foreign-born residents among the native-born population, where they would have more exposure to an "American" way of life.

The commission's housing division shared with the camp sanitation department the problems of indifference on the part of local authorities and opposition from property owners, builders, and real estate interests. While the camp sanitation program was relatively successful in challenging employers' right to an unregulated labor market, the commission's housing policy was tentative because of the commissioners' awareness of the strength of private housing interests and their reluctance to directly challenge the sanctity of private property ownership.

Internal constraints also limited the housing program. CCIH commissioner James H. McBride's distance from the main office in San Francisco (he lived in Pasadena) left the management of the division to the new executive officer, George L. Bell, who also had responsibilities running the commission's day-to-day operations.[1] Unlike the camp sanitation division, which had a growing staff and a hands-on, San Francisco-based commissioner in Paul Scharrenberg, the housing division had one inspector, twenty-two-year-old Caroline Schleef.[2]

Despite these limitations, the commission initiated its policy of housing reform in the spring of 1914. Armed with the authority to enter "tenement houses, buildings and dwelling places" to ensure compliance with state and municipal building ordinances, Schleef regularly toured the state inspecting conditions in both urban and rural areas, although she visited cities more often than she did small towns. Schleef's practice was to walk through neighborhoods, inspecting individual dwellings, talking to residents and sometimes property owners, and making lists of violations and what would be required for structures to come into compliance with state codes. These lists would be given to both the property owners and local health and/or building officials. Unlike labor camp inspectors, Schleef did not do cleanup work herself.

Schleef's initial surveys of working-class neighborhoods in San Francisco, Los Angeles, San Diego, Fresno, Stockton, and several smaller cities in 1914 and 1915 revealed just how large a task the commission had set for itself in trying to improve housing conditions in California. Even the smallest towns had "shack districts," and many small cities lacked sewer systems or garbage collection.[3] Indoor plumbing was a luxury for many Californians living outside of urban areas.

The state of California's regulation of housing was minimal in 1914. The only state legislation covering structures was the Tenement House and the Hotel and Lodging House acts, and the state left enforcement to municipal health and building departments. Privately owned, single-family dwellings were not covered by any state legislation, but they were the responsibility of the municipalities in which the structures were located. The state was responsible for dwellings in unincorporated areas but lacked inspection and enforcement mechanisms. Public housing had not yet been invented.

With the state lacking the will or ability to enforce its own housing laws, communities had little incentive to enforce the state codes or initiate their own. In 1914 few cities, with the exception of Los Angeles and San Diego, had any interest in or capacity for housing regulations.[4] Faced with these facts, the commission initially decided to concentrate on trying to secure the uniform enforcement of the state's Tenement House Act and the Hotel and Lodging House Act, mainly by lobbying cities to enforce the laws within their jurisdictions.[5]

As part of this effort, in 1915 commissioner McBride wrote two manuals for housing reform, "An A-B-C of Housing," and "A Plan for Housing," and used them to proselytize among community groups to improve housing and sanitation conditions and to lobby for more and stronger legislation. It was in the "A-B-C of Housing" and "A Plan for a Housing Survey" that the commission's progressive philosophy of housing reform and its relationship to Americanization, class relations, and citizenship were most clearly revealed.

Housing was a key element in the CCIH's approach to Americanization because the commissioners believed it was within the home that good citizenship was bred. Commission president Simon J. Lubin commented: "The home is most often a reflection of the house. It is hardly conceivable that an indecent house could cover a decent home."[6]

As environmentalists, the commissioners rejected the assertion by many conservatives that foreign-born residents naturally gravitated toward slum living, crime, and radicalism. Instead, the commissioners argued, the poor, criminals, and radicals were victims as well as products of their surroundings. The CCIH argued that "before a man should be asked to become a good American by being worthy of his surroundings, those surroundings should be made worthy of a good American."[7]

Good housing also reflected good Americanism on the part of landlords as property owners. The commission placed strong emphasis on the need for native-born residents to "Americanize" their foreign-born neighbors, workers, and tenants by being living examples of American ideals of democracy, equality, opportunity, and cosmopolitanism. Good citizenship was displayed in the physical condition of people's homes, yards, and businesses, and could be demonstrated by both citizens and aliens.[8]

Commission members possessed a Jeffersonian romanticism about rural areas, and considered cities a source of disease, crime, overcrowding, and social unrest. The commissioners shared an assumption of the importance of dispersing former European peasants onto the land to work as farmers, thinking this kind of life healthier than living in overcrowded urban areas. Immigrant resettlement to the countryside was deemed more healthful, economically efficient, and socially desirable. Furthermore, distribution of immigrants would match the agricultural skills of people who had once been farmers with California's need for a strong agricultural economy based on small family farms versus large corporate agriculture.[9] The commissioners' idea of good housing was one of clean, sturdily built, privately owned, single-family homes with yards and gardens.

In his manuals, McBride emphasized the need for large amounts of open space between dwellings, reflecting the California middle class's desire for lawns, gardens, parks, and the privacy that came with such space. However, the middle-class ideal of private family space was difficult to achieve in working-class neighborhoods where immigrants lived in cheaply constructed, overcrowded apartments with thin walls and no clear division between living, dining, and sleeping space. "The problem is to have detached homes with the conveniences of private bath, good plumbing and lot space at a price that laborers can afford to pay," McBride commented.[10]

As a doctor, McBride saw a direct relationship between housing conditions and public health, and he focused primarily on sanitation versus construction.[11] He frankly expressed his belief, that "it is less how a house is built, though this is important, than whether it is clean or dirty, sanitary or insanitary."[12]

This overarching concern about sanitation could also be seen in the commission's worry that poor neighborhoods negatively impacted the health of the larger community. In its publications about housing conditions, the commission actively tried to cultivate a sense of the threat of the dangers of bad housing on the part of the native-born middle class. The CCIH repeatedly argued that diseases refused to recognize the borders between rich and poor neighborhoods, and people living in unsanitary conditions spread illnesses. Most of these warnings centered around various cities' Chinatowns, where Chinese immigrants were segregated.[13]

To rectify this threat of disease, the commission insisted that communities take responsibility for their housing stock through the activism of private groups and municipal government.[14] The role of the state government was to legislate minimum standards for construction and sanitation and to enforce those standards proactively.

In progressive fashion, the CCIH relied primarily upon legislation to solve California's housing problems. Yet some things that impacted the housing market, such as low wages and racial discrimination, the commission was unwilling to challenge with legislation. The CCIH endorsed the minimum-wage crusade conducted Katherine Philips Edson, president of the Industrial Welfare Commission, but this support was qualified. While Edson directly challenged the employers' right to set low wages and insisted on the right of government to legislate economic ceilings and floors, the Immigration and Housing Commission relied on persuasion and the voluntary goodwill of employers, builders, and landlords to improve housing conditions.[15]

Racial discrimination was another area in which the CCIH was inconsistent. It firmly rejected racial prejudice and regularly urged that immigrants, especially darker-skinned ones, be treated equally with native-born whites. For instance, the commission opposed discrimination against Chinese immigrants, insisting, "The 'one standard for the Chinese, another for the white man' shall not be permitted in any civilized community." Such a statement was not often heard in California at the time.[16]

Yet the commissioners said nothing about restrictive lease or mortgage contracts designed to racially shape neighborhoods and communities that the real estate industry was beginning to use in California in the 1910s.[17] Nor did the CCIH loudly object to the racial discrimination that resulted in de facto segregation of Asian and Spanish-speaking immigrants and African Americans. Moreover, when the commissioners spoke of the importance for immigrants to become farmers and landowners, they were not talking about the Japanese immigrants who were eagerly buying and leasing farms throughout the state.

The commissioners also did not subscribe to racially essentialistic explanations for African-American, Mexican, and Asian ghettos. The dirt and overcrowding in poor communities was because of poverty and landlord prejudice, not biological or cultural peculiarities of different immigrant groups, as many white property owners argued. Residents had a right, regardless of skin color or nationality, to a uniform and healthy standard of housing, guaranteed and enforced by the state.

Although the commission sought state regulation of housing conditions, it believed it was ultimately the responsibility of citizens working individually and collectively to improve the quality of housing in California. Recognizing that inspections and enforcement of housing laws were reactive and ameliorative, the commissioners thought that the long-term solution to California's housing problems was public awareness and demand for strong laws, consistent enforcement, civic pride, and personal motivation to build and maintain good housing. These were the hallmarks of a strong "American" community.

This philosophy was also intertwined with the CCIH's ideology of Americanization: The foreign-born would be absorbed into American society by receiving the benefits of progressive social reform. This understanding of Americanization fit in with the commissioners' paternalistic view of immigrants as culturally and economically disadvantaged in American society. Not surprisingly, given the members' elite backgrounds, the one group whom the CCIH did not closely work with on housing reform was the foreign-born. Although the commission did consult with immigrant societies, it did not organize immigrants into lobbying groups to pressure municipal and state agencies or other power brokers to improve housing conditions or to reduce or stabilize rents, the high cost of which discouraged adequate maintenance.

In fact, the only instances in which the CCIH came into direct contact with immigrants in regards to housing was when Schleef inspected communities' "foreign quarters." It was in these encounters when the relationship between the state agency and the immigrant was most equitable. As a young woman, the housing inspector did not, in her physical appearance, give the impression of a powerful government official; and since it was months or even years before a neighborhood was reinspected, it was easy for foreign-born homeowners, landlords, and tenants to ignore Schleef's recommendations and demands.[18] Many property owners successfully avoided dealing with the commission housing staff entirely.[19]

At the same time, foreign-born tenants began to use the commission's housing division the way they used the Complaints Bureau: to file grievances against their landlords in the hope that the CCIH would pressure property owners to make desired changes.[20]

Despite the widespread publicity the commission attracted with its exposés of housing conditions throughout the state, McBride realized that going city by city to survey and then lobby to improve housing conditions were never-ending tasks. Although progressives controlled the state legislature and the governorship, conservative defense of private property rights and resistance to the imposition of state power over local prerogatives was still formidable.[21]

Ultimately, the CCIH gave up lobbying and proposing legislation at the local level and turned to consensus-building among public and private housing activists on behalf of stronger regulation and better housing construction. The goal was now to prevent the construction of inadequate shelter and encourage the building of good housing.

This required stronger legislation. In early May 1916 the commission invited representatives of the fourteen largest cities in California (twelve participated) to attend a "Housing Institute" to design a statewide bill to regulate the construction and maintenance of tenement houses, hotels, lodging houses, and other such dwellings.[22]

The primary purpose of the 1916–1917 Housing Institute was to work to amend tenement and hotel laws and combine with them a third bill for other dwellings. This new three-part law would cover all of California, not just unincorporated areas. The consolidated bill would then be submitted to the 1917 state legislature. A secondary goal was to bring housing in California up to one "American" standard set by the state.[23]

The CCIH was also eager to build stronger coalitions and networks with the building industry, which had previously lobbied successfully against the commission's efforts to strengthen the state housing codes. Architects, contractors, hoteliers, and real estate boards were invited to participate in the institute "to convince them that they should welcome, not oppose, housing laws."[24]

After meeting several times in May 1916–January 1917, the institute participants "practically unanimously" approved the final drafts of the bills written by the CCIH. Approved by the state legislature in late May, the institute's housing bills were signed by Governor William D. Stephens in June and became effective on September 1, 1917.[25]

With the passage of the 1917 state housing law, the commissioners could feel a sense of accomplishment, yet the triumph rested on shaky ground. Of all its programs, the commission's housing work was especially vulnerable to attacks from conservatives.

Although some farmers were unhappy with the camp sanitation program, labor camps were removed from the sight and minds of Californians, most of whom lived in urban areas. Housing reform, however, struck literally at home, potentially affected all California residents, and directly challenged the individual property owners' right to manage their property the way they chose.

In addition most Californians associated slums and tenements with eastern cities and refused to accept the fact that their communities also had these urban ills. The commission spent much of its energies in 1914–1916 simply trying to convince local authorities that housing problems existed in their communities. As the housing division increasingly relied on regulatory legislation to improve conditions, many private property owners and builders began to angrily criticize the CCIH for its challenges to property rights.[26]

The commission experienced much less public resistance to its education work, which focused primarily on immigrant women.

In April 1915 Governor Johnson signed Senate Bill 427, the Home Teacher Act, into law. Commissioner Mary Simons Gibson had written and lobbied for the bill, which authorized school districts to hire "home teachers," a new type of instructor responsible for assimilating adult immigrants through education. Home teachers were to work in the homes of their immigrant pupils, instructing them in English, sanitation and hygiene, home economics, and American civics and citizenship.[27]

With such a list of duties, the home teacher represented a new and a more overtly cultural approach to Americanization than the commission's housing and labor camp inspection programs. Those programs sought to assimilate immigrants indirectly by changing the environment in which the foreign-born lived and worked to meet an idealized "American" standard that reflected their adoption of middle-class values. The immigrant education program attempted to assimilate immigrants through state intervention into their homes, and directly addressed questions of national identity, citizenship, and cultural practices.

Of the various elements of the Americanization movement, the role of progressive women in immigrant education has received the lion's share of scholarly scrutiny because of its ideas about female citizenship and the power dynamics between native-born instructors and foreign-born and nonwhite students.[28] Yet the significance of educational Americanization is that it shifted responsibility for immigrant education from the private arena of settlements and women's clubs to the public school system. Educational Americanization programs promoted social stability through cultural homogeneity and class interaction, while helping to professionalize teaching and laying the foundation for adult education.

Although state support for education increased during the Johnson administration, California had no statewide policy of immigrant education to meet the needs of a rapidly growing foreign population in the 1910s, nor were education authorities eager to establish one.[29]

As the commissioner in charge of immigrant education, Gibson was the primary architect of the commission's education work, and she eagerly rushed in where state educational leaders feared to tread. She moved easily between the two worlds of public male politics and private female organizations, and it was her skill in both arenas that determined the initial success of the Home Teacher Act.

As with the other commission programs, educational Americanization was paternalistic, in accordance with Gibson's view of herself as "committed to the protection of the immigrant."[30] She believed strongly in the settlement house concept of "immigrant gifts," and she objected to racial segregation in the public schools.[31]

Another significant life experience deeply influenced Gibson's attitudes and policy toward immigrant mothers: that of infant death. Mary and Frank Gibson had four children, but only their son Hugh survived infancy; and he nearly died of polio at the age of four. Hugh's frail health as a child caused Gibson to tutor her son at home for several years. This experience reinforced Gibson's belief that as a parent she shared with other mothers a bond that transcended cultural, racial, or class barriers. The philosophy of the universality of the experience of motherhood was the cornerstone of Gibson's education program for immigrant women.[32]

Gibson designed the Home Teacher Act to support immigrant families and to enable foreign-born women to fulfill their roles as mothers and citizens. Unlike New York, Massachusetts, and other eastern states developing Americanization programs in the 1910s, California had granted women the vote in 1911. An alien woman married to a native-born or naturalized American citizen automatically became a citizen with the right to vote in California elections. Thus, immigrant women's political citizenship as well as their social citizenship were issues in Americanization in California.[33]

Gibson believed that as potential citizens, foreign-born women should be incorporated into the larger society, yet she viewed immigrant women more in terms of their roles as mothers than as potentially politically active citizens. In this way, Gibson belonged more to the nineteenth century's organized women's movement than to the emerging feminist movement of the early twentieth century. This was ironic, given Gibson's own vigorous political activism and her decision in 1920 to quit the Republican Party over its denial of leadership positions to politically active women.[34]

In addition, Gibson departed from progressive and conservative women active in women's clubs, patriotic societies, and settlement houses when she rejected their strategy of trying to Americanize foreign-born mothers through their more assimilated children.[35] Although she supported the assimilation efforts of the public schools and the kindergarten and playground movements, Gibson believed that immigrant women needed to be Americanized themselves through such programs as the Home Teacher Act.

As soon as Johnson appointed her to the CCIH, Gibson began to develop her ideas about how foreign-born women could be integrated into the English-speaking American community. She defined the problem of unassimilated immigrant women as one of isolation of the mother and a corresponding weakening of parental authority that threatened to undermine society.³⁶

This weakening of parental authority was supposedly caused by the assimilation of youth. As immigrant children learned English and adopted American cultural practices, they frequently came into conflict with, and sometimes felt alienated from, their less assimilated parents due to the adults' lack of understanding of, or resistance to, American culture. This alienation, progressives believed, led to juvenile delinquency and crime.³⁷

Immigrant children encountered Anglo-American culture in the local public schools, which became a source of intergenerational conflict within immigrant families. For example, Leonard Covello's teacher changed his name from Coviello to Covello, believing it would be easier to pronounce. Not surprisingly, his parents were outraged, his mother declaring: "A name is not a shirt or a piece of underwear. . . . Now that you have become Americanized you understand everything and I understand nothing."³⁸

American educators valued the public school for its power to assimilate, but Gibson believed that it was not enough to simply allow the school to inculcate immigrants into American culture; the school had to self-consciously promote American values through formal Americanization programs. The goal of Americanization education, Gibson argued was "to begin making the right kind of Americans—Americans who are on the way to become intelligent and broadminded citizens." Schools were to be "melting pots, from which shall come the metal of Americanism."³⁹ Teachers were encouraged to present "American," i.e., middle-class, standards of living and behavior, while emphasizing that immigrants brought with them important values and traditions that enriched the nation's cultural life. Instead of causing family conflicts, teachers were to reinforce parental discipline by teaching immigrant children to respect their parents' cultural heritages.⁴⁰

The negative consequence of the school's ability to assimilate the young was the danger of leaving the parents, especially mothers, culturally behind and dependent on their Americanized children. Gibson warned Americanizers who sought to influence foreign-born adults through their assimilated children: "Suddenly we discover that in our zeal to Americanize the foreign children we are destroying parental discipline."⁴¹

The home teacher was to be the solution to this problem of isolated, powerless immigrant women by educating the mothers to better understand American culture and to give them the cultural tools to enable them to reassert their traditional authority as parents. In addition to the practical matters of teaching English and Anglo-American-style home economics, home teachers were to uphold the proper place of the mother in the home—a place of authority and reverence. Gibson informed her colleagues in the California Federation of Women's Clubs (CFWC), "The Home Teacher steps squarely across the path of those who would Americanize foreign-born parents through their children," because "such a process of Americanization would give to those children the one added touch of authority needed to demoralize completely the relation between parent and child."[42] Thus, the goal of home teaching was to "educate the entire family instead of discriminating against that important member, the mother."[43]

The bill to create the Home Teacher Act passed overwhelmingly, but school districts were slow to embrace the concept of home teaching. The legislation authorized school boards to employ "teachers to be known as 'home teachers,'" but since districts were not required to, none immediately did so. The lack of state funding for local school districts to pay these new teachers also discouraged them from dipping into their own budgets to do so.[44] With the approval of Senate Bill 427, Gibson had her Home Teacher Act but no home teachers, no curricula, and no administrative structure responsible for recruiting, training, supervising, and paying visiting instructors. She also had only one assistant, former teacher and settlement house resident Ethel Richardson.[45]

With the Home Teacher Act now law, Gibson concentrated her efforts on convincing school officials that immigrant education and home teaching were necessary issues to which they should devote resources. She knew from her experience with women's reform projects, such as kindergartens, penny lunches, and pure milk stations, that if she could prove the value of home teachers, California's educational leadership would adopt it into the school system. Gibson chose Los Angeles as the place to experiment with the home teacher concept because it was her home, and its clubwomen were well organized. Also, the city's public schools already offered evening classes in English and civics, and diplomas from these courses were recognized by the Los Angeles naturalization courts as being part of students' citizenship work.[46] Richardson was also on hand to help from her home in Pasadena.

Gibson also heavily relied upon her women's club friends to lobby local school and city officials and to gather information about immigrants, illiteracy, and educational opportunities (or lack thereof) in their communities. Gibson then used this data to convince city leaders that spending more on education would reduce juvenile delinquency, which would, in turn, decrease overall tax expenses for preventing and punishing crimes committed by immigrants.[47]

Not willing to wait for August when Senate Bill 427 went into effect, Gibson used money from the Daughters of the American Revolution to hire Amanda Matthews Chase in June 1915 to be California's first home teacher and assigned her to the Amelia Street School in Los Angeles. Chase was a former resident of the Los Angeles College Settlement house and had taught at a girls' school in Mexico City for twelve years. Since half of the residents of the Amelia Street School's neighborhood were Mexican, the fact that Chase was fluent in Spanish was vital.[48] Gibson intended Chase's work to both demonstrate the need for home teachers, and show how domestic education of immigrant women might be done.

In Gibson's mind home teachers were to occupy a special place between the neighborhood school and the immigrant home, serving as a link between the two institutions. Although the connection could and should run both ways, home teachers were first and foremost teachers subordinate to their affiliated schools' principals, just as the day teachers were. In this respect, home teachers were more of an extension of the public school into the foreign home than a neutral conduit between the school and the family.

The home teachers were also to act as a connection between the immigrant family and social welfare agencies, yet they were to avoid overlapping the work of social workers to prevent agency turf wars.[49] Unlike evening school instructors, whose classes often included American citizens, home teachers were to teach aliens only.

In her home teaching, Chase fulfilled many of the functions of a social worker or visiting nurse. She began her work by simply going door to door around Amelia Street School, visiting the families of the school's students and informing them of her availability and services. She routinely visited these families, checking up on illness, parental unemployment, student truancy, and other family problems on behalf of the school's day teachers and social workers. Once she developed a relationship with the families, she organized classes, which tended to be segregated by nationality for linguistic and cultural reasons. Chase's first classes were comprised of Mexican and Japanese women.[50]

In her classes Chase emphasized speaking over reading and writing English, and focused on teaching words and phrases involving household tasks, shopping, and local travel, such as riding a street car to the grocery store. She also taught sanitation and gave housecleaning tips; took children to a local clinic for general examinations; helped people find jobs; and even distributed charitable aid.[51] Although Mexican and European immigrant women were eligible to vote if they or their husbands were naturalized, Chase did not teach the theories and mechanics of American citizenship, politics, and government.

With Chase at work in Los Angeles, Gibson next devoted her attention to the recruitment and training of home teachers. With the passage of the Home Teacher Act, a new subset of the teaching profession had been created; yet it first had to be formally developed. Of great concern to Gibson was that teachers of immigrants be properly trained in the pedagogical differences of instructing immigrants versus native-born Americans and in teaching adults versus children. The first home teachers were women who were already working as evening school instructors. However, evening schools were not exclusively for immigrants, and Gibson hoped to develop home teaching as a distinct field and to improve the quality of teaching in California's adult education classes. Without effective teaching, Gibson rightly feared that immigrant adults would refuse to attend evening English-instruction programs or to participate in home teaching.

To attract students of normal schools—teacher-training institutions—to go into immigrant education, and to assure school boards that home teachers would be properly trained and certified by the state, Gibson proposed in December 1916 that the California Board of Education issue a special certificate for teachers of English and civics in evening classes, which the board agreed to do.[52] But the superintendent of public instruction, Edward Hyatt, was unexcited about Gibson's ambitious plans; his office would provide publicity and textbooks for would-be home teachers, but little else.[53]

To persuade local communities, normal schools, and state education officials to more strongly support the concept of home teaching and to create a pool of trained home teachers from which school districts could hire, Gibson conducted a demonstration of home teaching in Los Angeles in the summer of 1917.

Working with the Young Women's Christian Association's International Institute and the Los Angeles State Normal School Department of Home Economics, Gibson, Chase, Richardson, and normal school professor Ruby Baughman organized almost thirty classes for immigrant mothers using thirty-seven students and recent graduates from the Los Angeles Normal School as instructors. The Los Angeles home teachers followed a program similar to the one that Chase had instituted two years earlier, with the teachers combining social service visits with English and home economics instruction.[54]

In addition to encouraging the special training and certification of home teachers, Gibson had to address the problem of the lack of textbooks and lesson plans for would-be home teachers. There was no developed curriculum or school supplies for the first home teachers, so Gibson and Chase began writing manuals. A booklet entitled *The Home Teacher: The Act, with a Working Plan and Forty Lessons in English* was published in October 1915. A report on *A Discussion of Methods of Teaching English to Adult Foreigners, With a Report on Los Angeles County* was issued in 1918. Chase wrote a two-part *Primer for Foreign-speaking Women* in 1918, and Mrs. H. K. W. Bent compiled *A Manual for Home Teachers* for the CCIH in 1919.[55]

In her manuals, Chase recommended that would-be home teachers divide their days into home visiting in the mornings, and teaching mothers in the afternoons and/or evenings, preferably in the school's home economics classroom or "cottage," which was to serve as a tangible model of middle-class Anglo-Saxon American life for immigrant women to emulate. She stressed the importance of being sympathetic; not gossiping; and never referring to poor immigrant neighborhoods as "slums." They were also not to refer to immigrants as "cases," as social workers did.[56]

Chase further instructed future home teachers in her *Primer for Foreign-speaking Women*: "Don't teach 'fancy cooking,'" and urged them to emphasize to their students the healthfulness of fresh fruits and vegetables, boiled and baked potatoes, and bread instead of tortillas and pasta.[57]

Food was an important reflection of national identity, but the CCIH did not consider diet to be a core aspect of culture as religion or language were, so the commissioners had no worries about trying to alter immigrants' eating habits. Chase's menus were based on Anglo-American cooking styles, but they were also more nutritious than those that many home economists and doctors were recommending in the 1910s and 1920s[58]

Progressive Americanizers' faith in "scientific" methods was most prominent in the area of childcare. In her manuals, Chase recommended that future home teachers instruct immigrant women not to feed or hold their babies whenever they cried because this interfered with the mothers' ability to do housework. The immigrant women were also told not to keep their children home from school when they were sick, but to let the school nurse take care of them. Home teachers were to give lessons on what to feed children (milk or cocoa, not beer, wine, or coffee) and how to put them to bed "the American way," in pajamas in a room with an open window.[59] In this respect, the home teachers' guidebooks read much like the pamphlets and brochures of the federal Children's Bureau, which also discouraged "excessive" infant cuddling and feeding, with the goal of standardizing childcare.[60] While Americanizers rejected the biological essentialism of the assumption that women "naturally" knew how to care for children, they also worked to replace traditional methods of childcare for more "modern" ones.

The manuals only briefly touched upon citizenship through their "patriotic lessons," which stressed the importance of reverence for the American flag, and offered homilies about the lives of Benjamin Franklin and Abraham Lincoln.[61]

The English lessons written by Gibson and Chase focused on teaching immigrant women a vocabulary useful and necessary for doing domestic service and selling handicrafts, such as lace or knitted items. Simultaneously, the guides inserted other, subtle value statements, such as teaching non-English speakers how to say, "The rent is too high," and "The landlord must mend the roof."[62] Through such a vocabulary and the home teacher's sanitation and hygiene lessons, the CCIH hoped to encourage immigrants to make their homes appear more like those of middle-class Anglo-Saxon Americans.

The curriculum devised by Gibson and Chase, and undoubtedly adopted by many home teachers, reflected the middle-class values and the assumptions of Americanizers, not the immigrant students, although these values sometimes conflicted or were confused. For instance, while the *Primer for Foreign-speaking Women* preached that husbands go to work, children attend school, and wives "get their houses in good order," the CCIH recognized that some immigrant women worked outside the home, and thus endorsed the progressive solution to the problem of working mothers: day nurseries for infants and small children too young to attend elementary school.[63]

While the primers were designed for women, and thus focused nearly exclusively on cooking, shopping, child rearing, housekeeping, and sanitation, *A Discussion of Methods of Teaching English to Adult Foreigners, With a Report on Los Angeles County* was tailored toward evening school teachers instructing immigrant men, and so focused more on citizenship and naturalization.[64] This difference in message to male versus female students reflected the CCIH's view of immigrant women as mothers more than as politically active citizens.

As the combination of the American entrance into World War I and the Los Angeles summer experiment drew public attention to the issue of immigrant education, the number of home teachers in California grew. Women's clubs, civic and charitable organizations, and school districts hired young women to bring the settlement house approach to Americanization to immigrants' homes in the name of national security and better citizenship. Normal schools began to develop specialized courses and certificates in immigrant education or "Americanization."[65] In July 1918 Gibson reported to the CFWC that there were ten Americanization instructors. In December 1918 CCIH staff member Christina Krysto informed *The Clubwoman* readership that California now had twenty home teachers, most of them working in cities such as San Francisco, Los Angeles, Sacramento, and Oakland; but others were in such areas as South Pasadena, Santa Barbara, and rural Tulare County.⁶⁶

The Home Teacher Act represented Gibson's and the commission's strong commitment to state action on behalf of immigrants. Gibson worked closely with city and county boards of education, the University of California's Extension Program, normal schools, the state superintendent of public instruction, and the state board of education to implement the Home Teacher Act. Although the California legislature was too parsimonious to appropriate any funds for the Home Teacher Act, and the state board of education refused to spend its own money to hire experts in immigrant education, resistance from either of these institutions would have made it difficult, if not impossible, for the commission to implement its proposals for immigrant education.

Gibson received little substantial support from California's educational leadership before World War I. Although the superintendents of the state and several large city and county school systems publicly supported the commission's educational programs, they still spoke of Americanization as yet another burden that progressives had placed upon the schools. Superintendent Hyatt's successor, Will C. Wood, argued as late as 1919 that he had no time or interest in training teachers for Americanization work.⁶⁷

The highly varied nature of home teaching also did not lend itself well to the development of a uniform profession. The practices and methods of home- and immigrant-education instructors varied enormously from teacher to teacher, depending on the individual and the circumstances. Normal schools were not required to offer immigrant education courses to their students, and there was no uniform curriculum for would-be home teachers. The lack of consistency in home teaching made it difficult to determine exactly how many home teachers there were at any given time; some instructors in evening schools, day schools, settlement houses, and other programs called themselves home teachers or "Americanization teachers" as the Americanization movement became more popular.⁶⁸

With the Home Teacher Act, the state government gained new power to intervene into its residents' lives by literally entering immigrants' homes. This interventionism was radical for the time, although not unprecedented. When she designed the home teacher program, Gibson was aware of the federal government's American Indian assimilation programs that used visiting nurses and teachers.⁶⁹

But the Home Teacher Act was distinctive from other visiting programs in that Gibson targeted adult women rather than children. Most female progressives active in "child saving" focused on assimilating immigrant mothers primarily through their children by teaching home economics in the public schools and encouraging daughters to participate in such programs as Little Mothers clubs that trained girls in middle-class Anglo-Saxon American housekeeping and parenting skills. The kindergarten movement also advocated child-directed assimilation programs.[70]

This issue of whether to first Americanize the child or the parents and Gibson's rejection of child-centered Americanization mark an important departure for her from many of her contemporaries who were involved in child welfare. While most progressive reform centered around the child—ranging from playgrounds to kindergartens to juvenile courts—Gibson focused on the immigrant family as a unit.

While the commission desired immigrants to adopt Anglo-Saxon American middle-class cultural conventions and values, its educational Americanization program was more social persuasion than social control or coercion. The commissioners recognized that immigrants could not be controlled if they did not want to be; and home teachers could neither compel adults to attend school nor cut off welfare services (though they might try).[71] There were limits to home teachers' power. Still, some home teachers did provide valuable services to immigrant women, particularly in the area of English instruction.[72]

Yet it was the combination of paternalism and state intrusiveness that caused many immigrants to reject immigrant education. Few immigrant women came into contact with home teachers; and of those who did, many refused to participate or dropped out.[73]

Despite Gibson's good intentions, and as much as Chase and other home teachers tried to model themselves as "friendly visitors" trying to assist their "neighbors," they were still cultural and often geographic outsiders trying to interfere with immigrants' lifestyles that were dictated by cultural tradition, individual choice, and economic necessity. Immigrants did not initiate or request home teaching; it was designed, created, and offered to them by middle-class Americans who had little understanding of immigrants' true wants or needs.

Home teaching, like investigations for mothers' pension programs and Sheppard-Towner nurses, also constituted a type of surveillance; Chase recommended to her fellow home teachers that their visits to their pupils' homes gave them the opportunity to look for signs of assimilation. "That these calls constitute a tour of inspection looking for evidence of cottage instruction in the houses will be the Home Teachers' professional secret."[74] Thus, the relationship between home teachers and their students, as in nearly all interactions between the middle and working classes in the progressive period, was a hierarchical one, with Americanizers asserting their right to investigate how well their immigrant pupils were adopting their recommendations.

Furthermore, the commissioners' perception of immigrants' cultural disadvantages permeated their educational literature. Although Gibson, Chase, and Richardson repeatedly argued that adult immigrants wanted classes and instructors who made learning English useful and relevant to their daily lives, they also believed foreign-born students wanted to be entertained. Classrooms were to be attractive, and teachers were encouraged to create a "social atmosphere." Recreation—teas, parties, dances—was a common feature of both evening schools and home teaching.[75]

While no one likes a boring class, especially adults not required by compulsory attendance laws to attend, the commission's stress on entertaining education arose from its view that many immigrants came from "folk" or "play" cultures. Mexican and southern European immigrants, especially, were not seen as serious people, but rather as overgrown children requiring entertainment.[76] Immigrants sensed this cultural condescension, and frequently chose not to participate in educational or social programs that did not take them or their cultures seriously.

The Home Teacher Act represented Gibson's and the CCIH's view that all California residents had a right to affordable, accessible education. Yet the education offered to women by home teachers was not what many immigrant women wanted or needed, if the low participation and high dropout rates are any indication. While many immigrants welcomed the commission's efforts to force employers or landlords to improve working and living conditions, the foreign-born resisted attempts to alter their cultural practices and beliefs.

Immigrant education was only a small part of the California Immigration and Housing Commission's overall Americanization policy. The CCIH continued to promote better housing through legislation and regulation. In this way, the commission sought to transform the immigrant home both inside and out. But the targeting of immigrants' cultures that underlay the Home Teachers Act was to become the driving factor in the entire Americanization movement during World War I.

5 ⭐ Wartime Americanization in the States

New York, California, and Massachusetts 1917–1918

The United States fought in World War I for less than two years, but those nineteen months between April 6, 1917, and November 11, 1918, were an intense and transforming period for America. On political, economic, and military levels, the nation prepared for and waged war; on social and ideological levels, it grappled with the fear that not all of its citizens were as one with the cause of defending democracy.

This new fear of disunity, diversity, and disloyalty affected state-level Americanization policies in different ways. New York's already uncoordinated approach to immigrant social welfare suffered from its equally disorganized mobilization effort, as the Bureau of Industries and Immigration and the Education Department competed for leadership of the state's Americanization's policy.

In California the Commission of Immigration and Housing continued to promote an environmental approach to Americanization, arguing that improving working and living conditions for immigrant workers was essential to increase wartime productivity and eliminate wasteful labor unrest. But the CCIH found itself frequently in conflict with the federal government about methods of Americanization. The commission was also swept up in the hysteria about labor radicalism, advocating the internment of members of the Industrial Workers of the World for their opposition to the war, a harbinger of the later, more effective federal prosecution of the IWW and other radical groups during the Red Scare of 1919–1920.

The Commonwealth of Massachusetts created a Bureau of Immigration (MBI) in the summer of 1917 as part of its general policy of mobilization. This bureau worked closely with the powerful Massachusetts Committee on Public Safety, which defined Americanization primarily in terms of English literacy. However, the MBI was able also to pursue a limited policy of social environmental reform as a way of aiding the war effort.

The wartime Americanization policies of New York, California, and Massachusetts reflected the diversity of the American war experience. But all of the states with immigrant social welfare programs had to respond to the demands of the federal government, which used Americanization agencies to ensure support for the war. President Woodrow Wilson's administration was slow to adopt formal Americanization programs, and when it did, it was in the area of education, not housing reform or labor relations. Americanizers who advocated environmental as well as educational approaches to Americanization were disappointed by the federal government's lack of interest in comprehensive immigrant social welfare.

Most histories of Americanization focus almost exclusively on the movement during World War I and, through that lens, see only xenophobia and coercive social control designed to eradicate foreign cultures in America and replace them with a bland Anglo-American conformity.[1] But Americanization as a form of immigrant social welfare policy was marked by real diversity, as Americanizers worked with varying degrees of success to integrate different policies into the larger war effort.

After declaring war on Germany on April 6, 1917, the federal government immediately put into place the limited mobilization plans it had developed in 1915 and 1916. Congress approved President Wilson's request for a military draft, and June 5, 1917, was declared Registration Day, when all men between the ages of twenty-one and thirty were to register for conscription. A week after war was declared, the Committee on Public Information (CPI) was organized to provide information and propaganda about the war effort. Other agencies, such as the War Industries Board, the Food Administration, and the Fuel Administration, were created over the next nineteen months to ensure greater productivity and efficiency in industries impacted by the conflict. To meet the needs of the American Expeditionary Force and the European Allies, the federal government both expanded and concentrated its power, especially over the economy, and influenced American public opinion through propaganda and censorship.

However, even with this additional power, the federal government's main tool for mobilization was *persuasion* rather than *coercion*. The Wilson administration depended upon volunteers, rather than a war-inflated bureaucracy, to achieve its wartime objectives.[2]

Congress passed and the president signed the Espionage Act of June 1917, the Trading with the Enemy Act of October 1917, and the Sedition Act of May 1918; and the Wilson administration revived the Enemy Aliens Act of 1798. But the government's ability to enforce these laws was weak. The U.S. Post Office, for example, had greater power to censor and control information by revoking mailing privileges and opening mail, and had far more personnel than did the Department of Justice, which depended on the 350,000-member American Protective League and other private "super patriot" organizations to augment its 300-man force.[3] The Wilson administration, already operating under ideological constraints of both traditional Democratic values of states' rights and antitrust and the New Freedom's advocacy of small-unit competition, found exercising many of its war powers difficult without public assistance.[4]

Ambivalent about the effect of a dramatically enlarged federal government on American society, cognizant of the bureaucratic limits of government power, and highly sensitive to the strong opposition to American entry into the war on the side of Great Britain and her allies, Wilson sought to turn these weaknesses into strengths. The chief source of power of the Wilson administration was its ability to exploit traditions of individualism, public opinion, and Anglo-Protestant cultural chauvinism to persuade Americans to volunteer their time and money, defer immediate gratification, and police their neighbors. Wilson knew that many Americans could be easily persuaded to participate in the war effort by appealing to their patriotism, and those who were less enthusiastic could be pressured by public opinion, incentives, threats, and, if need be, legal or extra-legal force. The Wilson administration embraced the preparedness movement's doctrine of "100 Percent Americanism"—universal conformity through a religiously fervent national loyalty—and Americans eagerly joined the new crusade to end war through war.[5]

When the United States entered World War I, the federal government had a weak Americanization policy based on the competing activities of the bureaus of Naturalization and Education.[6] Yet reflecting the priorities of the Wilson administration, the Bureau of Education spent the first year of the war more concerned with encouraging children to grow vegetable gardens and organize recycling drives than with immigrant education. The Bureau of Naturalization also did not go beyond its limited program of mailing out civics textbooks and scrutinizing naturalization petitions.[7] Neither agency worked with the departments of Labor, Agriculture, or Interior to reach non-English-speaking immigrants working in war industries, fields, mines, or forests.

The American war effort had two phases: the initial mobilization, which lasted from April 1917 to the spring of 1918, and the actual participation in the war in the summer and fall of 1918, when the United States began to commit large numbers of troops to the Western Front. Although the first U.S. troops arrived in Europe in June of 1917, it took most of the rest of that year and the first part of 1918 to induct, train, and transport the almost two million American soldiers who would be in Europe by November 1918.[8]

In the first phase of the war, the states found a role for themselves in the mobilization through state councils of defense. These groups, comprised of politicians and prominent citizens, were linked to the federal government through the National Council of Defense, which was responsible for coordinating the war effort at the state and local levels.[9]

Not all state councils were alike. The Massachusetts Committee on Public Safety was one of the best-organized and well-funded councils in the country.[10] The New York and California defense councils were weapons in state political battles rather than effective mechanisms for mobilization or Americanization.

The New York Council of Defense, chaired by Governor Charles S. Whitman, met infrequently and did even less. Unhappy with the Republican governor's appointments to the council, New York City Mayor John Purroy Mitchel, a Democrat, appointed his own city defense council, which refused to work with the governor's group.[11] The actual work of mobilization in New York was divided between the Resource Mobilization Bureau, which was managed by Adjutant-General Louis W. Stotesbury, who sat on the state defense council, and the New York Industrial Commission, which administered the Labor Department.[12]

In California the Council of Defense was an arena for struggles between progressives who continued to support Hiram W. Johnson, now in the senate, and those who backed the new governor, William D. Stephens.[13] Unlike New York, where committee weakness hindered more than it helped, the ineffectiveness of the California Council of Defense allowed the CCIH to manage its programs without outside interference. Here, the commission's superior funding made the difference: for 1917–1919 the CCIH received an appropriation of $90,000 as well as a special grant of $45,430 from the defense council, for a total of $135,430.[14] With such resources, the commission could afford to be independent of the Council of Defense.

In the first year of the war, President Wilson's administration did not see the need for a formal Americanization policy; its primary concerns were stimulating greater economic productivity and stifling dissent. To accomplish these goals, the administration used state Americanization agencies in four ways: disseminating information to immigrant communities about new wartime laws; monitoring alien opinion; regulating the immigrant labor market; and trying to increase industrial and agricultural productivity through improved working conditions, better safety, and English literacy.

The most important task Americanization agencies performed for the federal government was communicating with immigrants, especially those from nations with which the United States was now at war. This they did by holding informational meetings in immigrant neighborhoods; distributing thousands of posters, leaflets, and pamphlets; and partnering with (and sometimes pressuring) foreign-language newspapers to publish government propaganda.

With war came a whole host of new laws regulating the naturalization, military service, employment, and residency of non-citizens, particularly those from nations now at war with the United States. Remembering the Civil War draft riots, the federal government was particularly eager to ensure an orderly registration for the draft. Although non-citizens were exempt from conscription, alien men were still required to register for the draft. There was also great confusion among immigrants from Germany and Austria-Hungary about their new status as "enemy aliens."

While Americanization agencies had always viewed themselves as mediators between immigrants and mainstream society, wartime information dissemination was different in that the federal government dictated the message to be communicated.

The chief propaganda agency, the Committee on Public Information (or the Creel Committee, for its chair, George Creel) played a significant role in shaping American attitudes toward the war and toward immigrants. The CPI equated democracy with American ideals, and argued that democracy required a homogeneous population. This homogeneity was possible despite a racially and religiously diverse population if immigrants assimilated by adopting American cultural values and practices. These values were defined by the CPI to be a mix of the traditional and the new progressive political agenda: equal opportunity; religious toleration; universal education; labor's right to adequate wages; majority rule with respect for minority rights; respect for women, children and the elderly; respect for the home as the basis of society; free speech and press; and national idealism. There were, of course, limits to this language of inclusion: Immigrants who resisted assimilation were menaces to the stability of the republic because they threatened the homogeneity needed for democracy to survive.[15]

Rather than unify Americans around their civic nationalist principles of democracy, liberty, and self-determination, the war triggered a powerful racial nationalism based upon Anglo-Americans' sense of cultural superiority.[16] The CPI was a major articulator of this Anglo-conformist vision of American society through its argument that American culture was defined by a tension between "Puritanism," or self-control, and democracy, which was defined as external freedom. To be a good American was to recognize that liberty did not equal license, and that democracy was not simply majority rule with its tyrannical tendencies. Only when the individual acted with self-control and resisted acting upon his or her liberty could democracy thrive and create a harmonious society based upon consensus. On a more chauvinistic level, the CPI labeled English as the "American" language and branded all aspects of German culture (including food, place names, and even breeds of dogs) as "un-American."[17]

The CPI provided state agencies reams of material, including outlines of sample speeches; detailed lists of reasons the United States had entered the war and the goals the government wanted to accomplish; and explicit descriptions of the federal government's expectations of alien behavior. State Americanization agencies could create their own propaganda, and did, but the overall message was crafted by the CPI.

The information also flowed primarily one way: from the federal government to aliens. Federal officials were interested in immigrant public opinion, but only to avoid misunderstandings that could cause civil unrest or labor disputes that could disrupt the economy. Despite its rhetoric about democracy, the Wilson administration was not responsive to—and in fact, was hostile toward—lobbying by immigrant societies.[18] Such exercise of the right to petition the government was deemed as treacherous disloyalty by Anglophile Americans. The administration was not going to change its policies in response to the sentiments of foreign-born residents.

Despite the pressures from Creel and the national and state defense councils, state Americanization agencies had some leeway in crafting their communications to immigrants. Rejecting the national cry for "English only" as impractical, the California Commission of Immigration and Housing and the New York Bureau of Industries and Immigration organized informational meetings and lectures in the spring and summer of 1917 to explain the government's reasons for entering the conflict and provide information about the war effort to immigrants in their native languages.[19]

The Massachusetts Immigration Bureau also published brochures and posters in several languages and employed interpreters to answer immigrants' questions, but the bureau relied most heavily on volunteers it called "local correspondents" to communicate the expectations of the state defense council.[20] Local correspondents were primarily native-born Americans who were recognized as leaders of their communities and who provided the agency with information about the foreign-born in their regions.[21] By the end of the war, the bureau had recruited fifty-one local correspondents, six of whom were attorneys and sixteen of whom were women. The bureau also created advisory committees of Italian men and women, Greeks, and Lithuanians.[22]

All of the states relied upon the foreign-language press to spread government propaganda about the war effort among non-English speakers, but the MBI, NYBII, and New York Resource Mobilization Bureau's Division of Aliens relied upon foreign-language newspapers much more than did the California commission, which preferred to do its own advertising and could afford to do so.[23]

The federal government considered communication with immigrants crucial to ensuring a loyal, reliable, and productive labor supply for the American war economy. Progressives believed that the immigrant workforce could be made more productive by improving workplace safety and sanitation and ending the discrimination between foreign- and native-born workers that progressive Americanizers believed bred resentment and inhibited immigrants from adopting an "American" lifestyle.

But the federal government was primarily interested in productivity and efficiency, not immigrant assimilation through social reform. The fact that the only federal Americanization programs were located in the bureaus of Education and Naturalization, not the Department of Labor, revealed the Wilson administration's limited view of the uses of Americanization.[24]

This difference between state and federal governments over the potential role that Americanization could play in the war economy was most evident in the tensions that emerged between the California Commission of Immigration and Housing and the Wilson administration over contract labor from Mexico.

In California the commission's main concern in the spring of 1917 was that Draft Registration Day was scheduled for the same time that farmers were recruiting labor for the summer harvest. The immigration commissioners were disturbed by the arguments of large growers that the draft would cause such a dramatic labor shortage as to justify relaxing federal laws against contracting foreign workers. The commissioners were right to be concerned: Despite the objections of progressives, California's educational leadership had acquiesced when the state legislature argued that the state needed to relax its compulsory education and anti-child labor laws to allow children to work in agriculture and in other war-related industries.[25] With the state willing to roll back progressive protections of children, social welfare for foreign-born adults could be discarded even more easily. The CCIH also feared that employers would use the war as a justification for lowering sanitary standards in labor camps—standards the commission was still trying to maintain and raise.[26]

Against the commission's pleas that it or the federal government verify that a labor shortage existed before changing the contract labor policy, the Wilson administration responded to the growers' demands and suspended the newly enacted literacy test, the contract-labor law, and the recently raised $8–a-head tax for immigrants from Mexico.[27] In concession to the CCIH's protests, the federal government required large growers to meet the commission's standards for housing and sanitation. The CCIH also gained assurances from the U.S. Employment Bureau that the bureau would not refer workers to camps that the CCIH had not certified as meeting the commission's standards.[28] In the summer of 1917 more than 2,000 Mexican immigrants were brought in under the California Council of Defense's supervision and housed in special camps for the harvest.[29]

Despite its efforts to maintain sanitary standards and a newfound willingness to prosecute violators of the law, the commission began to receive large numbers of complaints from Mexican workers objecting to unsanitary conditions and misrepresentation of work by employers. In July 1918 the CCIH asked Commissioner-General of Immigration Anthony Caminetti for the names of large employers petitioning to bring Mexicans to California under the new rules, but the commissioners received little cooperation from federal officials.[30] It was not until December 1918, after the Armistice, that the U.S. Employment Bureau agreed to instruct its agents in California to pass workers' complaints on to the CCIH.[31]

Adding to the commissioners' anxiety about the importation of contract labor was the Industrial Workers of the World's strong opposition to the war and its agitation for workers to refuse to participate in the war economy. Surveillance of the IWW had been part of the commission's camp sanitation program from the beginning; with the Wobblies' outspoken opposition to the war, public fears about the radical union intensified. Leading the crusade against labor radicalism in California was Governor Stephens, who rarely made a public address about the war without also condemning the IWW.[32] Stephens created an atmosphere in which vigilantism was supported by state officials and prominent citizens, and any criticism of capitalism by organized labor was viewed as treasonous and a threat to social stability and the war effort. California state officials were so concerned about labor radicalism, especially among agricultural workers, that the Council of Defense spent most of its time speaking out against the IWW instead of fulfilling its primary responsibility of organizing the state for war.[33]

It was in this poisonous atmosphere of paranoia and hyper-patriotism that the CCIH proposed interning members of the IWW in the hope of finding a middle ground between the vigilantism being promoted by state leaders and the IWW's threats of industrial sabotage. In 1917 there were 4,450 strikes, most of them in the West; extralegal violence against labor radicals, often led by local authorities, exploded in the spring and summer of 1917.[34]

Afraid that civil liberties were being sacrificed in the name of national security and loyalty, commissioner Simon J. Lubin sent executive officer George L. Bell to meet secretly in July 1917 with the governors of Oregon, Washington, Nevada, Idaho, Montana, Utah, Arizona, Colorado, and New Mexico to discuss ways of preventing future industrial unrest in the West.[35] Bell convinced the governors that if conditions in the mines and fields were improved, workers would be more productive and loyal, and radicals would be unable to stir up discontent.

Bell then traveled to Washington, D.C., to lobby for federal support for the CCIH's proposal to clean up labor camps, intern en masse IWW members, and impose a "strong voluntary or forced censorship of the Press (including, particularly, A. F. of L. labor papers)" because the Wobblies were allegedly inspired by their pillorying in the press.[36]

Lubin and Bell feared that if the federal government did not neutralize the threat they believed the IWW posed, vigilante violence would continue to occur; internment was proposed as a moderate alternative to strikes and vigilantism.[37] Interstate coordination was needed to avoid the problem of local and state authorities deporting their labor problems into neighboring states, as had occurred in Arizona. The CCIH feared not only the IWW's ability to disrupt vital war industries—as it was doing in the southwestern mines and the northwest timber fields with its strikes—but also the violent anti-labor and anti-radicalism response by employers and other conservatives.

But the federal government did not respond to this proposal of mass internment or the improvement of Western working conditions. Although Immigration Commissioner-General Caminetti supported interning immigrant Wobblies, Labor Secretary William B. Wilson insisted upon proof of individual guilt before an alien could be interned. The Wilson administration was also reluctant to detain U.S. citizens, regardless of their political beliefs.[38] Refusing to support the CCIH's and the governors' plans, the federal government initiated its own prosecution of the IWW under new anti-syndicalism laws, using the military to raid IWW meeting halls and arrest members for disrupting the war effort.[39]

Unhappy with what they perceived as inadequate federal action, the western governors, led by the CCIH, agreed to clean up bad industrial conditions that the commission believed contributed to the IWW's success in organizing unskilled labor. The governors sent foreign language speakers (many of them the commission's employees) to immigrant communities to explain the government's position on the war. The western governors also agreed not to call out troops to deal with labor agitation unless they deemed it absolutely necessary. And, if troops were necessary, the governors would only call for federal troops to try to avoid the vigilantism that often occurred with state or local militias filled with hostile local citizens.[40]

The commission proposed its internment plan during a time of intense fear about radical interference in critical war industries such as agriculture and mining. But cooler heads did not prevail with the end of summer, as the commission had hoped. In fact, the fall of 1917 saw nearly as much violence and repression against the IWW as in the previous months. In September, Fresno police arrested 125 Wobblies in an effort to break up their network of farmworker unions in the Central Valley. That same month, vigilantes destroyed the IWW headquarters in Los Angeles. And in November 1917, twenty-five IWW leaders were indicted under California's new anti-syndicalism law; the charges were later dismissed.[41] In this atmosphere of hysteria and repression, the commission's idea of internment seemed mild compared to some of the more extreme proposals (and activities) of conservatives and the general public.

The wartime atmosphere of conformity made the transition from espionage to repression—ironically in the name of preventing vigilante violence—very easy for the CCIH. In their internment plan for the IWW, the commissioners applied a double standard in their definition of good citizenship: most of the commissioners had opposed U.S. entry into the war; yet after war was declared, they participated fully in the mobilization.[42] The Wobblies were to be punished for their ideological consistency.

The commissioners also continued to draw a clear line between acceptable and unacceptable types of labor organization. Throughout the war, the commission advocated unionization as a valuable tool in the assimilation of foreign-born workers. Yet the CCIH's pro-labor stance was selective and reserved only for mainstream, organized unions committed to working with and through the political process, such as the California Federation of Labor.[43] Through its rejection of capitalism, the political process, and now its active resistance to the war effort, the IWW stood outside the boundaries of social acceptability, according to the CCIH.

New York was also a site of conflict between the federal and state governments about mobilization in 1917. New York industries held one-quarter of all government war contracts, and the Wilson administration quickly became concerned that the political battles between Governor Whitman and Mayor Mitchel could disrupt the general war effort. To energize New York's mobilization, the federal government concentrated authority in the hands of industrial commissioner Henry D. Sayer, who was appointed federal director of employment for the state and director of the New York Council of Defense's Council's Industrial Division in late June 1917.[44] Although Sayer eliminated much bureaucratic confusion and competition, he did not give the Bureau of Industries and Immigration additional responsibilities, powers, or, most importantly, money. Compared with other divisions within the Labor Department, the NYBII's budget of $27,210 was pitifully small, especially since the bureau had the potential to be a valuable resource to the state as a liaison to New York's immigrant communities.[45]

Concerns about industrial and agricultural productivity raised new worries about inefficiencies, and gave progressives an opportunity to emphasize the relationship between safety and productivity. A key factor in workplace safety was the issue of illiterate and/or non-English-speaking workers who were unable to read safety instructions or understand warnings given in English. These concerns allowed American educators to interject themselves into the debate about how to effectively manage a predominantly foreign-born and often non-English-speaking workforce.

In order to prove that workers' lack of English fluency contributed to high accident rates, NYBII chief investigator Marian K. Clark reviewed 4,000 interviews with applicants for workers' compensation and found that 70 percent of the people applying to the state Industrial Commission for aid did not speak English. Tying illiteracy and non-English-speaking to lost productivity, she lobbied for more and compulsory English-language classes in New York's factories and greater teacher training to improve English instruction for adults.[46]

But while the NYBII sought additional funding to promote its own program of factory classes, the New York legislature preferred to rely upon the state Education Department, whose head of the Division of Vocational and Extension Education, Lewis A. Wilson, was named the director of Americanization for the state Council of Defense.[47]

As in other states, New York's wartime educational Americanization policy was a mix of persuasion and compulsion. The "carrot" was the Lockwood Act of 1917, which promoted teacher training for adult literacy and encouraged boards of education to host forums and organize community center activities by providing funds for such programs.[48] The "stick" was the banning of all foreign-language instruction—especially German—in the public schools, as well as the passage of three bills in the spring of 1918 that required compulsory school attendance for illiterate and non-English-speaking minors between the ages of sixteen and twenty-one; communities to provide public evening schools if they had twenty or more illiterate or non-English-speaking minors, and required the University of the State of New York to train teachers in Americanization and English literacy instruction. The state legislature appropriated $12,000 to pay for this training.[49]

The New York Board of Education also ordered public school teachers to attend weekly "Teachers Plattsburgs," camps run by the conservative National Security League where teachers were lectured on the league's views of citizenship and "Americanism."[50]

With the general public clamoring for "Americanization" instructors, the New York Department of Education intensified its training of instructors in the pedagogical methods of teaching illiterate adults. Immigrant education director William C. Smith and literacy experts Robert T. Hill and Henry H. Goldberger joined with Teachers College at Columbia University, the New York City Board of Education, and the mayor's defense council in the fall of 1917 to recruit teachers and others interested in immigrant education.[51]

The war caused New York to devote more resources to its evening schools, but the Massachusetts Bureau of Immigration was skeptical of the effectiveness of such programs (dropout rates were high), and instead emphasized factory classes. The benefit of work-based education was that instruction could be targeted toward the functions of the workplace, and thus helped reduce accidents and inefficiencies caused by communication problems. Plus, the student audience was captive in businesses where participation was mandatory or tied to incentives.

Factory classes, however, depended upon cooperation from employers and only reached workers in industrial plants, but not those employed in agriculture, shipping, industrial homework, or domestic service. Factory class students also tended to be men.

To develop an industrial Americanization program in Massachusetts, Immigration Bureau executive director Edward V. Hickey persuaded state education commissioner Payson Smith to hire Charles F. Towne to be director of immigrant education within the Division of University Extension. Towne developed curricula and trained teachers, and then worked with local school officials to organize English-language classes in factories. To gain support for this approach to Americanization, the MBI held a series of conferences with industry leaders in Boston, Worcester, and Springfield in January 1918 at which officials of the state's War Efficiency Committee, Education Department, and

Frances A. Kellor lectured business leaders about the relationship between English literacy, safety, and greater productivity. Industry support of the program was mixed; besides providing the students and the facilities, some Massachusetts companies paid their employees for the time spent in class, while others contributed nothing. Many employers who provided factory classes preferred to furnish their own instructors instead of using public school teachers so they could control the curriculum and instruction methodology.[52]

Americanizers received a major endorsement of support in the spring of 1918 when the Wilson administration finally moved to more firmly tie Americanization to the war effort through citizenship education. In April the U.S. Bureau of Education and the National Council of Defense jointly hosted a conference of immigration activists in Washington, D.C., where Americanization was defined in primarily educational terms. Simon Lubin's proposal that Washington create a federal Americanization department to promote progressive social reform on behalf of all Americans, both native- and foreign-born, was rejected.[53] As far as the Wilson administration was concerned, Americanization equaled immigrant education in English and civics, not a new approach to labor relations.

After the conference, the federal government began to encourage states to create Americanization committees to partner with the Bureau of Education to implement the bureau's adult education programs, focusing on non-English-speaking immigrants. States were also encouraged to work with the Bureau of Naturalization in its citizenship education work.[54]

Partly in response to this federal pressure, Massachusetts passed a law requiring citizenship training in its public schools. And the New York Education Department adopted the federal bureau's "Schedule of Standards and Methods in the Education of Immigrants," hiring a supervisor to train superintendents, principals, and teachers in these methods and standards.[55]

In 1918 Massachusetts education leaders partnered with the U.S. Bureau of Education to develop the state's civics and citizenship education program, organizing conferences with school administrators and teachers, and holding two teacher training courses in Boston and Springfield. Massachusetts also implemented the "Lawrence Plan for Education in Citizenship," which was directed by Lowell normal school principal John J. Mahoney, two Harvard University professors, and the Lawrence school superintendent; it was advised by education commissioner Smith and members of the National Security League.[56]

Most discussions of Americanization in the schools, however, focused on children, and openly advocated child-directed assimilation methods. Major emphasis was placed upon teaching patriotism in the public schools, with flag ceremonies and the Pledge of Allegiance finally becoming widespread and required in public schools nationwide.[57]

In California the CCIH resisted the national trend toward defining Americanization in exclusively educational terms. Although the California Department of Education convinced the state legislature to pass a law requiring non-English-speaking aliens to attend Americanization courses, the only English instruction program that the Commission of Immigration and Housing initiated during the war was one that taught English to non-English-speaking soldiers stationed at bases in the San Francisco Bay Area.[58]

The commission's insistence on viewing Americanization in terms of working and living conditions—not English literacy and citizenship—marginalized it from the larger Americanization movement, now firmly oriented toward immigrant education. Dissatisfied with the federal government's approach to Americanization, the CCIH decided to focus its efforts on California and began promoting Americanization through what it called "community organization."[59]

Community organization, according to the CCIH's interpretation, represented the complete mobilization of a community for progressive social reform, and included: "Democratic organization of the citizens by neighborhoods, for effective participation in and control of their community life, and the broadening of that life," and "extension, creation and union of social facilities and agencies, for discovering and meeting the community's need."[60]

The commission's community organization project was initiated in May 1918 after the federal government endorsed formal Americanization programs. The CCIH's project involved meeting with community groups, making speeches, and issuing public statements urging the improvement of living and working conditions, compliance with wartime measures, and tolerance for aliens (especially those from enemy countries).[61]

In this new model for statewide community organization, the CCIH helped to organize Americanization committees—comprising native-born citizens and representatives of the foreign-born, labor unions, employers, social service organizations, and educational authorities—in each county to coordinate activities at the local level.[62]

Schools, local industry, churches, and the local coordinating committees were the main institutions that were to be involved in local Americanization work. While county-based committees would be responsible for lecture series discussing the war, democracy, and other American values and practices, the schools would enhance community life by transforming themselves into social centers. Employers would encourage their employees to participate in Americanization work and practice "Americanism" themselves by improving conditions and eliminating the incentives for strikes and other labor discontent. Churches would add to their religious duties by focusing on the moral obligation of citizens to treat one another as equals and preaching against "race prejudice" and discrimination.[63]

The commission's plan for community organization envisioned each county committee first undertaking social investigation into the numbers, nationalities, status, and condition of its foreign communities, and then organizing Americanization programs in response to the particular needs of the local community. These programs could range from lecture series to community celebrations and festivals. The commission urged communities to provide their residents with Americanization propaganda, patriotic events, and education in English and civics, and to use farm bureaus and community organizations to reach more isolated rural districts. The CCIH also encouraged the continued development of home teaching and evening schools for English instruction and citizenship, home visiting for the purpose of fostering better neighborhoods and explaining the American position on the war, and constant vigilance in maintaining adequate sanitation in housing and workplaces.[64]

Most importantly, for successful community organization, Americanization had to be "thoroughly and sincerely democratic," with both native- and foreign-born residents actively participating in the community's reform.[65] This idea was new for the CCIH; before the war, it had emphasized the relative helplessness of the immigrant in the face of American society. Americanization was something done for the immigrant; now the commission was beginning to advocate mutual effort and joint cooperation between native- and foreign-born.[66]

But the commission's California Americanization plan was never truly democratic. Despite its rhetoric of democracy, the CCIH successfully sought to have county Americanization committee chairs appointed by the state Council of Defense, not elected or even nominated by the community's residents.[67] Most of the people the CCIH nominated in the fall of 1918 to head the county Americanization committees were elites: judges, college administrators, merchants, mayors, and newspaper editors.[68] The commission also favored native-born leaders, rather than foreign ones out of the belief that native-born Americans could "attract a more general following than a member of any foreign group."[69] Of the aliens who would sit on the panels, the CCIH sought the most prominent leaders of immigrant communities to form its

Advisory Americanization Committee.[70] Although the CCIH believed Americanization should be democratic, in progressive fashion it also relied upon the "best people" in a community to lead.

In California's new program of community-based Americanization, towns and organizations were encouraged to organize programs with native-born English speakers who stressed the responsibility that democracy placed on citizens and the belief that racial prejudice destroyed national unity. Foreign-language speakers were encouraged to emphasize the obligation immigrants should feel in return for the opportunities and freedoms of America, the advantages of democracy, the importance of learning English, and the need to contribute to American society. To aid with this, in 1919 the CCIH produced a brochure entitled "Americanization: A Suggestion for Speakers," which came complete with outlines of lectures. The CCIH also published a patriotic songbook, "The Spirit of the Nation" in 1918 to be used in community events and schools.[71]

"The Spirit of the Nation," according to the commission, could be found in the country's folk and patriotic songs and in the speeches of famous Americans. The pamphlet included the Declaration of Independence and the Pledge of Allegiance, Abraham Lincoln's Gettysburg Address, Alexis De Tocqueville's "Spirit of Republican Government," as well as several statements by President Wilson and Secretary of Interior Franklin K. Lane. The songs included the "Star Spangled Banner," "America," and "Hail Columbia." In an effort to be regionally balanced, the pamphlet included the "Battle Hymn of the Republic," "Dixieland," "Yankee Doodle," and "My Old Kentucky Home." Reflecting the racial attitudes prevalent in the 1910s, other Stephen Foster songs, such as "Massa's In the Cold Cold Ground" and "Old Black Joe" were also part of "The Spirit of the Nation," according to the CCIH.

"The Spirit of the Nation" reflected the change in the commission's wartime approach to Americanization. Before the war, when the preparedness movement was stirring up anxieties about security and prompting new demands for rapid Americanization, the CCIH preached caution and resisted calls for hurried assimilation. With "The Spirit of the Nation," the CCIH readily acknowledged that it was part of special war activities designed to "speed up" Americanization.[72]

The values being promoted by the California Commission of Immigration and Housing during the war contrasted with those being articulated by the new Massachusetts Bureau of Immigration.

Massachusetts finally launched its Americanization program in the early summer of 1917 under very different circumstances than when New York and

California had initiated their immigrant social welfare policies. Not only was the flow of migrants at its lowest point in decades because of the war, but the few immigrants entering the United States experienced more extensive forms of governmental control of human movement, involving passports, visas, and quotas that were instituted during and shortly after the war.[73] American perception of immigrants being a threat to society was at a high point not seen since the days of the early republic. Americanization in Massachusetts during World War I was more about cultural conformity as a type of loyalty test than a state of mind and emotion and certainly did not involve changing the behavior or values of native-born Americans, only those of immigrants.

The Massachusetts Bureau of Immigration was an executive commission with five members, one of whom was to be a woman, and two of whom were to be either foreign-born or the descendents of the immigrant groups most prevalent in Massachusetts. Bernard J. Rothwell, who had sat on the temporary commission of 1913–1914, was the chair. Besides Rothwell, who was an Irish Catholic immigrant, Pasquale Galassi represented Massachusetts' large Italian community, and Henry H. Chmielinski represented Polish and other Slavic immigrants. The other members were native-born Americans: Carroll W. Doten was head of the Research Department of the School for Social Workers at Simmons College, Harvard University, and a statistician at MIT; and Edith Prescott Wolcott was a descendent of Bunker Hill commander Col. William Prescott. The bureau was granted $10,000 in its first year to pay for an executive secretary and staff; the five gubernatorial appointees were to serve without pay but were reimbursed for travel expenses.[74]

The official legislative goal of the Bureau of Immigration was "to bring into sympathetic and mutually helpful relations the commonwealth and its residents of foreign origin, to protect immigrants from exploitation and abuse, to stimulate their acquisition and mastery of the English language, to develop their understanding of American government, institutions and ideals, and generally to promote their assimilation and naturalization."[75]

The MBI viewed the war as an excellent opportunity to achieve greater social and cultural homogeneity. Military service was to be a melting pot "for the fusing of these varied elements into an inseparable Americanism."[76]

Americanization was to be mutual and involved contributions from both aliens and citizens. The values of fairness, service, and moral examples on the part of native-born Americans were to undergird Americanization. Paternalism also infused the Massachusetts bureau: "The foreign born are much like children—imitative. If they note obedience on the part of the earlier comers in small matters they will develop respect for authority in larger affairs. Our foreign born must have the inspiration and encouragement of example if they are to acquire and maintain a respect for legitimate authority."[77] This meant that while Americanization required change on the part of the native-born, Americans were still to direct the assimilation of the foreign-born.

But immigrants' intense interest in the affairs of their native countries, particularly the lobbying of German and Irish nationals against the United States' alliance with Great Britain, threatened the bureau members, who were either native-born Americans (Doten and Wolcott), came from countries allied with Britain (Galassi), or were sympathetic to the Allied cause (Chmielinski). Only Rothwell, who had immigrated in 1869, represented Massachusetts' large Irish community, and he defined himself as an American without a hyphen. Like most native-born Americans, bureau members perceived German and Irish political activism as illegitimate while defining Anglo-American advocacy for support of Great Britain as solely American. The bureau insisted that "attempted coercion of the government or of officials, national, State, or municipal, through group action based solely on racial considerations, is little, if at all, short of treason, and should unmistakably be condemned by the American people."[78]

Much more than the California immigration commissioners, the Massachusetts Americanizers worried that without assimilation into a society predetermined by its English language, institutions, and heritage, America faced the violent social threat of pluralism. Americanism was defined as monolingual (English-speaking only), which meant that the largest groups of immigrants to Massachusetts, those from Great Britain and Ireland, had little use for the bureau's programs since they did not need to learn English. Linguistic diversity was viewed as "the menace of a polyglot nation," and reminders of the disintegration of the multilingual Austro-Hungarian and Ottoman empires were frequent. Americanization was also defined primarily in educational terms, with the primary goal being "a sound working knowledge of English and at least a comprehensive outline of the structure and aims of our government."[79]

The Massachusetts bureau members also supported immigration restriction, arguing that only those would-be immigrants who could prove that they knew the values of the Declaration of Independence and the U.S. Constitution should be admitted into the country.[80] Although this position did not favor or oppose particular groups, the preference for educated immigrants meant that northern Europeans would be more likely to meet the MBI's criteria for inclusion than southern and eastern Europeans and Asians.

The conservative approach of the MBI to immigrant social welfare—pro-restriction, anti-pluralistic, Anglo-conformist—reflected the direction that the Americanization movement was moving nationally during the war.

Despite California and New York's efforts to maintain environmental immigrant social welfare programs, the federal government's promotion of educational Americanization narrowed the scope of the movement and shifted it from the native-born to the foreign-born. Environmental Americanization programs had always focused on controlling the behavior of the native-born in order to create the right social conditions in which immigrant transformation could occur; immigrant education worked to change the immigrant directly. This understanding of Americanization as immigrant education was held by many Americans, who believed, as the Bureau of Naturalization argued: "The Americanism of a native American may be at a low ebb, but he cannot be Americanized. He may be inspired to higher ideals, but to view him as a candidate for Americanization means to make 'Americanization' meaningless. It remains, therefore, for the term to be applied to people not American."[81]

This focus on education reinforced the approach of conservative patriotic groups, such as the Daughters of the American Revolution and the National Security League, which had been active in citizenship education before the war. These organizations promoted a narrower definition of citizenship than progressives, one that stressed legal citizenship, naturalization, filiopietistic American history focused on the country's English heritage, and patriotic rituals, such as the Pledge of Allegiance and flag ceremonies. "During World War I, attitudes toward the flag became the litmus test of patriotism," with aggressive enforcement of flag protection laws and the frequent use of the flag in vigilante harassment of dissenters. The DAR, in particular, had long been active in promoting civic and patriotic education rooted in hostility to radicalism and labor organization.[82]

The nationalistic pressures of World War I caused state Americanization agencies to adapt their policies to meet the needs and the demands of the federal government, which defined Americanization primarily in terms of immigrant loyalty and compliance with national war aims. The more conservative vision of Americanization developing in Massachusetts, New York, and even California contrasted with efforts in Illinois, where Hull-House progressives attempted to craft a cosmopolitan approach to immigrant social welfare immediately after the war in the midst of intense national anti-immigration sentiment.

Figure 1. Immigrants at the Battery: cart men, immigrant passengers and baggage, circa 1901, Museum of the City of New York, the Byron Collection.

Figure 2. Tent or shelter, in the hop pickers' camp on the Durst ranch near Wheatland in the season of 1913, California Commission of Immigration and Housing Annual Report (1915), p. 16.

Figure 3. Immigrants outside the receiving room of the Immigrants' Protective League, Immigrants' Protective League papers, University of Illinois, Chicago.

Figure 4. Italian men in a classroom, from the Report of the Commission on Immigration regarding the problem of immigration in Massachusetts (Wright & Potter, State Printers, Boston, 1914), p. 161.

6 ✶ Cosmopolitanism Cut Short

The Illinois Immigrants Commission, 1919–1921

As the state with the largest immigrant population in the West and some of the nation's most famous progressive activists and institutions, Illinois was where one would expect to find an active public Americanization program. However, despite the presence of Jane Addams and Hull-House, Grace Abbott, Sophonisba Breckinridge, and the Immigrants' Protective League (IPL) and several other well-organized immigrant organizations, Illinois did not develop a public immigrant social welfare policy until after World War I. As the Americanization movement peaked in 1919, Illinois finally established the Illinois Immigrants Commission (IIC).

Like the New York Bureau of Industries and Immigration and the Massachusetts Bureau of Immigration, the Illinois Immigrants Commission had limited powers and a small appropriation, which limited most of its work to Chicago. Only in existence for two years, the IIC was created in the midst of the Red Scare and ceased operation just as the United States was implementing its first immigration restriction measure. For the short time that the commission was alive, it advocated a more cosmopolitan and pluralistic vision of American citizenship and national identity than most Americans were willing to accept in the early 1920s. The death of the IIC at the hands of machine politicians reflected the weakness of progressivism in Illinois and the strength of an alternative means of providing immigrant social welfare through patronage.

Since the establishment of Hull-House in 1889 and the founding of the University of Chicago in 1890, most progressive activity in Illinois was concentrated in Chicago, where most of Illinois' foreign-born residents lived. But progressives were politically weak in the Windy City. Kenneth Finegold notes that unlike in New York or Cleveland, Chicago politicians rejected progressives' approach to politics, which sought to build "an electoral coalition between elite 'traditional reformers' and 'municipal populists' supported by portions of the working class" and the city's "New Immigrants."[1] Central to those coalitions was a heavy reliance upon social science expertise and the new progressive middle-class values of professionalism, anti-individualism, and "scientific" objectivity. Chicago leaders instead practiced machine politics that traded individual socioeconomic benefits for working-class support. Unlike progressive social welfare, which sought to change recipients' behavior by modifying social systems and structures, machine social welfare was personal, tangible, and tied to specific instances of need, such as death or unemployment.[2]

Outside of Chicago, Illinois progressives were also unable to build an alternative political system that could transcend class, religion, national origins, and locality to pass new social welfare legislation at the state level.[3] So, despite creating and leading a national network of political activists and intellectuals, Illinois progressives were largely shut out of state politics. It took all of the nationalistic pressures of World War I to convince Governor Frank O. Lowden and the state legislature to create the Illinois Immigrants Commission in the summer of 1919.

The year 1919 was the high point of the Americanization movement, which coincided with mass national hysteria about alien radicals during the Red Scare.[4] In this politically and ideologically charged environment, the Illinois Immigrants Commission found few interested in a cosmopolitan approach to Americanization that gave immigrants the lead role in rejuvenating American democracy.

The IIC represented the transfer of personnel and ideas about immigrants, assimilation, and class interactions from private progressive groups affiliated with Jane Addams' Hull-House settlement to the public sector of state government. The direct link between these two sectors was the Immigrants' Protective League (IPL), a pro-immigrant organization directed by Hull-House residents Grace Abbott and Sophonisba Breckenridge.

The IPL had been established in 1908 by the Council of Jewish Women, the Chicago Women's Trade Union League, and several Hull-House residents and patrons to provide a wide range of social services to immigrants: meeting young women at Chicago's train stations to ensure that they went home with family or friends, not seducers or brothel procurers; providing new arrivals with information about housing, jobs, and social welfare services; and promoting immigrant education and citizenship. After the league began receiving complaints from immigrants about exploitive labor contractors, it lobbied successfully for state regulation of private employment agencies and better promotion of public employment offices.[5]

Progressives affiliated with Hull-House had long been scrutinized for their class-based paternalism and their promotion of Anglo-Saxon Protestant values in their interactions with immigrants, most of whom were Jewish or Catholic.[6]

Yet in Chicago, many IPL trustees were themselves Jewish, often of German heritage, and saw no conflict between their advocacy of cultural and social homogeneity and Judaism. Julian W. Mack, the father of the juvenile court concept; Julius Rosenwald, founder of Sears, Roebeck and Co.; Dr. Ernst Freund of the University of Chicago Law School; and the members of the Council of Jewish Women were all middle- or upper middle-class Jews who actively encouraged eastern and southern Europeans to assimilate into Anglo-American society. In Illinois, as in California and New York, Jews played an important, if often overlooked, role in the progressive Americanization movement.

The charge of paternalism against Chicago progressives reveals the underlying assumption that immigrants did not need progressive social welfare services and that the real motivation behind progressive reform was social control of the working class. It is true that only 25,000, or 5 percent, of the 400,000 immigrants who arrived in Chicago in 1909–1919 took advantage of IPL services. But what is unknown is how many of those 400,000 immigrants were in need of aid and able to obtain it on their own.[7] What is known is that some immigrants sought progressive assistance and did so on their own terms, with varying degrees of success.

Although Rivka Lissak is correct that Chicago progressives sought to eliminate small businessmen, such as labor contractors and immigrant bankers, from their roles as cultural mediators and community leaders, she misses the primary objection that progressives had to these immigrant entrepreneurs. Progressives' campaigns against the *padrone*, the saloon keeper, and the immigrant banker were not simply power struggles over who would supervise immigrants' assimilation; the conflict was over the direction that assimilation would take. According to progressive Americanizers, the problem with immigrant business leaders was that they had absorbed all too well nineteenth century values of political economy, and it was this ideology of laissez-faire that progressives were trying to overthrow.

Every aspect of the IPL's work rejected nineteenth-century definitions of liberty and equality. For the members of the Immigrants' Protective League, aliens were clearly disadvantaged by language, lack of urban experience, and unfamiliarity with local economic conditions. The suggestion that newly arrived immigrants had as equal an opportunity to succeed or fail in American society as the English-speaking native-born denied reality. But unlike Frances Kellor, who was primarily concerned about inefficiencies in the American marketplace, league members were more interested in providing immigrants with what they considered to be real opportunities to improve their socioeconomic condition. The IPL's emphasis on protection was paternalistic; yet, as the league's records indicate, thousands of immigrants in Chicago suffered real hardships of fraud, theft, unemployment, and socioeconomic injustice.

By World War I, the IPL had nearly ten years of experience assisting immigrants, but the organization was struggling financially. The abrupt decline in immigration in 1915–1918 had caused some contributors to assume (incorrectly) that the league had less demand for its services, and this—combined with competition with war bond drives—hurt IPL fundraising. Its largest contributor, Julius Rosenwald, objected to supporting the IPL to a greater extent than the $1,000 he had been contributing annually since 1909.[8] The league was also finding it difficult to promote its message of compassion, tolerance, and cosmopolitanism toward immigrants in a wartime atmosphere of fear, suspicion, and hatred of all things "un-American."

The proposal to create the Immigrants Commission came from Freund, who sat on the IPL's executive committee and had taught Breckinridge and Abbott law at the University of Chicago. In the fall of 1918 he drew up a plan for a state commission to be appointed by the governor. Noting that the federal government continued to resist the suggestion that it assume responsibility for immigrants beyond questions of entry-and-exclusion criteria, deportation, and naturalization, Freund proposed that Illinois follow the example of other states and develop a program to directly address issues of immigrant settlement, protection, and social welfare.[9] Such a public Americanization policy would also hopefully resolve the league's financial problems by transferring its functions to the public sector.

Freund's proposal was approved by the state legislature and signed by Governor Lowden in June 1919.[10] Lowden, a Democrat and an Irish-American Catholic, was more politically conservative than his predecessor, Edward F. Dunne, who had appointed Jane Addams and other progressives to high-profile positions. But the governor recognized the national trend toward public Americanization.[11]

The Illinois Immigrants Commission became operational July 1, 1919, (although serious work did not begin until January 1920, when Grace Abbott was hired as executive secretary).[12] Given the involvement of Freund and other IPL/Hull-House-affiliated individuals in the creation of the commission, there was never any consideration that the leadership of the IIC would come from any other group.

The new agency was located in the Department of Registration and Education, which was responsible for all of the state's education programs, including adult education and teacher training and licensing. The new agency, however, had several non-educational responsibilities, including making:

> a survey of the immigrant, alien-born and foreign-speaking people of the State, and of their distribution, conditions of employment, and standards of housing and living . . . examin(ing) into their economic, financial, and legal customs, their provisions for insurance and other prudential arrangements, their social organization and their educational needs; keeping in friendly and sympathetic touch with alien groups and cooperating with state and local officials and with immigrant and related authorities of other states and of the United States.[13]

The commission would also not be responsible for designing or implementing immigrant education programs similar to California's Home Teacher's Act. Nor would it involve itself in obviously non-educational issues, such as housing and labor conditions, beyond the required survey.

And, unlike the experience of the California Commission of Immigration and Housing with the Wheatland hop fields riot, the IIC's work was unaffected by the thirteen-day race riot that began July 27, 1919, in Chicago. Race relations among black and white Americans and European immigrants would not become part of the commission's responsibilities. This reflected the long tradition of Chicago progressives of bridging divides and breaking down cultural and class barriers between European immigrants and white Americans while largely ignoring the rigid separation of blacks and whites.[14]

As in California and Massachusetts, the Illinois commission had five gubernatorially appointed members who served without compensation. The commissioners were Helen Wooster (Harlan Ward) Cooley, president of the Chicago Women's Club and a close ally of Hull-House; Jewish banker and war hero Brigadier General Abel Davis of Chicago; Streator *Free Press* editor John F. Fornof; and Charles F. Harding, president of the Lakeshore National Bank in Chicago and a long-time IPL executive committee member. The new agency was chaired by Registration and Education Department director Francis W. Shephardson.[15]

In addition to executive secretary Abbott, the commission staff came from the IPL, which in March 1920 transferred to the new agency its records and three employees who spoke Polish, Russian, Lithuanian, Ukrainian, Italian, and German.[16]

Unlike the Massachusetts Bureau of Immigration, which relied upon local, native-born elites to serve as "local correspondents," the IIC organized a committee of representatives of the largest immigrant groups in the state to provide it with information about issues in those communities. These representatives included Dr. Rachelle Slobodinsky Yarros, a Russian obstetrician and gynecologist who lived at Hull-House; a Mr. Dusseffy, the editor of the Hungarian newspaper *Otthon*; Maurice J. Karpf, the superintendent of relief for the Jewish Aid Society; Peter S. Lambros, editor of the Greek newspaper, *The Star*; a Dr. Gaiczunas of the Lithuanian Red Cross; a Mrs. Berkman, chair of the Immigration Committee of the Council of Jewish Woman; a Mr. Palendesch, editor of the newspaper *Jugoslavia*; and a Mr. Berke, a Hungarian merchant.[17]

By the time the Illinois Immigrants Commission was created, several models of Americanization programs were in existence, and Grace Abbott knew, either personally or by reputation, most of the leaders of the Americanization movement, including Kellor, Simon J. Lubin of the California Commission of Immigration and Housing, and Bernard J. Rothwell of the Massachusetts Bureau of Immigration. By locating the commission within the state Department of Registration and Education, Illinois was mirroring the national Americanization movement, which was now focused primarily on immigrant education. The Illinois Department of Labor was also considered to be less politically friendly to the progressive programs Abbott envisioned; and Shepardson was willing to oversee the new office.[18]

Unlike Kellor or Lubin, who had eagerly sought to interject state government into Americanization before the war, Abbott had long been reluctant to involve herself or the IPL in Illinois state politics, which she considered to be dominated by anti-progressive machine politicians.[19] The main reason Abbott agreed to the idea of a public immigrant welfare agency in 1919 was the promise of steady and hopefully more generous funding than the private IPL had been able to raise. Although the commission would not assume any debts held by the league and the league would officially continue to exist, the IIC represented, in effect, the absorption of a private organization by the state.[20]

But Abbott's hopes of more generous public funding failed to materialize; the Immigrants Commission's first biannual appropriation of $15,000 was markedly less than what other Americanization agencies were receiving, as Abbott was well aware. For the same two-year period, 1919–1921, the California Commission of Immigration and Housing was granted $140,000, the New York Bureau of Industries and Immigration $51,200, and the Massachusetts Immigration Commission, established in 1917, was already receiving $66,200.[21] Public Americanization in Illinois would be as limited by finances as private Americanization had been.

The commissioners officially determined the agency's policies, but the ideology underlying the IIC's work came largely from Abbott, despite her position as executive secretary and thus, an employee. Abbott determined the IIC's agenda; managed the staff; supervised research; wrote reports, and successfully promoted her vision of progressive immigrant social welfare in commission meetings.

When she became the executive secretary of the Immigrants Commission in early 1920, Grace Abbott had been studying, working with, and living among immigrants in Chicago for more than ten years. A resident of Hull-House with her older sister Edith since 1908, the forty-two-year-old Abbott had grown up in Grand Island, Nebraska, in a family with strong abolitionist and suffragist traditions. The Abbotts were Quakers of English descent, but Grace and Edith Abbott had been exposed to a more pluralistic approach to American society by Grand Island's large German community. Although Grace's father, Othman Abbott, was an attorney and politically active in the Nebraska Republican party, the Abbotts were not wealthy. Abbott, her two brothers, and sister had all deferred their educations and worked to help pay off the family's debts when their father faced bankruptcy during the drought-and-depression years of the 1890s. It was not until 1907, when she was nearly thirty years old, that Grace Abbott was finally able to leave home to study political science at the University of Chicago, from which she earned a master of philosophy degree. She became the director of the Immigrants' Protective League in 1909, and two years later traveled alone through central Europe to better understand the cultures of the countries from where so many immigrants to Chicago had come. After serving as executive secretary of the Massachusetts Immigration Commission in 1913–1914, Abbott returned to Chicago and the IPL, refusing to join the national Americanization movement's embrace of military preparedness for World War I. Instead, Abbott, a pacifist, joined Jane Addams and Emily Greene Balch, among others, in 1915 as part of the American delegation to the International Congress of Women at The Hague to discuss international peace and ways of ending the war. After the United States entered the conflict, Abbott avoided working for the National Americanization Committee-controlled Americanization programs in the

Bureau of Education or for the Bureaus of Naturalization or Immigration. Instead, she directed the U.S. Children's Bureau's Industrial Division in Washington, D.C.[22]

Rejecting the coercive and culturally imperious trend in Americanization, Abbott continued to be guided by the cosmopolitan yet paternalistic values she had developed while living at Hull-House. In particular, she disagreed with the opinion of many native-born Americans that the "new immigrants" from southern and eastern Europe were unsuited for American citizenship due to race, religion, culture, and history, and so should be excluded.

Like other progressive Americanizers, Abbott recognized conservatives' vision of American society and citizenship as static and rigidly based upon a belief in Anglo-American cultural superiority. Dismissing eugenics-based arguments for immigration restriction, Abbott believed in the assimilability of immigrants and the malleability and flexibility of individuals, cultures, and societies. Like Kellor, Abbott rejected distinctions between "old" and "new" immigration as being based upon cultural prejudice, not social science. She noted that restrictionists' arguments against the "New Immigrants" were the same as ones that had been used against earlier groups, such as Germans and Scandinavians, who were now seen as desirable.[23]

Despite her disagreements with Kellor about the war, Abbott shared with her and Simon Lubin the belief that immigrants faced special disadvantages that stemmed from being foreign-born, non-English-speaking, and often lacking experience with urban life. With help in overcoming these barriers, immigrants could become productive citizens and had much to contribute to American culture and society.

Abbott also shared with other progressive Americanizers the belief that Americanization required the participation of both the foreign- and the native-born. Americans had a duty to protect immigrants from exploitation in order to foster a positive view of the United States on the part of foreigners; to provide the alien with educational opportunities "as would enable him to join us in the work of making the United States a really effective democracy"; and to reform politics and the economy to accommodate the needs of a diverse society.[24]

Although Abbott preferred to use the term "adjustment" to "assimilation" and she was more receptive than most Americans to cultural diversity, she was, nonetheless, an assimilationist. Through her advocacy of English as a common language, and her efforts to break down social barriers between foreign- and native-born communities and raise immigrants' standards of living closer to that of native-born Americans, Abbott sought a more homogeneous society.[25]

Unlike the intellectuals Randolph Bourne and Horace Kallen, Abbott never advocated a pluralistic model in which American society was comprised of distinct, autonomous, and unaltered groups.[26] Living in a diverse urban environment, Abbott saw how the foreign-born had adapted their cultural traditions to meet the social and economic demands of American life, and she viewed these adjustments as positive evidence of immigrants' assimilation.

A social scientist first and foremost, Abbott emphasized the importance of conducting methodical research into immigrants' European heritages and American situations before crafting ameliorative policies. "(We) must take account, first, of those traditions and characteristics which belong to the immigrants by reason of their race and early environment and, second, of the peculiar difficulties which they encounter here," Abbott insisted. "These two elements in the problem must be known before we can hope to reach conclusions."[27]

What distinguished Abbott from other progressives was her skepticism of programs designed to distribute immigrants from coastal urban areas to rural hinterlands; her insistence that it was the foreign-born, not the native-born, who sustained American democracy; and her refusal to view immigrants as a threat to American social stability or culture.

Most progressives active in Americanization programs advocated the distribution of immigrants from cities to rural areas where their labor was alleged to be in demand (and where assimilation was thought to more likely occur). Abbott flatly rejected the supposed economic benefits of distribution, saying: "This is not in accordance with the facts. . . . If the immigrant were not industrially 'wanted' he would not go to the city or to the mill town."[28]

Yet Abbott also believed that leaving the distribution of immigrants to market forces was inefficient because the newly arrived foreigner relied upon other immigrants with only slightly more experience in the United States. Immigrants were thus often underemployed and/or employed in the wrong field, and thus unable to maximize their economic potential. Therefore, Abbott advocated public employment offices, believing that private agencies were economically inefficient and often engaged in immoral or fraudulent practices.[29]

Abbott defended immigrants who did not speak English and lived in foreign enclaves, arguing that the immigrant neighborhood was not a place of cultural isolation, but rather a dynamic but temporary institution essential to immigrants' transition and adjustment to American life. The immigrant neighborhood protected immigrants against native-born discrimination and prejudice and sheltered newcomers against the "culture shock" of American society. And there were practical economic as well as social and cultural reasons for newcomers to settle in foreign colonies, Abbott argued.[30]

Yet these neighborhoods were also the sites of crime and vice as well as inadequate housing and city services, such as schools, health care, and sanitation. For this, Abbott blamed machine politics and discrimination by native-born Americans who successfully demanded better services from city leaders for their middle-class neighborhoods while refusing to pay for them in working-class districts.

Abbott believed that immigrants came to the United States with expectations and preconceived ideas about the meanings of democracy and liberty, but they were often disappointed with life in the United States. The America that immigrants encountered tolerated gross inequality, economic exploitation, racial discrimination, and political corruption. Conservative rhetoric about equality of opportunity simply allowed native-born Americans to take advantage of immigrants' unfamiliarity with the mechanisms of American society, economy, and government. In response to conservatives who defined Americanization in terms of teaching immigrants civics and American history, Abbott argued that the principles of democracy and republican government could not be learned through book learning but through active civic engagement, beginning at the local level. "The immigrant does not need to be taught American ideals so much as he needs to be given the facts concerning our organized community life which will enable him to apply those ideals."[31] This meant information about the American legal and political systems and fair access to jobs, housing, education, and other social services.

For Abbott, it was the immigrants' faith in American democracy, liberty, and opportunity that sustained those values; it was native-born cynicism that allowed political corruption and economic fraud to occur. In testifying against the literacy test before Congress in 1912, Abbott argued: "If it were not for the thousands who come every year expecting to find a real fulfillment of the 'promise of American life,' I am afraid the goal of real democracy would have been forgotten long ago."[32] Thus for Abbott, immigrants were central to the progressive rejuvenation of American society and political economy.

Yet living in a city known for its machine politics, Abbott did not believe that immigrants should be left alone to absorb the political and economic values of Chicago's bosses, who corrupted American civic and political life. Along with other Hull-House-based activists, Abbott advocated such middle-class progressive reforms as the short ballot and the referendum, measures that sought to limit working-class democratic action and shift local politics away from individual personalities to impersonal issues. Unlike other political progressives, however, Abbott also advocated bilingual campaign information. Abbott explained foreign-born support for machine politics as evidence of a lack of viable political options. If given the choice, working-class voters would choose progressive social welfare instead of machine assistance. Abbott did not believe that foreign-born voters might derive real or imagined benefits from Chicago's ward bosses or from participating in a more intimate form of politics.[33]

Although Abbott called for greater immigrant involvement and inclusion in the democratic processes of American cities, she did not propose concrete measures for how this would be achieved. Should non-citizens be allowed to vote in municipal or state elections? Should the principle of "one man, one vote" be changed to proportional representation? Or was the solution to be found in organizing immigrants into interest groups based upon religious, national, occupational, or class lines? Beyond advocating greater social services using progressive standards of fairness and need, Abbott did not articulate how her vision of a stronger democracy was to be achieved.

There were other hazards in allowing immigrants to determine their own adjustment. Most progressives, including Abbott, believed that assimilation could occur too quickly, with negative consequences for the individual and society. This negative form of Americanization happened when the immigrant rejected stabilizing traditional values and mistook American values of liberty and freedom for license and irresponsibility. This harmful assimilation was most commonly seen with more experienced immigrants exploiting the American free market to take advantage of newcomers unfamiliar with U.S. wage rates, rents, and banking and other business practices.

The problem of accelerated assimilation most seriously threatened young women, who faced the moral dangers of abandoning the conservative Old World values that protected them. "A too rapid Americanization is dangerous, and the girl who leaves her own people and eats strange American food, learns a new language, and modifies her old country clothes and manners, often wrongly concludes that all her old world ideals are to be abandoned and that in America she is to live under a very different moral code from the one her mother has taught her," Abbott argued.[34]

Thus, assimilation needed to be gradual, methodical, and conducted under the supervision of experienced social workers who could assure that the immigrant learned to distinguish between positive and negative values and behavior. It would be progressive social scientists, such as Abbott, who would determine the value and appropriateness of immigrants' contributions to American society.

Abbott's middle-class background and values were most evident in the league's and the commission's work with immigrant women. Fears of white slavery, seduction, and the moral dangers of taking in boarders and lodgers were continuous themes in IPL and commission discussions of their efforts on behalf of young women.

Abbott's solution to the perceived problem of single women living with relatives and unrelated male boarders was to try to persuade such girls to move out of their immigrant neighborhoods and take live-in jobs in middle-class areas where, theoretically, the girls would not be exposed to such potential moral threats. But she conceded, "We have not been able to persuade many to move, because we have no alternative to offer."[35]

Despite recognition of the economic demands that required most working-class women and children to work, Abbott still encouraged the adoption of the middle-class ideal of working father, stay-at-home mother, and school-attending children.

In one incident, she encountered an Italian family in which the mother and twelve-year-old daughter worked while the unemployed father stayed at home and cared for two younger children. According to Edith Abbott, "Grace had asked the Bureau of Charities to visit the family and see why the man wasn't at work instead of the mother and Carmella. Relief might be needed to keep the mother at home, and, anyway, the twelve-year-old Carmella must go to school."[36] Further investigation revealed that the father was an unemployed carpenter who refused to continue doing unskilled labor after he had paid for his family to join him in Chicago.

Finding the family arrangement unsatisfactory, Abbott arranged for Hull-House to lend the father enough money to join the carpenter's union, which enabled him to go to work and allowed the mother to stay at home and care for the younger children while the older child went to school.[37]

As a long-time resident of Hull-House, Abbott was familiar with alternative family arrangements: the divorced Florence Kelley leaving her three children in the care of friends for weeks at a time; Jane Addams and Ellen Gates Starr and other women living in "Boston marriages"; unmarried childless women living and working cooperatively—that was the core of the settlement concept. Grace and Edith Abbott never married. However, Grace Abbott did not believe such non-traditional family arrangements were possible or desirable for the immigrant working class.

In a time of increasing support for immigration restriction and other conservative approaches to Americanization, Abbott strongly rejected what she considered coercive efforts to get immigrants to adopt American customs. "Compulsion by law or social pressure would fail here just as it has failed in Poland, in Bohemia, and in Lithuania," she argued during World War I. "Americanization means much more than learning to speak the English language under a compulsory school attendance law. While the barrier of language must be removed, it can never be successfully done by autocratic and coercive methods."[38] Yet Abbott had proposed compulsory half-day schools for illiterate aliens between the ages of fourteen and seventeen and evening schools for those ages seventeen to twenty-one in Massachusetts.[39]

Abbott's concerns about anti-immigrant sentiment also did not extend to defending political and labor radicals in the postwar period. During the Red Scare of 1919–1920, when approximately 10,000 people, including hundreds of foreign-born Chicagoans, were arrested for suspected labor radicalism, Abbott was silent.[40] The Immigrants' Protective League and Chicago's United Charities investigated several cases of individuals arrested, and they helped free some men who had been wrongly imprisoned. But as a new government agency just getting organized, the Immigrants Commission did not involve itself directly in helping aliens accused of radicalism.[41]

Abbott had not always been so reluctant to involve herself in political causes. In 1908–1909 she and other Chicago progressives had worked to gain asylum for Christian Ansoff Rudovitz, a Russian émigré whose extradition Russia had demanded for alleged crimes committed during the failed 1905 revolution.[42] But ten years later, Abbott distinguished between protecting immigrants and defending radicals, and carefully avoided controversy.

For much of the 1910s Abbott had been aware of the Americanization activities of other states, particularly Massachusetts, California, and New York. Recognizing that each state had unique immigration histories and patterns as well as differences in agency structure and funding, she was still influenced by other states' immigrant social welfare programs, particularly complaints resolution (which Abbott called "protective case work"); education, including compulsory education laws for illiterate and/or non-English speaking adolescents; and outreach to immigrants.[43]

The IIC was charged with conducting a statewide survey of the conditions under which immigrants lived, but Abbott decided that such a study was impossible with the commission's small budget. Instead, the agency would do targeted studies and assist newly arrived immigrants—not surprisingly, the same type of work the IPL had done. In March 1920 Abbott and the commissioners agreed upon a course of action for the agency for the next year:

Besides monitoring conditions at Chicago's train stations and collecting and resolving complaints, the commission would study mining communities and the educational opportunities available to immigrants in Illinois.[44]

Like other Americanization agencies, the Illinois Immigrants Commission provided complaint resolution services as a way of discovering the problems that immigrants faced and then proposing policy solutions. Although the commission's small budget prevented it from having an extensive complaints department with offices outside of Chicago, the agency did provide valuable services to Chicago's immigrant communities. Many of the nearly 1,950 complaints the IIC received in 1920 involved consequences of the war—problems with transmitting money to Europe (particularly Poland), difficulties in bringing family to the United States, and naturalization questions.[45]

By the fall of 1920 the number of immigrants giving Illinois as their intended final destination had reached prewar levels, and the IIC and the IPL began to devote more time and resources to reuniting families and aiding new arrivals at Chicago's train stations.[46]

The IIC also used its advisory committee and staff investigations of immigrant banks, mutual aid, and benevolent associations as means of making and maintaining contact with Chicago's many immigrant societies. "These societies constitute a means by which contacts can be established with organized groups of the foreign-born," Abbott wrote in the spring of 1920. "They ought be utilized in securing night school enrollment, in state and city health campaigns, in civic undertakings and in spreading information as to state laws, etc., etc."[47]

The education and mining studies gave Abbott the opportunity to demonstrate the advantages and uses of progressive social science research, which she believed was an essential foundation of successful policymaking and social reform. Communities were surveyed and socially mapped, visits and interviews conducted, and reams of statistics collected and analyzed according to the progressive social science methodology Abbott had learned at the University of Chicago.[48]

The education report was also an opportunity for Abbott to promote her vision of Americanization and immigrant education. She lobbied for an "organized and scientific" program that would include training for teachers of adult immigrants; the establishment of standards of achievement to measure community success or failure; the use of foreign-born and fluently bilingual instructors, especially for beginning classes; and special programs for immigrant women and older people, who Abbott believed had different educational needs from those of working men or children.

By 1920 Illinois was experimenting with a program similar to the California Home Teacher Act, and Abbott believed that such a program could potentially be an effective method of educating foreign-born women. She favored a curriculum similar to one the CCIH was promoting that taught the cultural contributions of different immigrant groups, but she disagreed with the suggestion that examples of past American heroes, such as George Washington or Abraham Lincoln, would be useful or meaningful to the foreign-born.[49]

Abbott believed English-only educational programs were ineffective, but she still advocated the adoption of English as the country's primary language. "Removing the language barrier is perhaps the most concrete beginning which can be made in reducing the complications which result from our complex population," she argued.[50] But she also criticized the message of "100 Percent Americanism" as vindictive, insincere, and ineffective. Abbott wrote of the wartime Americanization movement: "A distorted enthusiasm made some believe that apart from the very great individual and community advantages of a common language, a knowledge of English was in and of itself a proof of worth and character; and that a refusal to recognize or tolerate any national culture except our own would result in a united America."[51]

Abbott also believed that educational Americanization programs should not undermine the structure of the immigrant family. Like California commissioner Mary S. Gibson, Abbott feared that public schools' zealous Americanization of immigrant children had the harmful consequence of undermining parental authority and thus the stability of the family. "What is really needed is a reestablishment of the parents in the eyes of the immigrant child," Abbott argued, lobbying for adult education programs that would meet the needs of adult, non-English-speaking foreigners.[52]

After handling almost 2,000 requests for assistance and receiving positive reviews of the education and mining studies, the Immigrants Commission intended to expand its work in 1921, both in terms of the number of studies conducted and in the nature of the services provided to foreign-born residents. In preparing its budget request for 1921–1923, the IIC asked for $53,670 to hire one expert each in domestic science and childcare, social administration, and immigrant education. Abbott also wanted to conduct new studies of immigrant settlement across time and throughout the state; housing conditions in railroad camps; immigrant girls; non-family groups of men; and immigrants working in agriculture. In addition, the commission proposed more immigrant education services and housing regulation, and opening two new offices—one in central Illinois and the other in southern Illinois—to collect complaints. Finally, the commission wanted to open a publicity division to communicate with immigrant institutions, particularly the foreign-language press.[53]

Governor Lowden responded favorably, encouraging the legislature to grant the IIC $58,000 for 1921–1923.[54] But Lowden would not be governor for much longer. In November 1920 conservative Republican Lennington 'Len' Small was elected governor. Eager to establish his own patronage machine in Illinois, Small demanded that Abbott provide him the political affiliations, wards, and precincts of her employees. When Abbott refused, saying that she had hired the staff according to civil service rules and that the IIC was apolitical, Small responded by eliminating the commission's appropriation, effective July 1, 1921.[55]

With the IIC still legally alive but fiscally dead, Abbott moved the office to Hull-House and wrapped up the remaining casework over the next few months. The Immigrants' Protective League—dormant since the spring of 1920—resumed its work, although hampered, as usual, by a lack of funds. When the league ran out of money, it gained financial and political support from the Young Women's Christian Association and the Chicago Americanization Council, a group of civic organizations and social agencies that took over the league's work, using IPL staff. Then Illinois progressives began a campaign to reinstate the commission's appropriation, an effort that continued until as late as 1929. Eventually, in 1926, the IPL officially reconstituted itself and resumed helping immigrants.[56]

Meanwhile, Abbott briefly served as chair of the labor committee of the Illinois State Children's Commission before returning to Washington, D.C., in 1921 to replace Julia Lathrop as director of the U.S. Children's Bureau.

From the start of the campaign to establish the Immigrants Commission to the reactivation of the Immigrants' Protective League's work in 1926, Illinois's progressive Americanizers were highly conscious of the policies and ideas of reformers in other states, especially California, New York, and Massachusetts. They collected reports from other states, corresponded with Americanization activists around the country, and imitated each other's policies. But the Illinois Immigrants Commission pursued its own agenda, reflecting Grace Abbott's paternalistic optimism about immigrants' adaptability and worthiness of inclusion in the larger society.

The commission also faced political barriers that Americanization agencies in New York, California, and Massachusetts did not. By 1919–1920 New York and California had had between seven and ten years to develop their immigrant social welfare policies and build constituencies to help defend their Americanization agencies against conservative attacks. Massachusetts established its immigrant welfare program around the same time as Illinois, but its policy was limited to education and naturalization, aspects of the movement that had been embraced by even the federal government.

The Illinois Immigrants Commission was a product of Chicago's progressive community, but that was a community largely shut out of politics, particularly in Chicago. And after the election of Governor Small, Illinois progressives had no access in Springfield either. When Small cut the commission's funding, he had no concern about progressives' ability to retaliate politically. Nor did he attack the IIC because he objected to its work or Abbott's ideas about immigration and Americanization. Rather, Small killed the commission's appropriation because the agency would not operate according to the rules of Illinois politics.

Illinois' abandonment of its public Americanization policy in 1921 and the resumption of the provision of immigrant social welfare by the Immigrants' Protective League and other private organizations represented the option of private social services common in the Progressive Era that would continue until the New Deal. Meanwhile, the other states that maintained Americanization programs—New York, California and Massachusetts—faced new challenges in sustaining their policies in the face of growing political opposition.

7 ✵ Schooling the Immigrant

Americanization and Adult Education, 1919–1929

During World War I and in the immediate postwar period, state Americanization policies shifted emphasis from reforming the social environment and altering the behavior and attitudes of the native-born to trying to assimilate the immigrant through education. English language classes gave the immigrant a new language; citizenship courses taught him the history, ideals, and mechanisms of American government; factory classes taught him how to work more efficiently and safely. Meanwhile, home teachers instructed immigrant women in English and "American" ways of housekeeping and childcare.

Inspired in part by new federal funding for education after the war, New York, California, and Massachusetts expanded their immigrant education programs. With their efforts to assimilate immigrants through education, progressive educators deepened their knowledge of adult learning, strengthened teacher training, and greatly expanded educational opportunities for adults not destined for higher education. Educational Americanization was a means by which progressives tried to both professionalize and democratize education.

But enrollment in immigrant education programs was always low, even as states tried to attract the foreign-born through a more diversified curriculum, better teaching, and compulsory attendance laws. With alien adults apparently disinterested in immigrant education, justifying such programs became more difficult, and classes were cut. By 1923 New York, California, and Massachusetts were among only eight states in the country that supported Americanization programs, most of them focusing on education.[1] By 1929, when the United States instituted the National Origins Quota Act restricting immigration to northern Europeans, immigrant education programs had been largely replaced by adult education, as educators sought to broaden their constituency from undesirable aliens to upwardly mobile, working-class Americans, both foreign- and native-born. The curriculum was often juvenile and the teachers ill-trained, but immigrant education in the United States laid the foundation for adult education, based upon the progressive belief that an educated citizenry was essential for a stable and democratic republic.

Immigrant assimilation through education had been endorsed by the Wilson administration in the spring of 1918, but the federal government abruptly withdrew from the Americanization movement after the war by terminating most of its Americanization programs and directing federal funds away from projects specifically for immigrants to ones that benefited U.S. citizens, particularly in the middle and working classes.

Federal support for Americanization ended in 1919 after Congress banned public agencies from receiving private support, thus cutting off the U.S. Bureau of Education from National Americanization Committee funds. The bureau tried to get special funding for its Americanization programs, first through the Smith-Bankhead Bill, and then the Kenyon-Vestel Bill. The Kenyon-Vestel Bill, which passed the Senate in January 1920, would have granted the U.S. Bureau of Education $12.5 million annually to distribute among the states to promote literacy and English-language instruction in 1920–1923. But the House version died in committee, and efforts at reintroduction in 1921 failed. By that time, the Bureau of Education had already closed its Americanization division. In November 1919 the bureau published the last issue of its *Americanization* bulletin, an important source of information about national immigrant social welfare activities.[2] The U.S. Bureau of Naturalization was able to continue funding its distribution of citizenship training materials to public schools only because it had access to naturalization fees.[3]

Instead of funding immigrant education, Congress devoted large sums to vocational and agricultural education through the Smith-Hughes National Vocational Education Act, passed in 1917.

The great advantage of Smith-Hughes over the Bureau of Education's proposed immigrant education bills was that it theoretically provided services to more people, and particularly to more citizens than aliens in both rural and urban areas. Americanization activists had made much ado about the many illiterate, non-English speakers drafted into the Army during the war. However, wartime intelligence tests had also revealed large numbers of native-born illiterates, particularly from the South, a region that was culturally inclined toward immigration restriction and had leadership entrenched in Congress.[4]

With federal funds available for *adult* education, many states, including New York, Massachusetts, and California, initiated new educational programs or expanded existing ones. Initially, these programs targeted non-English-speaking adults, but they developed a broader constituency as the decade progressed.

In 1919 the New York legislature appropriated $100,000 to expand the state's adult education programs offered by the Department of Education's Division of Vocational and Extension Education. Although the funds were nominally for adult education, in practice the money was used to fund New York's educational Americanization policy. Education officials divided the state into fifteen zones and appointed a director to oversee adult education and Americanization in each zone. In addition to a director, each zone was assigned teachers; an organizer responsible for recruiting students and publicizing the program in the zone; and "specialists in the various fields of administration, supervision, community organization, teacher training, factory and home class instruction and teaching in evening or day classes."[5]

Significant pressure to expand New York's adult education program in 1920–1921 came from the anti-radical state Committee to Investigate Seditious Activities, chaired by Republican state Senator Clayton R. Lusk. Looking for a way to shut down the socialist-affiliated Rand School of Social Science in New York City, Lusk shepherded through the legislature five bills that mandated Americanization classes in factories and community centers; required the University of the State of New York (the administrator for all state education programs) to license secular private schools; directed state commissioners of education to examine and certify the loyalty of public school teachers; instituted specialized teacher training in adult education; and created a state bureau to investigate and prosecute groups and individuals under the state's criminal anarchy statute. Though these bills were vetoed by Governor Al Smith, the private school licensing and teacher loyalty certification bills were reintroduced, passed, and signed by conservative Republican Governor Nathan L. Miller in 1921 after he defeated Smith in November 1920. (The Lusk laws were repealed in February 1923 after Smith regained the governorship by campaigning against them.)

Although the New York City Teachers' Union, settlement houses, civic organizations, and religious schools opposed the private school licensing bill out of fear that it would be selectively applied against their educational programs, the Department of Education supported the Lusk laws as a way of increasing its authority and responsibility. New York education officials also used the January 1920 Lusk committee hearings on education as an opportunity to lobby for more resources and to link the training and qualifications of teachers to the assimilation of immigrants.[6] Unfortunately, the association of

Americanization with Red hunting also tainted immigrant education in the eyes of many foreign-born New Yorkers.

One of the many tensions within progressive education was over the question of segmenting students and differentiating curricula based upon ability versus providing a common core of knowledge to everyone. Many progressives advocated providing specialized education to students based upon their needs and interests, yet others clung to the value of a common core in the school curricula. Progressive Americanizers sought to reconcile this tension by providing immigrant students with a core curriculum of English literacy and American history supplemented by a curriculum supposedly tailored to aliens' needs and abilities. This combination of specialization and core curriculum could be found in adult education policies in New York and Massachusetts.

In New York, adult education encompassed several different programs: evening classes teaching commercial, industrial, and traditional academic subjects at both the elementary and secondary levels; immigrant education, comprised of English literacy and preparation for naturalization; factory classes, which often included training specific to plant or industry conditions, as well as English instruction; classes for immigrant women in their homes or nearby community centers; and part-time day classes for illiterate and non-English-speaking minors between the ages of sixteen and twenty-one. In 1921 more than 245,000 New Yorkers were registered in some type of public adult education program, and one-third of them, about 82,500 people, were enrolled in immigrant education programs offered in evening schools, factories, community centers, and private homes.[7]

But that year the New York legislature changed its funding mechanism for adult education, cutting back the large appropriations it had been giving the University of the State of New York since 1917. Instead, the state legislature authorized the Department of Education to reimburse local school districts for one-half of the salaries of evening and extension schoolteachers working with illiterate and non-English-speaking adults, up to $1,000 per instructor.[8]

This change in funding hurt immigrant education programs in New York City, where nearly 70 percent of the state's illiterate and non-English-speaking residents lived. Despite the cutbacks, the Department of Education continued to promote instructional services for immigrants; and initially, New York's foreign-born seemed receptive.[9]

In 1922 the number of students enrolled in immigrant education classes in New York increased to nearly 94,500, but this increase only occurred in the larger cities; enrollment in adult education classes in smaller towns declined.[10] In 1923 enrollment in immigrant education classes dropped to 85,700 before jumping to more than 102,300 in 1924, as the presidential election and the debate about restriction spurred immigrants' interest in naturalization and the growing number of benefits that came with American citizenship.[11]

By the mid-1920s students enrolled in New York's immigrant education classes studied U.S. history, geography, hygiene, and current events, as well as English and civics. Specialized courses prepared students petitioning for citizenship for naturalization court interviews.[12] In 1920 the Bureau of Naturalization reported that it was working with 183 New York communities to develop and sustain citizenship education programs. Only Minnesota, Pennsylvania, Washington, and California exceeded New York in the number of communities participating in citizenship education projects.[13]

In the 1920s the Massachusetts Department of Education also expanded its Americanization instruction through its Division of University Extension, which provided correspondence courses and in-class extension lessons for adults not enrolled in colleges or universities.

In January 1919 the Division of University Extension produced a guideline, *The Federal-State Program for Immigrant Education,* under the theme "One Language, One Country." Not surprisingly, the division defined Americanization as "essentially a problem of education"; and, as such, responsibility for it belonged to the Department of Education. Other agencies, such as the Massachusetts Bureau of Immigration, could play important roles, but they were to be subordinate to the Department of Education.

The goals of the Massachusetts Federal-State Program were to make English the prevailing language of the commonwealth and nation; to foster better relations between native- and foreign-born residents; "to preserve the best contributions brought from the Old World and unite them with the best ideals of the New"; to prepare aliens for naturalization and citizenship; and "to make a united people, loyal to America."[14]

Assimilation was to be measured primarily in terms of English adoption. That 62.5 percent of illiterates had lived in Massachusetts for six years or longer was "strong evidence that the assimilative processes have not worked very rapidly."[15]

But the Massachusetts Department of Education also believed that there were different degrees of assimilation. Big business had taught the immigrant American industrial work habits, but "the process still left him an alien in his relation to the other citizens of the commonwealth, and in his understanding and appreciation of the fundamental ideals and purposes which form the groundwork of American democracy," the Division of University Extension argued.[16] Courses in citizenship would make the immigrant a more well-rounded individual, better able to appreciate his relationships and obligations to the larger society outside of the workplace.

Believing that evening schools attracted only the most ambitious of the foreign-born and left many others unschooled, the Division of University Extension lobbied for the development and expansion of three types of classes: day and evening, factory, and home.[17]

In July 1919 the Massachusetts legislature endorsed the division's Federal-State Program and approved an "emergency" law "to promote Americanization through the education of adult persons unable to use the English language." Local school boards were to provide the classes and teachers, and the state would pay for up to half the cost of a community's immigrant education classes, as the 1913 Immigration Commission had recommended. Instruction was required to be in the English language and to incorporate the principles of American government and citizenship. In September 1919 Education Commissioner Payson Smith hired Lowell Normal School principal John J. Mahoney to be the state's supervisor of immigrant education.[18]

The combination of state monies and increasing demand for classes caused many Massachusetts towns to initiate adult education programs for both foreign- and native-born adults. In 1920 Mahoney reported that sixty-three communities had organized immigrant education classes, and enrollment had jumped from 3,281 to 9,030 between December 1918 and December 1919. Enrollment in evening school classes, which included English language instruction, citizenship, as well as other subjects, was even higher, with more than 27,600 students in eighty-five cities and towns in 1919. By 1922–1923, enrollment in immigrant education programs in Massachusetts was more than 27,650 students, most of them (20,425) in evening schools, but a sizable minority (4,100) in factory schools.[19]

Most of these immigrant education classes were initiated and directed by local businesses, usually large employers of immigrant labor, and by women's clubs through a program of "cooperative classes." In cooperative classes, the organizer of the course paid for the instructor and the Division of University Extension paid for lesson materials, supervised instruction, and provided graduation certificates. The division also fostered what it called "certificating classes," which were courses provided by private organizations but that had curricula and instructors approved by the division.[20] This method allowed the local chapters of a wide range of organizations to effectively control immigrant education courses without much state supervision after the division approved the initial course outline.

For example, the Daughters of the American Revolution had fifty chapters in Massachusetts active in Americanization work. Believing that the foreign-born would learn good citizenship by studying U.S. history and civics, singing patriotic songs, and reenacting historical events, twenty-five DAR chapters provided local classes with teaching materials, flags, and pictures of presidents; and they helped organize social, musical, and theatrical events. Individual members also donated time to help prepare alien students for naturalization interviews. Massachusetts DAR chapters did such volunteer work into the late 1920s.[21]

Mahoney's assistant, and later replacement, Charles M. Herlihy attributed the steady rise in student enrollment to the state's willingness to invest in teacher training and subsidize communities' adult education classes.[22] In 1920 the legislature reimbursed Massachusetts communities for their immigrant education classes for a total of $71,637. By 1923 that figure had jumped to $149,983.[23]

Nevertheless, the number of aliens enrolled in immigrant education programs in Massachusetts and New York was quite low when compared to the number of foreign-born in each state. Massachusetts had more than a million foreign-born residents in 1920, while New York had 2,786,112 foreign-born residents. According to the U.S. Census of 1920, Massachusetts had 135,720 foreign-born illiterate residents, while New York had 389,603. Both achieved their highest enrollments in immigrant education classes in 1924, with approximately 32,300 students in Massachusetts and 102,300 students in New York, respectively. This was about 3 percent of each state's total foreign-born population. Even if one assumes that all immigrant education students were illiterate (and not all were), immigrant education was reaching only about 23 percent of illiterate aliens in Massachusetts and 26 percent of illiterate aliens in New York.[24]

In California, meanwhile, in 1920 the illiterate immigrant population was 69,768, only 2.4 percent of the nearly 2.9 million Californians ages ten or older. Yet, as in other parts of the country, enrollment in immigrant education programs was low: Only 2,080 foreign-born Californians twenty-one years old or older were attending some type of school in 1920.[25]

Low enrollment in immigrant education courses reflected the fact that after several years of policy development, educators were still struggling to overcome problems of inappropriate curricula, ineffective and uninspiring teaching, and weak enforcement of compulsory school laws for minors. Although immigrant education courses failed to attract large numbers of non-English-speaking foreigners, state educators persisted in maintaining their educational Americanization policies.

Factory classes were particularly unsuccessful, yet remained popular with Americanizers. Ever since the war, both educators and some employers believed that factory classes were an effective way of improving workplace safety and productivity, while reaching those men who found evening school inconvenient or were not interested in pursuing education on their own. These industrial education programs of the early 1920s were part of the larger welfare capitalism movement in which business leaders attempted to woo employees away from labor unions by providing such benefits as health care, pensions, stock purchase plans, subsidized housing, and even recreational and social activities.[26]

Even the industrialized Northeast had few workplace programs. In New York, school districts and businesses partnered in 1920 to offer instruction in English and job skills to approximately 5,000 men and women in 262 factory classes in thirty-five cities and towns—a very low number given the immigrant population of the state.[27] These programs were vulnerable to economic conditions, and the number of immigrants enrolled in New York factory classes dropped to nearly 3,500 men and women in 1921 as the economy went into recession and employers cut programs.[28]

When businesses withdrew from Americanization programs, some of their foreign-born employees turned to industrial education offered in public evening schools. In New York enrollment in these courses rose in 1921–1922 to 30,795 students, as the public schools stepped in to meet student demand and to fill the vacuum left by industry.[29] By 1923 immigrant education classes offered by businesses were most commonly found in New York City, Rochester, Buffalo, Syracuse, and a handful of smaller industrial towns where Americanization programs had been established before the war.[30]

In Massachusetts, industries' support of factory classes was even weaker, despite the efforts of the Division of University Extension and the Bureau of Immigration during the war. Just under 3,300 immigrant workers were enrolled in Massachusetts factory classes at the end of World War I.[31] A survey of the state's employers in 1919 found that classes were being held in only about thirty factories, with ten more businesses sponsoring their workers' education outside the plant. About seventy-five businesses employing fifty or more non-English-speaking workers were willing to consider instituting classes in their shops.[32]

In response to this lack of enthusiasm on the part of business, the Massachusetts Department of Education intensified its efforts to increase industry's participation in factory schools. Between 1919 and 1920, the Division of University Extension hosted three educational Americanization conferences, two of them in partnership with Associated Industries, a trade organization that represented 1,600 firms. At these conferences, business leaders pledged themselves to a program of voluntary (and uncompensated) English-language instruction for their non-English-speaking employees.[33] In November 1920 the division also hired Cambridge Assistant Superintendent Charles M. Herlihy to promote and supervise factory classes.[34]

The combination of publicity, increased availability, and anti-immigrant sentiment during the Red Scare caused enrollment in Massachusetts factory classes to jump from 3,200 in November 1918 to 15,320 in November 1920. "It is worthy of note that the increase was in a period (September, 1919, to Nov. 30, 1920) during which industry was almost stagnant, and that, at the time of the writing of this report (January, 1921) new classes are being opened weekly in cities and towns heretofore only mildly interested in immigrant education," University Extension director James A. Moyer reported to the Massachusetts legislature.[35]

Although many manufacturers withdrew from industrial Americanization programs and other progressive welfare capital projects, businesses belonging to the Associated Industries maintained an average of 250 factory classes into the late 1920s.[36]

Factory classes had the potential of reaching a significant minority of immigrant men, and even some women, who worked for large- or medium-sized businesses. Employers could—and some did—make class attendance mandatory or offer incentives for participation, and the curriculum could be made relevant to workplace conditions. But factory classes, like all welfare capitalism programs, always came with a cost-benefit analysis: When the economy tightened, factory English classes were among the first frills to be cut. Employers also increasingly sought to shift the cost of training their workforces to the local public schools. Larger school districts welcomed the opportunity to expand their vocational and evening school programs, as New York City did, after the recession of 1921. Massachusetts employers who continued to offer internal factory classes into the late 1920s were unusual in their willingness to sustain their immigrant education programs.

New York education officials did attempt to promote factory classes for women—given the large number of immigrant women working in New York City factories—but most educational services for foreign-born women continued to follow the model of home teaching established in California. While English fluency was an important goal, American-style home economics was an equally valuable part of the curriculum. Although women were on the verge of achieving the vote and the full benefits of legal citizenship, progressive Americanizers, including those who supported woman's suffrage, continued to conflate women's roles as wives and mothers with that of voting citizens.

After traveling to Los Angeles in 1919 to observe the California Commission of Immigration and Housing's home teaching project, New York City school officials established the position of "visiting teacher," and by 1920 the city had eight such instructors.[37] But unlike in California, these teachers did more social work than provide adult education for immigrant mothers; they targeted families whose children were considered potential juvenile delinquents. In California, home teaching was seen as an antidote to juvenile delinquency, yet all immigrant mothers were targeted—not simply those with deviant or potentially delinquent children. But the goal of reaching the allegedly isolated immigrant mother was the same in New York as it was in California.

New York education officials believed that home classes for women were effective tools for Americanization, specifically because of the intrusive nature of the visiting teacher's work. "A more direct influence is brought to bear, wherever this is needed, for better hygienic and sanitary conditions, cleaner and better prepared food, more balanced diet, greater attention to proper care of babies and children, and other strictly home affairs."[38] As in California, visiting teachers sought to convince foreign-born women to exchange their native customs for an "American" lifestyle as defined in Anglo-Saxon cultural terms.

Initially, significant numbers of foreign-born women participated in New York's immigrant education programs, particularly after the passage of the woman's suffrage amendment in 1920 and the Cable Act of 1922, which separated a woman's citizenship from her husband's. In 1921, 29,210 women were enrolled in immigrant education classes (35 percent of enrollment); in 1923, nearly 34,000 were enrolled (almost 40 percent).[39] The federal Bureau of Naturalization's Division of Citizenship Training reported that public schools were cooperating with private organizations, many of them women's clubs, to prepare foreign-born women for naturalization and suffrage.[40]

The New York Department of Education also offered home economics programs in evening schools, but these lost their popularity in the early 1920s as women enrolled in immigrant education classes that were more specifically tailored to their needs and interests. In 1920–1921, 21,775 immigrant women were enrolled in 628 homemaking classes in thirty-four New York communities. This number dropped to 19,000 in 1923.[41] These courses covered "such phases of homemaking as the nutrition of the family, clothing of the family, health of the family, selection, furnishing and care of the house, care and rearing of children, management and expenditure of the income, the social, moral and civic obligations of the home"—things that most immigrant mothers believed they already knew.[42]

Home classes for immigrant women began more slowly in Massachusetts because the Division of University Extension did not embrace the home teacher concept until 1923. But by 1927 the state had more than 200 home classes in thirty cities. As in California and New York, Massachusetts' approach to home teaching was based upon the perception of the foreign-born woman as culturally and physically isolated, burdened with children and household responsibilities, and requiring exposure to Anglo-American social customs and housekeeping methods.[43]

Ever since California had pioneered the concept of home teaching for immigrant women in 1915, the methodological debate about whether child-directed Americanization programs undermined the immigrant family or assisted in its assimilation had continued unresolved into the 1920s. The progressive administrators of the federal Sheppard-Towner Maternity and Infancy Act, passed in 1921, promoted "little mothers" classes for adolescent girls in hope of influencing parents who were resistant to American cultural practices. On the conservative end of the spectrum, the DAR, the National Security League, and the new American Legion began to aggressively promote citizenship education in public schools. These groups believed that children could more easily be inculcated with feelings of loyalty through patriotic rituals involving flag ceremonies, loyalty pledges, singing, pageants, and parades than could adults.[44] This conservative approach to Americanization defined loyalty to the nation as obedience to the nation-state, and explicitly identified "Bolshevism" and other variations of socialist theory as "un-American."[45] Through "patriotic education," children were to be taught to "oppose any revolutionary movements, such as Bolshevism, anarchism, I.W.W.-ism, or any movement antagonistic to the laws of the United States or tending to subvert the Constitution of the United States," as a proposed 1919 pledge of loyalty for the New York City schools read.[46]

But conservatives became active in citizenship education for children primarily because they were increasingly skeptical of their ability to influence immigrant adults. By 1921 most patriotic organizations that had been active in Americanization during and immediately after the war had scaled back their immigrant education programs and endorsed immigration restriction as the best solution to the perceived problems of labor radicalism and undesirable foreign cultures in America. Only the DAR continued its Americanization work among foreign-born adults even as it withdrew its support from a wide range of progressive projects and embraced immigration restriction in the mid-1920s.[47]

Immigrant youth who had avoided the assimilating influences of the American public school through truancy or employment were a new target of Americanization activists in the 1920s. Continuing the trend toward coercion established during World War I, states began passing compulsory education measures in the immediate postwar period. In early 1919 California passed a law that required non-English-speaking immigrants between the ages of eighteen and twenty-one to attend school for four hours each week. In 1921 the law was amended to require high schools to provide classes if twenty or more non-English-speaking minors lived in the district. In 1923 the education law was revised again, this time requiring non-English-speaking adult aliens to attend citizenship classes and directing districts to provide classes when requested by twenty or more students.[48]

In 1920 New York required local school boards to open part-time or continuation schools for minors between the ages of fourteen and eighteen who had not graduated from high school and had ceased attending school. These youths, if working, were required to attend day classes four–eight hours per week for thirty-six weeks. If unemployed, they were to attend for twenty hours per week.[49]

Progressives had long been willing to use the power of the state to compel minors to attend school, believing that a common public education would create the educated citizenry needed to sustain a democratic republic. New compulsory education laws in the 1920s that targeted young people under the age of twenty-one were an extension of earlier progressive efforts to keep children in school longer. Yet, like previous compulsory laws, the key was enforcement, and enforcement was frequently weak. States might require non-English-speakers to attend immigrant education classes, but few would actually be forced to do so. Instead, the threat of compulsion, combined with an increase in educational services, pressured immigrants to enroll in classes.

More immigrants enrolling in classes meant more demand for more teachers. Reflecting the broader movement within American education for professionalism and specialization, education officials emphasized the necessity of developing instructors who were specially trained in identifying and meeting the unique pedagogical needs of non-English-speaking adults.

In the fall of 1919 the New York Division of Vocational and Extension Education received a special appropriation of $12,500 for teacher training and promptly turned to literacy expert Henry H. Goldberger and Union College professor Dr. Robert T. Hill, who had co-led teacher training institutes for New York's Department of Education since 1915.[50] Goldberger, who had authored the 1919 U.S. Bureau of Education bulletin, *Teaching English to the Foreign Born: A Teacher's Handbook*, also developed an adult course of English as a Second Language that focused on teaching practical English, including lessons on opening bank accounts, visiting the doctor, making purchases, and asking directions.[51]

In Massachusetts the Division of University Extension offered two, one month-long professional development courses on immigrant education techniques at the State Normal School in Hyannis in July 1919 and January 1920. Taught by immigrant education director Charles F. Towne and entitled "Americanization: One Language—One People," the July 1919 seminar focused on "Methods of Teaching English to Immigrants," and "Organization and Supervision of Americanization Work." The January 1920 workshop was "for Supervisors and Organizers of Americanization Activities" and provided "an Elementary Course for Teachers."[52]

In California the Commission of Immigration and Housing worked closely with the state superintendent's office and the University of California's Division of Extension to produce more immigrant education teachers to meet the demand caused by the state's new compulsory education laws. First, in the summer of 1919 commissioner Mary S. Gibson persuaded Superintendent of Instruction Will C. Wood to hire Los Angeles Normal School professor Ruby Baughman (who had worked with Gibson on the 1917 home teachers demonstration) to train teachers to work with non-English-speakers.[53]

Next, the CCIH collaborated with University of California Extension director Leon Richardson and the superintendent's office to plan a series of six-week teacher training courses to be held in Los Angeles, Fresno, and San Francisco in the fall of 1919. Ethel Richardson acted as Americanization supervisor, overseeing the fieldwork for the classes. The 150 students who completed the seminars received a special certificate indicating their advanced training in immigrant education.[54]

But Gibson's coup was in December 1919 when she got Ethel Richardson hired as the assistant superintendent of immigrant education.[55] In this position, Richardson became responsible for overseeing the state's Americanization program in the public schools and the normal school training of home teachers and other instructors working with immigrants. She also helped to organize immigrant education instructors into the California Association of Americanization Teachers, and contributed regularly to its journal, *Community Exchange Bulletin*.[56] Most importantly, she provided a close personal and bureaucratic link between the Commission of Immigration and Housing and the state Department of Education. This connection was maintained in part because the CCIH continued to pay her salary until the state legislature increased the Board of Education's appropriation.[57] But Richardson, Gibson, and the other commissioners also shared the opinion that immigrant education, and home teaching in particular, needed to be professionalized and imbedded in the state's education system.

With Richardson in the superintendent's office, the number of home teachers and immigrant education classes in California grew rapidly. In 1918, twenty home teachers were at work; by 1923, Los Angeles alone had forty-seven home teachers.[58] In 1920, thirty-five school districts in twenty-seven cities offered immigrant education, mostly in evening schools; by 1922, 140 districts offered classes for the foreign-born.[59] Now the state's challenge became to sustain its capacity to produce enough immigrant education instructors to meet the new demand.

To attract and train more immigrant education teachers, the commission organized and hosted a second series of seminars in the summer of 1920. Richardson and New York community organization leader John Collier oversaw a second round of teacher training courses at the University of California–Berkley; the University of California–Los Angeles; the University of Southern California; and teachers' colleges in San Jose and San Francisco. In addition to these formal courses, several short-session institutes were held for instructors already teaching immigrants.[60]

It was in their teacher training materials that Americanizers most clearly articulated their ideas of American citizenship. These ideas and the methods used to encourage good citizenship on the part of their foreign-born students were hardly a monolithic program of coercion and elitism.[61] Rather, the educational philosophies and pedagogies underlying immigrant education programs, particularly in California and Massachusetts, were diverse and represented the persistence of paternalistic yet cosmopolitan values of pro-immigrant progressives. Building upon its home teachers' manuals, the California Commission of Immigration and Housing published "Heroes of Freedom" in early 1919 during the Paris peace talks and the signing of the treaty at Versailles. "Heroes of Freedom" was designed to be a tool for California teachers to educate their students about famous individuals, such as Pocahontas, Abraham Lincoln, Wilbur Wright, Charlemagne, Joan of Arc, and Beowulf, who exemplified desired American values. Non-Western "heroes," such as Confucius, and recent military celebrities (although none from Germany) were also included on the "Heroes of Freedom" list. Even the contributions of American Indians, and "the negro," and Japanese folk stories of exploring the Pacific (and possibly discovering California) were cited. (Mexicans were subsumed under "Latin peoples," meaning Spanish colonizers). A bibliography of "hero tales" focused on Europeans but also included Chinese and Japanese epic works that teachers could use to demonstrate heroic and noble deeds of various nationalities. The commission hoped that by learning such stories, native-born children would come to appreciate "immigrant gifts," while foreign-born children would regain respect for their parents' cultures, thus reinforcing immigrant parents' authority in the home.[62] And with Ethel Richardson now assistant superintendent for immigrant education, CCIH teaching materials were guaranteed to be widely distributed among immigrant education teachers.

The values upon which the United States was founded, according to "Heroes of Freedom," included love of liberty, courage, honor, justice, human equality, and loyalty. Children were to be taught a sense of cosmopolitanism and the idea that although they came from other nations, they were also Americans. The commission emphasized its belief that through immigration America was "neither Latin nor Slav, Celt nor Anglo-Saxon," but becoming a new nation through cultural mingling.[63] "American hero stories should bring out that the greatness of America is due to the mixture of peoples, that Democracy is dependent upon freedom from race prejudice and class distinctions, that the great men of America have usually been those who have risen from poverty, through their own efforts."[64]

To accompany the "Heroes of Freedom" booklet, the CCIH designed a "Family Tree of America" that charted the nationalities of the world that came together through immigration to make up the United States. The commission argued, "The story of our United States of America is a story of the foreigner, his adventurous spirit of discovery and exploration, and his courageous spirit of colonization. It is the story of the interdependence of peoples."[65] Thus, the CCIH continued to view Americanization in racially inclusive terms, even including the Chinese and Japanese, who were legally excluded from American citizenship, in their vision of the American community. (How teachers were to explain discriminatory laws and practices to their Asian students was not addressed.)

The commission also continued to defend communicating with immigrants in their native languages and on the need to have foreign-language speakers involved with local Americanization efforts. The CCIH argued that Americans should learn from the examples of European monarchies, such as Austria-Hungary, that linguistic compulsion did not work, and in fact, alienated immigrants from mainstream society and the government. Valuing immigrants' native languages was a key way to gain the foreign-born's loyalty and love of country. Furthermore, Americanization could not wait for the immigrant to learn the "American language." Instead, the immigrant had to be reached in his or her native language and through the immigrant press.[66]

Although Massachusetts educators did not go so far as to endorse bilingual education, they did articulate similar progressive ideas in their teaching materials. Within the Division of University Extension, progressive pedagogy was clearly expressed in a teacher's handbook of forty-five "Standard Lessons in English for American Citizenship," produced in 1919.

In the handbook, the Division of University Extension articulated a view of educational Americanization that was increasingly common among pro-immigrant progressives late in the 1910s: The effective immigrant education teacher was sympathetic to foreign-born residents; knowledgeable about his or her students' national heritages; and most importantly, not condescending or patronizing. "The friendly attitude of the teacher will bring out the best of these contributions which the newer arrivals from the Old World are constantly bringing to the New," the teacher's handbook advised.[67] Thus, the university extension staff shared with the California commissioners the progressive idea that American society was a dynamic mix of cultures and was constantly in the process of evolving.

Teachers were advised to segregate students based upon ability, sex, and "race" ("because of the lack of a common language, racial prejudice is perpetuated and sometimes intensified"), but were informed that once students had a rudimentary English vocabulary, this separation was no longer necessary. "Democracy means that individuals must learn to live in harmony with those about them. Such harmony is impossible where individuals are unable to communicate with one another because of the barrier of language," the handbook instructed.[68]

The teacher's handbook also provided specialized lesson series for teachers working with immigrant women and an industrial series for factory classes. Both series conveyed certain core middle-class values. The "Lessons in English for Women with Home Interests" covered a wide range of homemaking activities, including making breakfast, shopping, and writing and mailing letters. The lessons also promoted children attending school (rather than working); the importance of serving children milk rather than coffee or tea; calling a doctor instead of a midwife in the case of illness; housekeeping; infant care; and the importance of frugality, thrift, and budgeting expenses. Lessons also were designed to teach the societal functions of the police and fire departments, library, and post office. The industrial series taught workers to wash their hands and faces with soap before eating lunch, and emphasized safety measures; efficiency; how to resolve such disputes as mistakes in wages; and the role of the U.S. Employment Service in helping people find jobs.

Another aid for immigrant education teachers in Massachusetts was "Civics of Naturalization," which the university extension division initially published in 1917 and re-released in 1919 and 1921 after women had been granted the vote. The booklet listed a series of questions about U.S. government and history that immigrants applying for citizenship could expect to be asked by federal naturalization examiners, and described Massachusetts and city government structures and commonwealth history. Similar to California's "Heroes of Freedom" pamphlet, the "Civics of Naturalization" publication explored the idea that the United States had pluralistic origins by noting the historical contributions of several European nations—Italy and Spain (Christopher Columbus' discovery of America); France (early explorers and Huguenot settlers); the Netherlands (Henry Hudson and New Amsterdam); and Germany and Scandinavia (early settlers)—to American society.[69]

The teacher's handbook and "Civics of Naturalization" were produced under the guidance of Mahoney, who introduced a more cosmopolitan approach to the university extension division's Americanization policy during the critical years of 1919–1922.

Although still focused on education and English literacy, Americanizers in Massachusetts now began to speak of Americanization as a transformation of the native-born as well as of the foreign-born, an idea the CCIH had been proselytizing since the mid-1910s. "We have found that we must first Americanize ourselves before attempting to make good American citizens of our foreign population," the division noted. "Experience has taught us that everything touching the immigrant's life is an instrumentality for his Americanization, or the reverse." Thus, Americanization was as much about preventing exploitation; providing good housing; "clean milk for babies"; "adequate wages"; "satisfactory industrial conditions"; and the "spirit of neighborliness" between the native- and foreign-born as it was about learning English.[70]

This idea of Americanization being a total way of life has been interpreted as treating immigrants like children who needed to abandon all aspects of foreign culture and remake themselves into would-be "WASPs."[71] Yet it was this approach to Americanization that placed responsibility for immigrants' living and working conditions on the native-born, who, through the powers and privileges of legal citizenship, held considerable political and economic power over aliens. Immigrant education had always focused on trying to change the immigrant directly by teaching him or her English and American customs. By exploring the idea of Americanization as mutual assimilation, Mahoney began to move the Division of University Extension toward a broader understanding of citizenship that involved both rights and obligations on the part of citizens and aliens.

Mahoney also reflected that "Americanism must come through the efforts of the immigrant himself; it cannot be imposed from without. Attachment to the United States does not take away from the immigrant his religion, language, social customs."[72] These views were markedly different from the "America First"-type of language that the division had extolled in early 1919 and that conservatives continued to use in advocating immigration restriction. American democracy and society were now described as dynamic and reciprocal, the United States as a nation in the process of being created by both the native- and the foreign-born. Most importantly, Americanization should not be coercive. "The Great War has made a great many people hysterical," Mahoney noted disapprovingly of the anti-radical hysteria of the Red Scare. "The Americanizer, of all people, needs to remain sane."[73]

Under Mahoney's leadership, the division broadened its concept of citizenship and changed the way it prepared teachers to teach civics and history. Instead of focusing on historical facts and the mechanics of government, Mahoney emphasized the goal of creating a good citizen and designed lessons around the core questions of: What is American democracy? How did it develop? How does the U.S. government and American democracy work and serve the American people? Encouraging immigrant students and their teachers to explore these questions was a radically different approach to citizenship education than was commonly found in American schools. Despite this new theoretical foundation, the purpose of the course was to prepare aliens for naturalization, and legal citizenship was to be the measure of students' Americanization.

The course, "Thirty Lessons in Naturalization and Citizenship," was designed for literate and English-speaking students, and emphasized class discussion and examples of citizenship in daily life. The course outline emphasized a definition of democracy as cooperation and that "every American is an immigrant or a descendent of an immigrant."[74] While this definition effectively excluded American Indians and black Americans and their descendents from membership in the national community of immigrants, it also rejected the restrictionists' claim that native-born, Anglo-Saxon Protestants were the only true Americans and all others were hyphenates and second-class citizens. Mahoney reiterated the argument that "making English the language of all Americans" did not mean immigrants giving up their native languages. Instead he envisioned English would become a type of national "lingua franca" (a common language) that a diverse people would use to communicate with one another.[75] These thirty lessons were to be taught in special courses for advanced students preparing for naturalization.

The new naturalization and citizenship course also reflected the middle-class values of Mahoney and his staff in the Division of University Extension. The pioneers of America were described as "hard-working, thrifty," middle-class people who valued liberty, education, and property ownership. Foreign-born students were encouraged to vote against political machines; prolong their children's education; keep their homes clean and tidy; and engage in healthful outdoor recreation and play.[76] In a state with contentious labor relations, the course outline advocated the view that while strikes sometimes benefited workers, they always hurt the general public, and often both labor and capital. Working-class immigrants were to be taught the benefits of arbitration, union collective bargaining, and "industrial democracy," which was defined as being when "employer and employee learn to pull together in a spirit of friendly co-operation."[77]

California progressives had pioneered educational Americanization, yet ironically state commitment to immigrant education began to weaken once Ethel Richardson joined the state superintendent's office in late 1919. This was primarily because the Commission of Immigration and Housing was no longer in charge of California's immigrant education policy, and California education leaders had other priorities besides Americanization.

Although the CCIH's teacher training institutes had attracted a large number of participants in the summer of 1920, by the fall education officials were beginning to lose interest in the project. Richardson spent most of October attending conferences of educational leaders, trying to persuade them to continue the seminars and implement the commission's proposal for a certificate in Americanization and immigrant education.[78]

The lack of interest in educational Americanization on the part of state officials meant that local school districts were left largely on their own in developing their immigrant education programs. Cities and towns with active women's clubs and elite civic organizations were much more likely to have strong immigrant education programs than other communities.[79] The lack of strong state coordination also meant that great variation existed in quality and method of immigrant education in the communities that had such programs, and state supervision was minimal.

Although the CCIH, the University of California, and normal schools trained Americanization teachers by the dozens, the state Department of Education never completely embraced the concept of *immigrant* education. Richardson was assistant superintendent for immigrant education, but she was only one person with a staff of one half-time stenographer.[80] In 1923 when conservative governor Friend W. Richardson cut deeply into the state's education budget as part of his "economy" campaign to destroy progressive social welfare programs, Ethel Richardson was laid off for six months until commissioner Archbishop Edward Joseph Hanna persuaded the governor to restore funding. When Ethel Richardson resumed work in 1924, it was as the supervisor of the new Division of *Adult* Education.[81] She realized that the Education Department would have to focus more on adult versus immigrant education if it were to survive future conservative attacks.

In New York the availability of immigrant education classes declined in the mid-1920s, despite the efforts of the Division of Vocational and Extension Education to maintain the policy. As the federal government imposed immigration restrictions and Americans tired of progressive exhortations to "Americanize" the immigrant, communities began to cancel their evening and factory schools and home classes—programs that had been specifically designed for the foreign-born. In small towns the decline began even earlier; in 1920–1923 the number of New York cities and towns that offered such classes dropped from 128 to 114, and the decline was most sharply felt in smaller communities.[82]

Shrinking availability also reflected declining student interest in immigrant education. Enrollment in immigrant education classes in New York peaked at 102,382 students in 1924. In 1925 enrollment in such courses dropped down to 83,331. Part of the decline was due to illiterate youth attending part-time day schools rather than evening schools, but New York's enrollment numbers also reflected the nation's debate about immigration restriction and immigrants' negative reaction to compulsory and condescending Americanization programs. By 1929 only 72,300 students were enrolled in Americanization classes.[83] "The discontinuance of evening school in some communities was due to the failure of pupils to attend in numbers large enough to warrant the expenditure; in other communities the failure to carry on the work was due to lack of local initiative," Assistant Commissioner for Vocational and Extension Education Lewis A. Wilson noted.[84]

Despite the best efforts of progressive Americanizers and educators to retain students through improved teaching and specialized curricula, enrollment in immigrant education classes was driven mainly by external political factors.

In New York enrollment in immigrant education courses initially rose in response to federal immigration restrictions and a New York voter literacy law. In November 1921 New York voters approved a constitutional amendment that imposed an English literacy test for voting starting in 1922. The law mandated that local election officials require all new voters, upon registering to vote, to read a fifty-word excerpt from the state constitution and then legibly write ten words in English from the passage. A certificate of literacy issued by local school officials was an acceptable substitute for the test and was granted to individuals who had completed the fifth grade or equivalent or who had passed the New York State Regents literacy exam.[85]

This law quickly ran into problems of implementation, however, as educators complained that the test given by election officials was inconsistent, both in terms of content and administration, and did not match the academic rigor of the regents exam. Also, few New Yorkers enrolled in English classes in order to pass the voter literacy test, and election officials kept no record of the number of people who took the registrars' tests. In response to complaints from the Department of Education, the New York legislature amended the voting law in 1923, requiring that all new voters unable to present evidence of having completed the eighth grade must attend school and get literacy certificates. "The school authorities are now in consequence the sole agency for administering the literacy test law," the New York Department of Education proudly announced in 1923.[86]

Massachusetts had required English literacy for voting since 1857; and since 1895 California had required men seeking to register to vote to be able to read the U.S. Constitution in English and to write their names. By the mid-1920s, New York was among twenty states that had adopted literacy tests, all intended to discourage voting by certain segments of the population.[87]

Voter literacy tests reflected the progressive middle-class belief in the need for an "educated" voter. In the case of New York's law, this literally meant someone who had spent time in a classroom studying English and civics and/or who had passed an exam. Educating one's self by reading newspapers or participating in political campaigns was no longer an adequate demonstration of citizenship. Voting now required book learning.[88]

In 1929 Lewis A. Wilson commented that the voter literacy requirement "has been the greatest single factor in attracting pupils to classes in the evening school for elementary English and citizenship."[89] Increasingly, illiterate New Yorkers chose to gain their voting literacy certificate by attending immigrant education classes rather than taking the regents' literacy exam and risk not being able to vote if they failed. But immigrant education course enrollment and regents' literacy exam applicants surged in 1924 and then again in 1928 when New York Governor Al Smith ran for president.[10]

Immigrant education course offerings and enrollment in such classes also declined in Massachusetts in the mid- to late 1920s. In 1923 the Massachusetts Division of University Extension raised the fee for classes and the enrollment minimum from twenty to thirty to form a class, both of which caused enrollment and the number of classes offered to decrease. In 1923–1924 enrollment in immigrant education classes in evening schools, factories, and community centers was approximately 32,300; in 1929–1930 it was 23,460.[91]

After World War I advocates of Americanization through education were in an excellent position to promote their ideas and methods of immigrant education. Although the federal government quickly abandoned its immigrant education programs, its support for adult education allowed states with large immigrant populations to increase educational services for the foreign-born by expanding their adult education programs. Educational Americanization programs strengthened adult education in the United States, as progressive educators refined their courses and curricula and better trained teachers.

Nonetheless, enrollment in immigrant education classes was low when compared to the number of aliens and illiterates in the United States. Immigrants resisted both the coercive and intrusive nature of many immigrant education programs and objected to the underlying motivation behind them: that foreign cultures were inferior. Only such harsh policies as tying voting rights to literacy and exchanging immigration benefits for legal citizenship induced many immigrants to participate in educational Americanization programs.

But as the Americanization movement lost momentum in the mid-1920s, the foreign-born also felt less pressure to attend English language classes than they did immediately after the war. In addition, immigrants began demanding more diverse curricula than simply English and American civics and enrolled in other adult education courses to help them improve their socioeconomic status. An increase in federal and state government support for adult education provided opportunities for more citizens as well as aliens, and so had broader political and social appeal beyond Americanization.

The other component to Americanization policy, social-environmental change, was also increasingly attacked, but by native-born Americans who objected to state interference in their businesses, property, and labor practices.

8 ✺ Americanization versus Restriction

Immigrant Social Welfare Policy in New York, California, and Massachusetts, 1919–1929

In the 1920s, as the national obsession about immigrant loyalty and the meaning of American citizenship peaked and then ebbed in favor of immigration restriction, pro-immigration progressives suffered attacks on their policies of Americanization. As the country became more politically conservative, immigrant social welfare agencies in New York, California, and Massachusetts struggled to maintain programs designed to reform the social environment to facilitate immigrants' adoption of a more "American" way of life. But native-born Americans rejected Americanizers' efforts to stabilize society by raising the standards of living of both the foreign- and native-born.

Instead, the United States reversed one hundred years of immigration policy, adopted a policy that dramatically reduced the number of southern and eastern Europeans admitted, and totally barred Asian immigrants. This new immigration policy defined American citizenship and national identity in racial terms that progressive Americanizers had rarely used. To be an American no longer meant subscribing to certain political values, such as democracy, liberty, or equality. Rather, according to Congressional restrictionists, to be "American" meant to be of northern European descent; and since the "national origins" of true Americans were northern European, northern Europeans should be given preference as immigrants and future citizens over other, less desirable peoples. With the imposition of the first quotas in 1921, most Americans considered formal Americanization programs unnecessary; the few remaining state immigrant social welfare agencies survived by adapting themselves to new political conditions and significantly reducing the scope of their ambitions. The ultimate decline of progressive Americanization policies in the mid- to late-1920s was caused by the combination of repeated conservative attacks and the loss of political support caused by those attacks.

A cursory glance at the 1920s indicates a strong and resurgent conservatism in American society—the Red Scare, immigration restriction, passive presidents calling for "normalcy," the Ku Klux Klan, and virulent racial violence. Some historians have cited the Americanization movement as further evidence of the country's rightward shift toward nativism and conservatism in the 1920s. Yet the Americanization policy movement, with its emphasis on reforming the social environment, was a leading driver of progressive social activism after World War I.[1] Eugenics and scientific racism influenced the 1921, 1924, and 1929 quota laws, but state Americanization programs were implemented independently of federal immigration policy and continued to focus on the settlement and adjustment of immigrants already in the country even after the adoption of immigration restriction.[2] The new immigration policy's primary effect on state immigrant social welfare agencies was to cause an increase in immigrants requesting legal advice and assistance in dealing with the new federal rules. Neither the new conservative political climate nor immigration restriction changed the attitudes of progressive or conservative Americanizers. It was only in the late 1920s when some progressive Americanization activists began to qualify their pro-immigrant stance in favor of some types of restriction, and this shift in position was in direct response to the demographic changes caused by the quota acts.

World War I ended just as the United States had finally achieved full mobilization and was sending large numbers of troops to Europe. Reluctant to lose the feeling of national unity, Americans transferred their wartime zeal away from "swatting the Hun" to a new enemy, "the Red," almost immediately after the declaration of the Armistice on November 11, 1918. Led by conservative law enforcement officials, patriotic organizations, and anti-union business leaders, the Red Scare offered a clear alternative vision of Americanism to that promoted by progressive Americanizers. "Red hunters" sought to maintain public opinion's wartime insistence on "100 Percent Americanism," which was now defined as opposition to labor organization, immigration, progressive political economy, and anything else that deviated from provincial, Anglo-Saxon American culture.

The anti-radical hysteria affected state-based Americanization policies in different ways, depending on how the Red Scare unfolded in each state. In Massachusetts several dramatic strikes—including those by Lawrence textile workers, New England telephone operators, Boston elevated train operators, and the Boston police—directly contributed to Americans' irrational fear of a communist revolution in the United States. The Massachusetts Bureau of Immigration was not immune to the anxieties felt by many Massachusetts residents. Fear of the "Red Menace" combined with hostility toward the undesirable immigrant, and the MBI railed against both disloyal aliens and Americans who supposedly fostered that disloyalty through exploitation of the foreign-born. The bureau responded to the state's many strikes in 1919 by distributing placards printed in Russian, Yiddish, Finnish, Italian, Lithuanian, Polish, and English that compared the virtues of American democracy to the evils of communist dictatorship. "This Bolshevistic attack on the immigrant residents of the Commonwealth, wherein 'freedom of speech' becomes 'license of treason,' is the form of exploitation even more dangerous to the alien than the activities of individual swindlers," the Immigration Bureau declared.[3] Yet propaganda posters would not do much to prevent violent Bolshevik Revolution.

More effective was the MBI's partnership with the state military intelligence department to collect "evidence of the activities of various foreign-born revolutionary groups who aim at the destruction, by violence, of the existing political and social system—the overthrow of law and order."[4] Like the California Immigration and Housing Commission's response to the Industrial Workers of the World, the Massachusetts Immigration Bureau targeted radicals more for their rhetoric and beliefs than their actions and was quick to define dissent as disloyalty. The MBI was even willing to advocate the deportation of "those native-born harebrained sentimentalists" who encouraged foreign-born radicals' advocacy of violence, the type of strong language frequently heard from "100 Percenters."[5]

The Massachusetts Bureau of Immigration's fears of disloyal aliens and treasonous Americans distracted the agency from its primary mission of immigrant assistance. While the bureau leadership worried about the connections between immigration and radicalism, the staff spent the immediate post-war months re-investigating the immigration situation in the state since the Massachusetts Immigration Commission of 1913–1914. The bureau discovered that except for promoting immigrant education, the state had enacted few if any of the policies recommended by the temporary commission.[6]

To design a new Americanization policy to address the state's perceived new problem of immigrant labor radicalism, the Immigration Bureau co-hosted a conference with the Department of Education's Division of University Extension in May 1919. But before it could begin work on the plan developed at the meeting, the MBI found itself reorganized into the Department of Education, becoming, briefly, the Division of Education of Aliens and then the Division of Immigration and Americanization (MDIA) in 1921.[7] Immediately after the reorganization, the new division confronted the problems of integrating noneducation functions—that is, social investigation and complaint resolution—into an education bureaucracy.

In California the transfer of educational Americanization work to that state's Department of Education freed up resources for the Commission of Immigration and Housing's labor camp and housing inspection programs. But the transfer of the Massachusetts Immigration Bureau to the Department of Education meant an immediate loss of the autonomy the bureau had had in the governor's office and the end of non-educational activities. In California the CCIH continued to exist; in Massachusetts the MBI as an executive agency was eliminated and turned into one more division in the Department of Education. But at least the new division in Massachusetts was adequately funded: $36,500 in 1920 and then $45,300 in 1923. After the Immigration Act of 1924, funding was cut back to $43,000–$36,000, but rose back to $45,000 in 1926 and then $48,000 in 1929.[8]

The new Division of Immigration and Americanization was headed by Pauline R. Thayer, who reported to education commissioner Payson Smith. Besides Thayer and her staff, the new division was required to have an advisory board comprised of six individuals who were members of various immigrant groups and from different parts of the state. None of the bureau members was retained to serve on the new advisory committee.[9] The Italian representative, Domenic D'Allesandro of Quincy, had been a member of the Immigration Bureau's Italian Advisory Committee in 1919—before the bureau had been dissolved—and was the only committee member with a previous connection to the MBI.[10]

In eastern states the Red Scare centered upon foreign-born communists and socialists, with immigrants from eastern Europe and Italy being particular targets of suspicion. In California, conservatives' chief target was the anarcho-syndicalist IWW, although the state was more than willing to prosecute socialists and other radicals under its new criminal syndicalism, sedition, and "red flag" statutes.[11] But this time, the California Commission of Immigration and Housing did not lend its investigative expertise to the state and the federal governments' prosecutions of Wobblies. With the war over, the commission no longer considered the IWW a danger to domestic security.

The California commissioners took the opposite approach to that of the Massachusetts Bureau of Immigration, dismissing the supposed threat of radicalism as conservative political self-interest masked by the fears of an easily manipulated general public. But while the commissioners considered the Red Scare to be irrational, they were also not complacent about conservatives' use of the rhetoric of Americanism.[12] In protest of the rightward direction the national Americanization movement was moving after the war, commissioner Simon J. Lubin and his assistant Christina Krysto published five articles in the progressive social work journal *The Survey* between December 1919 and February 1920 entitled "The Strength of America."[13]

In the first piece, "Cracks in the Melting Pot," Lubin and Krysto criticized the hostility and disdain native-born Americans displayed toward foreigners, and urged that immigrants' traditions be appreciated and integrated into mainstream American culture. They argued further that such cultural blending was necessary, inevitable, actually occurring, and, in fact, had always existed in American society. Rejecting a definition of the melting pot as a process that stripped immigrants of their cultural traditions and replaced them with native-born, Anglo-Saxon customs, Lubin and Krysto proposed a model of mutual assimilation in which cultural pluralism was celebrated because American nationality was recognized as ideological, not racial or religious. Thus, American citizenship and identity was theoretically open to all, regardless of race, religion, or national origin. (The difficulties posed by Asians' exclusion from American citizenship were once again not discussed.)

In a piece entitled "The Menace of Americanization," Lubin and Krysto protested against those who sought to capitalize on the Americanization movement for political gain, particularly business groups that used the rhetoric of "Americanism" to promote the anti-union "American Plan." Industrialists, patriotic organizations seeking to preserve Anglo-American hegemony, and eugenicists advocating exclusion based upon race or nationality were "perverting" the "soul of our nation, the spirit of America."[14] Coercive Americanization methods cheapened American citizenship, alienated the foreign-born, and actually discouraged assimilation. If Americanization were to have any meaning as a concept, it had to be about more than controlling immigrant workers and teaching them English.

The Survey series was preaching to the converted, but the commissioners were also unwilling to allow conservatives to attack the agency directly without a firm rebuttal. In May 1920, after anti-radical hysteria had died down in California, a new Los Angeles-based business organization, the Better America Federation (BAF), emerged and immediately began criticizing the CCIH. Using the tactics of the Red Scare, the BAF aggressively campaigned for the open shop and a return to laissez-faire social welfare policies by attacking the commission, the Los Angeles Young Women's Christian Association, and other progressive and labor organizations. The BAF singled out Lubin and commissioner Paul Scharrenberg in particular, accusing them of IWW sympathies, a laughable yet politically hazardous suggestion in 1920s California.

The commission fought against these attacks by partnering with commissioner Mary S. Gibson's friend and fellow progressive, Dr. John Randolph Haynes, to investigate and expose the BAF's close connections to California's private utilities industry (the BAF had lobbied against raising taxes on the industry in 1921).[15] Although the commission revealed BAF members' self-interest behind their conservative rhetoric, the federation's mantra that progressives were really revolutionary Bolshevists helped conservatives defeat the progressive wing of the California Republican Party in November 1922. Despite the commissioners' best efforts, the political ground was beginning to shift beneath their feet.

As Todd Pfannestiel has noted, the anti-radical crusade in New York lasted until 1923, much longer than did the national Red Scare.[16] New York's chief "Red hunter," state Senator Clayton R. Lusk, thought Americanization could be an antidote to communism and anarchism, but he defined Americanization in exclusively educational terms. Uninterested in the protective work of the New York Bureau of Industries and Immigration, Lusk's Joint Legislative Committee to Investigate Revolutionary Radicalism spent most of its time in 1919–1922 trying to close the socialist-affiliated Rand School of Social Science and combating the alleged dissemination of radical propaganda in the public schools by socialist teachers.[17] This emphasis on education further marginalized the NYBII and reinforced the public's perception that Americanization equaled immigrant education, an idea that the New York Department of Education encouraged because it reinforced the department's leadership of the state's Americanization policy.

Ignored by Lusk and the Department of Education, the Bureau of Industries and Immigration sought, unsuccessfully, to realign the immediate postwar debate about immigration from political questions of ideology and loyalty to those of biology and national identity. In doing so, the NYBII almost completely abandoned the concept of Americanization as a means of providing social welfare and settlement assistance to New York's many immigrants.

Instead of describing the actual work the NYBII did in her 1919 annual report—inspecting more than 1,100 lodging houses and 400 labor camps; investigating 1,164 frauds and 832 employment agencies; receiving nearly 2,400 wage claims, etc.—chief investigator Marian K. Clark launched a polemic advocating a eugenics-based immigration policy.[18] While Clark's support for eugenics was not new, the stridency and completeness of her statement was. The bureau's efforts for social justice on behalf of the foreign-born were unworthy of any discussion or analysis in Clark's eyes.

Clark had two goals in writing her 1919 annual report: to attack the federal government for the alleged admission of "defective" aliens and to reject progressive claims that assimilation was desirable. Instead, Clark continued to promote eugenics as the best and only solution to America's "immigrant problem."

Rejecting ten years of immigrant protection work by the NYBII, Clark declared that Americanization was a question of "the established relationship of the indigent to heredity and to point out that through the admission of excludable alien stock an inequitable burden of unfit defective and criminal dependents is created that threatens the very fabric of our civic, social and national existence."[19] Although the chief investigator had complained for years about what she considered to be lax screening at Ellis Island, she now attacked the U.S. Bureau of Immigration for admitting on bond potentially excludable foreigners during the war, and then failing to hunt them down and deport them after the Armistice. As evidence, Clark claimed that 3,923 excludable aliens had been admitted into the United States between 1914 and 1918, a number that was less than 2 percent of the more than 2.25 million immigrants who entered the country during the war years, a low point in immigration to the United States.[20]

Clark also rejected the suggestion that the vast majority of patients and inmates in New York (and U.S.) hospitals, prisons, and other institutions were native-born Americans, a statistical fact that had been well documented by progressives as well as by the pro-restriction Dillingham Commission. She did not consider the possibility that the adjustment to American society had caused some foreigners to suffer from mental illness or that American industrial conditions disabled many workers, both foreign- and native-born.

Although Clark was careful to not identify just which of the many national groups in the United States were undesirable, her blanket statements about how the United States had become "'the dumping ground' of the world's defectives" for a "quarter century," and that Italians and Russian Jews made up 50 percent and nearly 29 percent, respectively, of the inmates at Sing Sing prison suggest that Clark had a low opinion of the "New Immigration."[21]

For a eugenicist, Clark's understandings of heredity, race, and mental illness were unsophisticated. She gave little thought to the differences between social and physiological causes of mental illness—beyond the traumatic experience of war—and she subscribed to the Lamarckian view that mental and physical disability would be passed down to descendents, a theory American eugenicists were moving away from in the late 1910s.[22] "It has been conclusively demonstrated that the feeble-minded child will remain feeble-minded, also it is true that insane tendencies are hereditary and that crime and pauperism are inheritable traits," Clark declared, assertions that few social scientists and even fewer biologists believed at the time.[23] Even many eugenicists, particularly those with scientific training, acknowledged that the social environment played some role in fostering or inhibiting deviancy, but Clark was convinced that biology was destiny.

Clark also made little to no distinction between physiological or neurological conditions, such as mental retardation, epilepsy, or schizophrenia, and those influenced by social conditions, such as depression, alcoholism, and socially deviant behavior. The number of suicides, according to Clark, was because "the defective and semi-defective offspring of our prohibited class of admissions are too neurotic to stand the strain of constantly increasing complexity of existence."[24] Thus, suicide, mental illness, mental retardation, physical disability, disease, criminality, and anti-social behavior were all thrown into the catch-all category of defective and undesirable.

Although the national eugenics movement was gaining momentum after the publicity about the results of the Army's wartime intelligence testing, Clark had picked a bad time in which to so publicly lobby for a eugenics-based immigration policy. Democrat Al Smith had been elected governor of New York in November 1918, and Smith knew where much of his support came from: foreign-born New Yorkers.

By 1920 Clark realized she had gone too far with eugenics and her criticisms of Ellis Island commissioner Frederick C. Howe and other federal immigration authorities. In her 1920 annual report, Clark made no mention of eugenics for the first time since 1914. Instead, she described the Bureau of Industries and Immigration as a clearinghouse for immigration problems. The bureau returned to its original mission of Americanization, defining assimilation as the product of social welfare and social justice. But Clark's vision of immigrant social welfare had narrowed significantly. She "conceded that the State owes a duty to the newly arrived immigrant in exchange for his economic value to the State," but the chief investigator did not explain what that duty was or how it should be fulfilled.[25]

Although Clark had muted her advocacy of a eugenics-based immigration policy, by 1920 criticism of the Bureau of Industries and Immigration was growing louder, particularly among those who argued that the bureau's responsibilities were redundant and/or could be transferred to other agencies. The New York Department of Health, especially, had long competed with the NYBII over the responsibilities of inspecting labor camps and enforcing the state's sanitation code. In the early 1920s the Department of Health increased its pressure to take from the bureau the power to inspect and license immigrant lodging houses. Clark fought to keep her agency from being broken up and distributed among the other divisions of the Department of Labor, arguing that the bureau prevented immigrants from becoming "fertile soil for the 'made in America' brand of 'Reds'"; but few were listening to her anymore.[26]

In November 1920 Smith lost the governorship to Republican Nathan L. Miller, who rode to Albany on Warren G. Harding's coattails. The following year Miller reorganized the New York Department of Labor, and the effects were devastating for the NYBII. Industrial commissioner Henry D. Sayer eliminated the NYBII and created a Division of Aliens within a new Bureau of Industrial Relations. The new Division of Aliens, still headed by Clark, lost the power to inspect immigrant lodging houses and labor camps to the new Bureau of Inspection, but it retained the responsibility of licensing immigrant lodging houses and doing social research into the living and working conditions of immigrants.[27]

The 1921 reorganization represented a dramatic overhaul of New York's labor policy and upset many progressives who objected to the concentration of power in the hands of the industrial commissioner and, by extension, the governor, who appointed the chief commissioner. Progressives and labor leaders feared that the elimination of specific powers and responsibilities belonging to each bureau—powers that represented hard-fought victories over the previous twenty years—would weaken state protections for workers and other disadvantaged groups, such as working women and immigrants.[28]

Progressives were right to be concerned. The 1921 reorganization of the Department of Labor was led by conservatives upset by the growing costs of social reform and progressive interference with private property rights. Miller was a former U.S. Steel attorney who had signed the Lusk laws regulating private schools and certifying teacher loyalty over progressive objections. In his first message to the state legislature, Miller noted that the Department of Labor had grown from a staff of 619 employees and a budget of $1.1 million in 1916 to 1,147 employees and a budget of more than $2.6 million in 1920.[29] Miller and other conservatives believed it was time to significantly prune the progressive welfare state that had grown since Charles Evans Hughes was elected governor in 1906.

In the cutbacks that followed the 1921 reorganization, the Division of Aliens' budget was slashed from $24,453 in 1920–1921 to $10,160, which paid for three investigators and two stenographers, plus Clark.[30] With such a budget, the former NYBII was back where it had started under Frances A. Kellor in 1910.

It was ironic that the most serious political attack on the Bureau of Industries and Immigration came from fiscal conservatives rather than from alienated progressives or immigrant societies, but Clark's eugenics advocacy had come back to haunt her. Her anti-immigrant sentiments weakened the political position of the NYBII at a time when conservatives were looking to reduce the size and scope of the progressive welfare state. New York progressives were unwilling to defend the bureau because of Clark's embrace of eugenics and restriction. The result was that Americanization beyond immigrant education was almost totally eliminated in New York in 1921.

The replacement of the Bureau of Industries and Immigration with the weaker Division of Aliens occurred just when New York's immigrant communities most needed help navigating the legalistic and bureaucratic complexities created by the first of a series of immigration restriction laws passed in 1921. This radical new policy limited immigration to 350,000 entries for 1921–1922, with quotas of 3 percent of each nationality living in the United States in 1910; immigrants from Canada, Mexico, and other Western Hemisphere countries were exempt from the quotas. Alien children of U.S. citizens were also exempt, and close relatives of citizens and immigrants in the process of naturalizing were given preference in the quota queue. In May 1922 the Quota Act was extended until 1924.[31]

The 1921 quota law affected Americanization agencies in very different ways, depending on the way that immigration had traditionally occurred in those states. As major ports of entry, New York and Massachusetts immediately experienced the consequences of a poorly designed immigration policy.

The Quota Act went into effect May 19, 1921, and created immediate chaos in the international migration flow, largely because the United States continued to admit immigrants on a first come, first served basis. People in war-torn regions of the world sought to escape to the United States, arriving only to find that they would not be admitted because the quota for their particular nation had already been filled. Steamship lines raced across the Atlantic in the hopes of getting their passengers to the United States first, even though only 20 percent of the annual quota for any one nationality was admissible in a given month. A typhus scare in New York in the spring of 1921 caused further confusion as ships were redirected to Boston and passengers disembarked at a port where no family and friends were there to meet them.[32]

In New York the political turmoil surrounding the reorganization of the Department of Labor meant that the new Division of Aliens was ill prepared to provide assistance to the 209,778 immigrants who passed through the Port of New York in 1921–1922.[33] In Massachusetts the new Division of Immigration and Americanization was overwhelmed trying to monitor dock conditions. Only twelve ships had arrived in Boston Harbor in 1920, and the majority of their passengers were Italian, Greek, Portuguese, and Syrian immigrants who had lived in Massachusetts before the war or were family members of Massachusetts residents.[34]

In 1921, division field secretaries Mrs. Herbert J. Gurney and Mary E. Power met forty-eight ships carrying immigrants from all over Europe, and all of them desperate to enter the United States.[35] The new quotas caused the MDIA to work much more closely with federal immigration officials, who began to contact the division when it appeared that the quota for a particular country was close to being full. The Division of Immigration and Americanization would, in turn, publicize this through the foreign-language press and immigrant societies in the hope that this news would quickly reach Europe, and would-be immigrants would be discouraged from attempting to squeeze in under the quota. The division also worked closely with societies trying to help immigrants who had relatives in federal detention, usually because of health or quota reasons. These cases were handled directly by division chief Thayer, who was appointed to the federal commission that was responsible for immigration stations in 1921.[36]

Immigration issues soon made up the bulk of the cases the division staff handled in the early 1920s. Besides helping people fill out visa paperwork, the MDIA's field officers devoted much of their time to explaining the position of the federal government in enacting the quota laws, which immigrants immediately recognized as discriminatory. The MDIA staff saw its role as defending the new policy and countering what it considered "anti-government propaganda," i.e., statements against immigration restriction. Division director Thayer commented:

> By taking time and patience we have been able to make such people see how it happens that under the present policy many American citizens are bound to be disappointed [in bringing family to the United States]. We show the evidence of effort being made all over the country to evolve a law that will cut such hardships to a minimum and still protect this country for future generations. We explain the impossibility of having that law perfect at the start. By drawing comparisons with things the man knows about, we finally give him knowledge of the problem and he loses his hostile attitude in spite of the fact that he cannot bring his people here.[37]

This statement summarized the Massachusetts Division of Immigration and Americanization's policy toward immigration in the 1920s: Immigration restriction, with all of its racial discriminations and its biases toward northern Europeans, was not to be opposed or organized against, but rather, was an inevitable policy to be tolerated and accepted.

In California the new restrictions had little effect on either immigration to the state or the state's Americanization policy. Few immigrants besides Asians entered at the Port of San Francisco, and the 1921 law banned all Asian immigration. Immigration from the Western Hemisphere (which in California meant immigration from Mexico) was exempt from the quotas. In 1922 the Commission of Immigration and Housing received ten complaints related to immigration and six deportation-related requests for assistance out of a total of 1,500 complaints and 1,427 requests for information.[38] In 1924 the commission handled seven immigration cases and twenty-four deportation cases, still a fraction of the 2,262 complaints the CCIH received that year.[39]

The California commissioners had always maintained strict neutrality on the question of restriction, and they had long argued that Americanization programs needed to focus on immigrants already in the country, regardless of what the federal government's immigration policy was. It was with this attitude, then, that the commission spent the early 1920s trying to strengthen California's housing laws rather than interjecting itself into the national debate about immigration restriction. But achieving its goal of better housing and stronger regulatory legislation was difficult, and the CCIH struggled just to maintain its policy of inspections and sustain the legislative reform of the 1916–1917 Housing Institute.

The purpose of the commission's second Housing Institute, held shortly after the November 1922 elections, was to strengthen and consolidate the tenement and hotel laws that the CCIH had revised in 1917 into one state housing code.[40] The entire institute endorsed the bill developed by the legislative committee in January 1923. Once passed by the state legislature, Governor Friend W. Richardson signed it in May 1923.[41]

The success of the 1923 amendments was ironically the commission's last attempt at housing reform. Even more ironic was the new governor's willingness to sign the legislation. Richardson's election in November 1922 had marked the resurgence of conservatives in the California Republican Party, and the new governor immediately attacked the progressive social welfare state that Hiram W. Johnson had built and William D. Stephens had maintained over the previous twelve years. In his proposed 1923–1925 "economy" budget, Richardson sought to eliminate the CCIH entirely by slashing its budget and shifting its functions to the Bureau of Labor Statistics. Richardson claimed (inaccurately): "The Americanization work of this commission has been voluntarily surrendered to the Board of Education and is now in that department budget."[42]

The commission barely survived Richardson's budgetary attack in 1923; only after Archbishop Edward Joseph Hanna lobbied a few influential friends was the commission itself spared and some of its appropriation restored.[43] For 1923–1925, the CCIH received $125,000, a respectable amount, but far short of the $186,576 it had received in 1921.[44]

Far more disastrous to the political strength and morale of the commission than the budget cut, Richardson removed Paul Scharrenberg in April 1923, nominally for improperly trying to influence legislation, specifically, the 1923 Housing Institute bill.[45] Richardson claimed that Scharrenberg had violated state ethics rules by lobbying for the housing bill. But the labor activist received no compensation for his work for the CCIH or for any other agency; and he had long lobbied for legislative support for the commission's projects, as had all of the other members. (Lobbying was, in fact, one of Lubin's primary responsibilities on the commission.) Scharrenberg—who had taken every opportunity to criticize Richardson in *The Seamen's Journal* about the 1923 budget—responded to his removal by saying, "I have read the Governor's statement and cheerfully plead guilty to the charge of lobbying for good housing laws. If that is a crime I want to be classed as a criminal."[46]

However, the purge did not end with Scharrenberg's removal. In response to the governor's attack on the CCIH, Lubin issued a challenge, published in the *Sacramento Bee*: "If Scharrenberg is guilty of the charges you publish, then I, too, am guilty. If I am innocent and worthy to be retained on the commission, then he, too, is innocent and should be retained."[47] Richardson was silent to this demand, but waited six months until Lubin was out of the country before removing him from the commission.[48] Archbishop Hanna became president of the CCIH.

With Mary Gibson resigning in July 1922 because of ill health, the loss of Scharrenberg and Lubin caused the character of the CCIH to change dramatically within eighteen months.[49] Richardson's new appointments to the commission—state comptroller and *Sacramento Bee* editor John S. Chambers, Berkeley telephone executive Gilbert B. Ocheltree, and San Francisco labor leader George S. Hollis—were more conservative in their politics. Ocheltree had been president of Berkeley's Chamber of Commerce, while Hollis was president of the San Francisco Labor Council and former president of the San Francisco Typographical Union. Chambers, who died in November 1923, was replaced by orange grower Charles C. Chapman of Fullerton in 1925. Chapman was active in Southern California Republican politics and horticulture industry boosting.[50] Of the prewar members, only Hanna and Dr. James H. McBride remained, and McBride died in 1928. Although Jackson Putnam is correct that 1922–1923—when conservatives controlled both the governorship and the state legislature—was an aberrant period in California politics, immigrant social welfare policy as implemented by the Commission of Immigration and Housing became less ambitious after 1923.[51]

About the same time that the CCIH was fending off Richardson's attacks, a limited form of environmental Americanization was being revived by the administration of New York governor Al Smith. Marian K. Clark had not quietly accepted the elimination of the NYBII in 1921; she immediately began campaigning to have the bureau's old powers restored and a larger appropriation granted.[52] In 1922 the Division of Aliens' budget was increased to $13,000, which paid for Clark, three investigators and two stenographers. Despite this increase, Clark continued to be highly public in her criticisms of the diminished authority and powers of her agency.[53] She argued that the lack of funds meant that the division could not even fully report on "all of the predatory conditions that have been described in previous reports of the division."[54]

Smith reclaimed the governorship from Miller in 1922, and in April 1923 pro-immigrant members of the New York legislature formed a joint committee on the exploitation of immigrants. The committee reflected the urban interests of the New York Democratic Party in the 1920s. It was chaired by Democratic state Senator Salvatore A. Cotillo of Manhattan (18th SD) and was comprised of Democratic state Senator Henry G. Schackno of the Bronx, Assembly Speaker Nelson W. Cheney (R-Erie County), Democrat John Joseph O'Connor of Manhattan (12th AD), and Republican Russell B. Livermore of Yonkers (Westchester County).

The chief impetus for the creation of the special committee was the difficulties many eastern European immigrants experienced trying to send money back to Europe during the war. But the panel also examined many of the same issues Frances A. Kellor and Lillian D. Wald had studied for the temporary Immigration Commission of 1908: notaries public, transportation issues, worker's compensation, and employment agencies. Only "medical exploitation" (that is, malpractice and fraud) and Americanization were new areas of investigation. But unlike the Lusk Committee in 1920, the Committee on Exploitation defined "Americanization" as protecting the immigrant from crime and fostering a respect and value of American law and citizenship.[55]

Clark testified before the panel that the reorganization had stripped the Bureau of Industries and Immigration of all its effective powers, and she urged legislators to re-establish the bureau with its old authority and responsibilities.[56] On the recommendation of the special committee, the Division of Aliens regained some of its statutory powers in 1924; but by that point Clark had left the Department of Labor. She was replaced by Democratic Party activist Lillian R. Sire, who wisely stuck to immigrant assistance and avoided eugenics and immigration restriction as topics for advocacy.

Under Sire's leadership, the New York Division of Aliens rededicated itself to social research and the protection of immigrants. In 1926 the division's appropriation was nearly $16,000, and the office was again investigating complaints, licensing lodging houses, and helping immigrants and native-born Americans resolve wage claims against employers. The authority to inspect immigrant lodging houses and labor camps, however, remained with the Bureau of Inspection, although the Division of Aliens did begin to investigate brickyards in 1927.[57] The attention that Kellor and Clark had paid to conditions at the Port of New York and the Battery was not renewed, however.

In 1927 the division was granted $16,675, but the staff of three inspectors and two stenographers remained the same as it had been before the 1924 restoration of powers. Frustrated by the size of her budget, Sire began to argue as Clark had that the federal government should direct some of the monies collected in head taxes to New York to pay for the social costs of immigration.[58] Although she used the same argument that Clark had—that since the state had no say about which immigrants were allowed into the country and into the state, it should not have to pay for immigrants with mental illnesses—Sire wisely used a quieter tone.

A year later Sire continued to complain about the division's lack of resources and authority to collect withheld wages.[59] In 1929 the division gained one more investigator, but the appropriation remained just under $17,000. (In 1930, under industrial commissioner Frances Perkins, that figure rose to $18,300).[60]

The lack of funds and staff significantly limited the work the Division of Aliens could do on behalf of New York's foreign-born residents, but the agency had a vision as limited as its budget. The theory of Americanization that Kellor had originally developed—that providing immigrants with a safe, clean, and healthy living and working environment would encourage the adoption of white American middle-class values—had left with Kellor in 1913 and was not revived under Sire. Sire and the Division of Aliens would engage in the mechanics of immigrant social welfare policy, but would offer no ideological explanation for that policy.

This reflected Governor Smith's successful effort to subsume Americanization into his broader program of urban liberalism. Uninterested in changing the values of his working-class constituents, Smith instead partnered with such progressives as Frances Perkins, Mary E. Dreier, and Wald to improve living and working conditions for working-class New Yorkers in general, regardless of birthplace or citizenship status. In the eyes of Smith, industrial commissioner Perkins, and division chief Sire, the Division of Aliens was simply one branch of a much larger state social welfare bureaucracy.[61]

The immigration Quota Act of May 1921 had its desired effect: Within one year the number of immigrants who entered the United States dropped dramatically (805,000 people were admitted between July 1, 1920, and June 30, 1921, while only 309,556 entrants were accepted in July 1, 1921–June 30, 1922). By 1923 the Massachusetts Immigration and Americanization Division's field secretary, Mrs. Gurney, noted that the apparent rapid assimilation of Boston's newcomers was because most were skilled textile workers from Great Britain who blended easily into the city's white population.[62] But the hardships imposed by both the quota system and the continued political violence and economic problems in Europe placed the MDIA in an increasingly uncomfortable position. Massachusetts Americanizers had long supported immigration restriction, yet the staff daily faced the individual trauma that the new policy created for immigrant families.

In 1924 after surprisingly little debate, Congress passed, and President Calvin Coolidge signed, another Immigration Act. This legislation tightened the restrictions established in 1921 by reducing the quota percentage from 3 percent to 2 percent and the basis of the quota from the census of 1910 to the census of 1890, when far fewer eastern and southern Europeans lived in the United States. Under this formula, the total quota for 1925 and 1926 was 164,667; after three years (this was extended by two years, to 1929), the quota would be reduced to 150,000, with each national quota to be based upon "the whole white population of the United States, with due regards to the national origin of that population."[63] Also for the first time, would-be immigrants were required to have visas issued by Department of State consulates in their home countries, and travelers' identities had to be documented by photographs. Aliens who wanted to leave and then re-enter the United States without being subject to the quotas were required to obtain a re-entry permit. Within four years, the United States went from a system of relatively open immigration—in which the burden of proof for exclusion belonged to the federal government, which conducted its inspections at immigration stations such as Ellis

Island—to a highly bureaucratic regime in which aliens had to prove their desirability to consular officers in their home countries before being granted visas that allowed them to enter the United States.

In addition to the new restrictions imposed on overseas migration, the United States also began to tighten up its border with Canada, which had long been unregulated. While the new law exempted Canada, Mexico, and the independent nations of Central and South America from the overall quota, it did require a consular visa for Western Hemisphere immigrants as well as the payment of the $8 head tax and inspection at the border. Canadian citizens living in the United States who wanted to become American citizens found themselves at a disadvantage compared to European immigrants because the lax border regulation prior to 1924 made it difficult for Canadians to document when they had first entered the United States. Failure to properly document entry could result in a permanent bar to naturalization and the increasing number of social welfare benefits that came with American citizenship. The Massachusetts Division of Immigration and Americanization spent considerable time advising and assisting Canadian nationals in dealing with the new regulations governing border crossings.[64]

The Massachusetts division's work on behalf of Canadian citizens differed markedly from that of the California Commission of Immigration and Housing's interactions with Mexicans seeking to cross the southern border. California's close proximity to Mexico discouraged many Mexicans in California from spending the time and money ($9 for a visa, an $8 head tax) to become legal permanent residents. Rather, migrant laborers bought a $3 re-entry permit, which was good for one year, and crossed the border almost as freely as they had before 1924.[65] The commission's complaint staff did spend more time advising and assisting aliens with immigration-related paperwork after 1924, but few of these immigrants were from Mexico.[66] Unlike the Massachusetts division, the California commission continued to think of itself as an *immigrant* welfare agency, not an *immigration* office.

Although the new immigration law did not change the CCIH's work as much as it did that of the MDIA, the 1924 immigration act did help transform California's migratory labor force, particularly in agriculture. When the Commission of Immigration and Housing began inspecting labor camps in 1913, it found a highly diverse workforce of native-born whites and immigrants from all over Europe, China, Japan, the Philippines, and Mexico. Mexican immigrants comprised only 4.4 percent of the state's population in 1910; in 1920 they were 12.7 percent.[67] The exemption of Western Hemisphere immigrants from the 1921 and 1924 quota acts caused large growers and the railroads to recruit more labor from Mexico, while the Mexican Civil War pushed more Mexicans north. Migrant farm labor and unskilled work, in general, was increasingly reserved for Mexicans in the 1920s.

This demographic change in the state's migrant labor force so worried Archbishop Hanna that the CCIH publicly spoke out against immigration for the first time in its history. "While the Commission realizes the fact that it is necessary to use unskilled labor in our state, nevertheless it believes that unrestricted immigration from Mexico should be stopped," the commissioners reported in January 1927.[68]

In a 1920 article entitled "Nation Building" in *The Survey* series "The Strength of America," Simon Lubin had proposed, among a long list of progressive Americanization ideas, the creation of a Bureau of Selective Immigration. This bureau, staffed by progressive experts in immigration and labor, would recruit immigrants based on skill level and economic need. This proposal had the potential for being restrictive in that it sought to replace the then current policy of granting entry to all immigrants except for those who fell under certain categories for exclusion.[69] In fact, former executive officer George L. Bell had first proposed the idea of "selective immigration" at the May 1919 Bureau of Education Americanization conference in Washington, D.C., and was promptly criticized for advocating a restrictionist policy.[70]

Yet "selective immigration," with its goal of economic efficiency and market rationalization and dependence upon bureaucratic expertise, was progressive. On the other hand, immigration restriction, with its racially based quotas, was not. Furthermore, the CCIH hinted in 1921 that it opposed restriction when it suggested that a strong Americanization program would do more to attract desirable immigrants than restriction would because immigration was stimulated by letters written by immigrants already in the United States to family and friends abroad.[71] Thus, the commission's 1927 statement in favor of restriction was a significant departure from its past position on immigration, which had always been carefully neutral and reflected the members' desire to maintain consensus on important matters of policy. Yet in 1927, the commission's membership was considerably different from what it had been in 1921. The quotas' exemptions for Western Hemisphere migrants, combined with continued political violence in Mexico, caused a surge in Mexican immigration to California in the 1920s, and it was this increase in unskilled Mexican labor that caused the CCIH to finally support restriction.

Governor Richardson's attack in 1923 had severely weakened the commission. The final blow came in 1927, when the commission lost its policymaking powers and became the Division of Housing within the state Department of

Industrial Relations. The camp sanitation and housing programs were maintained, but complaints resolution and Americanization—programs designed specifically to meet the needs of immigrants—were abandoned. Americanization through improvement of the social environment was over in California.

Of all the states that implemented Americanization policies in the mid-1920s, Massachusetts went the farthest in adapting its immigrant social welfare programs to help aliens deal with the requirements of U.S. immigration policy. Before 1924 the Massachusetts Division of Immigration and Americanization had promoted citizenship education among aliens who had begun the naturalization process; and it investigated complaints, particularly of immigrant banks failing to transmit money overseas and of fraudulent investment schemes.[72] After 1924 most of the division's time and resources went toward assisting aliens negotiate the bureaucracy of the U.S. Bureau of Immigration. However, the MDIA did continue to encourage immigrant education, naturalization, and limited social reform in the communities of the foreign born through its branch offices in Springfield, New Bedford, Fall River, and Lawrence.

Immigrant social welfare policy in Massachusetts developed with fits and starts as Americanizers tried to adjust the state's approach to Americanization to better match the direction of the national movement toward immigrant education. But the political difficulties experienced by the New York Bureau of Industries and Immigration and the California Commission of Immigration and Housing were the result of repeated attacks by conservatives whose vision of American society was based upon a definition of "Americanism" that was distinctly anti-progressive.

Conservatives objected to two central components of progressivism: government interference in private property rights and labor markets and the use of government to protect special groups, such as women or immigrants. Progressives' reluctance to trust in the self-correcting properties of the free market and their willingness to use government on behalf of groups—particularly undeserving ones, such as aliens—angered conservatives, who continued to believe in nineteenth-century ideas of individuals competing in an unfettered marketplace. Government involvement in the economy for the sake of promotion was as the founders intended; government restriction of the property rights of individuals to assist undeserving groups of people who failed to succeed on their own merits was, according to conservatives, fundamentally "un-American." Conservatives were also unhappy with the growing financial cost of the progressive social welfare state.

According to conservatives such as Governor Richardson in California and state Senator Lusk and Governor Miller in New York, "Americanism" was fiscally conservative, individualistic, and rooted in Anglo-Saxon Protestant cultural values. It was distinctly *not* multilingual or multicultural, socially inclusive, or politically pluralistic.

Progressives had long portrayed immigrants as a potential threat to the stability of American society, thus requiring Americanization and other progressive social reforms to aid immigrants in their adjustment to American life. Yet most progressives also opposed immigration restriction, so clearly the foreign-born were not so great a threat as to require exclusion or deportation.

Conservatives also viewed immigrants as a threat, but one to American culture, and they proposed an easier and cheaper solution: the exclusion of all foreigners from countries deemed culturally incompatible with the United States. As Daniel J. Tichenor has noted, immigrants from Mexico were also deemed culturally undesirable, but they were needed economically in the Southwest and were seen as transient; and so an exception was made in the new policy of restriction.[73] As early as 1921 conservative groups active in Americanization, particularly the American Legion and the Daughters of the American Revolution, began supporting immigration restriction, using the argument that the nation needed to first assimilate those immigrants already in the country before allowing more immigrants to enter. The Massachusetts Bureau of Immigration and its successor, the Division of Immigration and Americanization, also made this argument throughout the 1920s.

With immigration restriction, Americanization as immigrant social welfare was unnecessary, according to conservatives. Undesirable foreign elements were greatly reduced, time and exposure to American conditions would work their assimilative magic, and existing immigrant groups would be cut off from continuous contact with their home cultures, thus encouraging further assimilation. By allowing only immigrants from northern Europe, where literacy rates were higher, the need for immigrant education was also largely eliminated.

By the time of passage of the 1929 National Origins Act, Americanization as an expression of immigrant social welfare policy was politically dead in most states. Americanization as immigrant social welfare policy ended as the United States shut the gates to immigration.

✴ Conclusion

The Americanization movement of the 1910s and 1920s was a unique phenomenon in American history. High rates of immigration have often been accompanied by reactions of nativism, but only once have Americans attempted to define their national identity through positive social reform rather than through discrimination and exclusion. The result, the Americanization movement, was deemed such a failure by both foreign- and native-born Americans that by the late 1920s the effort was abandoned in favor of immigration restriction. This taint of failure has been long-lasting; Americans have not attempted a similar large-scale program to promote American citizenship among immigrants since the 1920s. Even the term "Americanization" remains so distasteful that it is not used to describe the myriad public and private programs that encourage naturalization and assist immigrants today.

Americanization obtained this sorry reputation because of its connections to the nationalism of World War I. Progressive Americanizer Frances A. Kellor made a fatal political error when she tied her cause of immigrant assimilation through social welfare to the military preparedness movement. Nationalism was central to progressivism, yet Kellor and other progressive nationalists failed to recognize that their newfound conservative allies were not interested in expanding definitions of American citizenship and national identity to include immigrants, and that they were hostile to the progressive argument that immigrant assimilation required the transformation of both foreign- and native-born through progressive social reform.

The association of Americanization with the spirit of "100 Percent Americanism" that was pervasive during World War I has prompted scholars to view Americanization as a product of the war. This perspective has, in turn, caused historians to examine only the educational programs that dominated the post-war movement and miss the social environmental reforms that progressive Americanizers initiated in the early 1910s.

This understanding of Americanization as both a wartime phenomenon and as education policy comes from the pioneering work of John F. McClymer. McClymer was one of the first scholars to recognize Americanization as progressive social policy in his analysis of the activities of the U.S. Bureau of Education and Naturalization. He was the first to draw attention to the gender dynamics within the Americanization movement and to the critical role of middle-class women as both leaders and foot soldiers in Americanization programs.[1] His insights into Americanizers' faith in "scientific" expertise and social engineering, their politicization of culture, and their eagerness to ascribe great meaning to the trivialities of everyday life are reminders of the many weaknesses of the Americanization movement.

World War I had a profound influence on the Americanization movement, but Americanization as immigrant social welfare had existed long before the war in both the private and public sectors. Neither a product of the war nor a monolithic program of coercion through education that emerged during the Red Scare, Americanization was a diverse set of social welfare policies initiated and implemented by progressives before and after World War I to foster immigrant assimilation and define American identity along middle-class lines. Americanization policies also encompassed more than immigrant education; they also included the reform of the social environment through such activities as labor camp and housing inspection, complaints resolution, and dock monitoring.

Looking at Americanization through the lens of education reveals invasive, paternalistic, and sometimes culturally condescending programs that some scholars, particularly Gary Gerstle and Desmond King, have deemed coercive and require a "disciplinary state."[2] However, a close examination of Americanization policies, before and after the war, reveals low participation rates by immigrants, inadequate funding, and spotty enforcement of laws that technically made immigrant participation compulsory. Progressive Americanizers were more willing to compel native-born employers, contractors, hoteliers, and landlords to uphold employment, licensing, housing, and sanitation laws than they were to force foreign-born adults to attend English-language classes.

The most distinctive aspect of Americanization policy— progressives' attempt to reform the social environment by regulating the behavior of Americans in the name of good citizenship—has been largely ignored except by Daniel A. Cornford and Gilbert González, who examine the California Commission of Immigration and Housing's labor camp sanitation program. Frank Van Nuys's study of the Americanization movement in the West is a step in the right direction, Considering the educational and social environmental components of the progressive immigrant social welfare policies that comprised the Americanization movement.³

This study of immigrant social welfare policies in New York, California, Massachusetts, and Illinois argues that Americanization was a core component of the larger progressive movement of social reform, and as such sought the stabilization of American society through greater homogeneity of both socioeconomic status and cultural practices, defined in terms of middle-class values.

An analysis of Americanization from the perspective of public policy addresses central questions of problem definition, method of implementation, and measurement of success. How did Americanization activists translate their theories of assimilation, national identity, and citizenship into public policy? Why did they explicitly link social welfare to citizenship? Why did the Americanization movement emerge when it did, and what was its relationship to the larger effort for progressive social reform? How did immigrants respond to the Americanization campaign, and why did it ultimately fail? These are the questions one must ask to effectively analyze—and judge—the Americanization movement of the early twentieth century.

Americanization activists developed their portrait of a "good American" in reaction to the surge in immigration at the turn of the twentieth century. The presence of literally millions of foreigners in virtually every state in the Union—living in "foreign colonies" and creating parallel institutions of churches, schools, newspapers, banks, and other businesses—gave Americans a highly visible "Other" against which to compare, contrast, and measure ideas about national identity and citizenship. And increasingly by the 1910s, Americans of a wide variety of political leanings found the newcomers deficient.

Americans defined high levels of immigration as a multifaceted problem of cultural diversity, widening economic disparity, and the threat of continuing alien isolation from mainstream society. Although political pluralism was built into the Constitution, tolerance of differing political opinions (within a narrow range of liberal and republican political values) was not the same as accepting cultural, linguistic, or even religious diversity.

Americans responded to the socioeconomic consequences of immigration in a variety of ways that reflected their disagreements about the nature of American citizenship, the type and amount of pluralism acceptable in an already diverse society, and the role of government in the economy.

The progressive solution to "the immigration problem" was to assimilate immigrants through ameliorative social welfare and the promotion of legal citizenship. Progressive immigration activists translated their vision of good citizenship into public policy by codifying minimum standards of health, sanitation, public safety, and education into state law in order to improve the living and working conditions of both working-class aliens and citizens alike. Yet the standard of living progressives called "American" was an idealized version of their own middle-class values and lifestyle; the "American" standard most immigrants experienced was whatever the labor and housing markets could endure.

According to progressive Americanizers, to be truly "American" was to be an English-speaking legal citizen; have financial stability with a private family life and clearly defined gender roles; practice contemporary housekeeping and child-rearing methods; invest one's money in the mainstream economy; and balance frugality and temperance with regular consumption of popular culture. Many Americanizers also advocated the observance of Anglo-Saxon customs and traditions, including an Anglo-American diet. Most importantly, "Americanism" meant having a particular ideological outlook and strong emotional connection to American political values.

According to this ideological understanding of Americanization, true Americanism was defined by a higher standard of ideals, and to be an American meant that one had to live up to these ideals; birthplace, race, and religion were irrelevant. Since American idealism did not belong to any particular group, it was possible for immigrants to maintain their cultural traditions and still be good Americans by upholding the spirit of Americanism—obeying the law, treating others fairly and decently, and thinking of themselves as Americans. Gerstle has called this ideology "civic nationalism" and emphasizes the contradictions within Americans' conception of national identity, particularly in regards to the exclusion of Americans of African descent and other nonwhites from full American citizenship.[4] Yet progressive Americanizers faced the greatest challenge to their civic nationalist understanding of citizenship in their interactions with Asian immigrants, who were legally excluded from naturalizing, yet still were included in Americanization programs.

This progressive ideology of "Americanism" ultimately lost out to a more conservative and racially nationalistic vision of the United States as a country that belonged only to those descendents of the original white immigrants of the seventeenth and eighteenth centuries. The "national origins" quotas of the 1921, 1924, and 1929 immigration acts enshrined cultural and social traditions of Anglo-Saxon Protestantism into immigration law, and explicitly discriminated against southern and eastern European and Middle Eastern immigrants. Immigrants from Asian countries were excluded completely while the entire continent of Africa was granted an annual quota of 1,200 entrants.

Although conservative Americanizers agreed with progressives about the general components of good citizenship, they objected to progressives' racial inclusiveness and their methodology of encouraging immigrant assimilation. Progressives believed that all immigrants, even Asians legally excluded from naturalization, could become Americanized by subscribing to American political ideals and adopting a progressive middle-class lifestyle. Progressives described American society as a dynamic "melting pot" that incorporated through mutual assimilation the "immigrant gifts" of southern and eastern Europeans and possibly even of non-whites to create "a new race" called "American." Through Americanization, this "American race" would be as culturally and biologically distinctive as European or Asian nationalities.

According to conservatives, however, this "American race" already existed and was comprised of the descendents of the original colonists from Great Britain and northern Europe. The introduction of new, more foreign elements into American society threatened to contaminate the cultural and biological integrity of this already-established "American race." To prevent this contamination by undesirable immigrants, conservatives favored restricting immigration from southern and eastern Europe and maintaining the ban on Asian immigration. Some conservatives went even further and advocated the use of eugenics in immigration policy to exclude genetically "unfit" people from entering the country.

Conservatives also firmly rejected progressives' insistence that Americanization first required the reform of the social environment by changing the attitude and behavior of native-born Americans. They objected specifically to progressives' interference in the labor market and in private property rights in the name of assimilating immigrants, and they resisted progressive efforts to introduce pluralistic and even socialist ideas into American society. According to conservatives, Americanization required immigrants to change, not the native-born. Thus, conservatives emphasized education as the most effective way of assimilating immigrants.

In addition, conservatives strongly objected to the progressive argument that immigrants needed to become citizens to be able to help reform society. Whereas progressives spoke of citizenship as a tool for social reform, conservatives viewed citizenship as an end unto itself. Conservative Americanization programs tended to focus on rituals involving the flag and the new Pledge of Allegiance, not on the practical exercise of citizenship in a democratic republic.

These disagreements between progressives and conservatives about the nature, theory, and methodology of Americanization were part of a larger debate in American society about the proper relationship between government and industrial capitalism, and the nature—pluralistic or homogeneous—of American society. Americanization was thus a central component of the progressive movement to transform America from a country in which an individual's pursuit of self-interest was revered as the definition of a good American to one in which the collective interest of society and the needs of interdependent groups were recognized and valued. Although conservatives came to play an important role in the Americanization movement, there were important philosophical differences about citizenship, national identity, and assimilation—concepts at the very heart of the Americanization movement.

But there were areas of agreement. Americanizers of all political persuasions linked social welfare and protective legislation to citizenship and national identity because they believed the cultural assimilation and political integration of aliens into the American polity was the only way to sustain the experiment of a democratic republic. America's unique system of government required an engaged citizenry; and having a large number of aliens who were ignorant of and detached from the moral and civic responsibilities of republican government was dangerous. In addition, republicanism had always argued that the state is obligated to consciously create citizens through education and the cultivation of civic virtue. Creating citizens includes the right to judge who is a good citizen and who is not. By the early 1900s, progressives were no longer willing to leave the cultivation of virtue to chance, nor allow the creation of citizens through naturalization without an accompanying program of civic and moral education.

Furthermore, progressives were unhappy with many working-class Americans' persistence in defining liberty as freedom from government restraint, and, in turn, seeing nothing wrong in taking advantage of immigrants' unfamiliarity with American society, economy, and law. Progressives sought to both protect aliens and educate them in American cultural mores and political practices, while at the same time adjusting working-class Americans to a new ideology of political economy based upon positive liberty and an interdependent society.

Like other progressive social welfare programs created to both benefit and socially control the poor and working classes, Americanization policies reflected the middle-class values of their designers in several ways. Educational Americanization programs, particularly home teaching, were often explicit in their efforts to teach foreign-born women Anglo-Saxon Protestant housekeeping, cooking, and childcare methods. Other programs that taught vocational skills in addition to English emphasized the belief that education was the best means for upward mobility. Adult education courses were designed to provide immigrants with the tools to succeed as individuals, rather than through group effort, as with labor unions or immigrant societies.

Some environmental Americanization programs, such as housing and labor camp regulations, also promoted middle-class standards of living. While the New York Bureau of Industries and Immigration and the California Commission of Immigration and Housing worked to improve sanitation in labor camps to reduce disease, accidents, and labor unrest, the inspection programs also tried to teach foreign-born workers how to live like white middle-class Americans.

Other environmental programs, such as the regulation of immigrant bankers, notaries public, immigrant lawyers, and doctors, promoted participation in the mainstream economy and the use of middle-class American professionals versus immigrant entrepreneurs and institutions. The most common forms of environmental Americanization—dock monitoring and complaints resolution—promoted the middle-class faith in the equality of law and trust in political authority. These programs also represented progressive efforts to counter more traditional American business practices and to discourage immigrants from adopting the "wrong" kind of American values of individualism and self-interest before community interest.

From a policymaking perspective, environmental Americanization programs were easier to implement than educational programs because the real goal was to change the behavior of the native-born; the immigrant was almost extraneous. Only complaint resolutions needed immigrant engagement. Immigrant education required immigrant students, and the reluctance of the foreign-born to participate greatly hindered educators' aspirations for education to be the primary method of Americanization.

Yet the popularity of home teaching among educators was due to programs that intruded only upon immigrants' homes and sought to change immigrants' cultures; the behavior and attitudes of native-born Americans were left alone. Native-born Americans were much more resistant to the progressive argument that they were responsible for encouraging immigrants to assimilate by improving the conditions under which the foreign-born lived and worked.

Paternalism was a middle-class sentiment that was ubiquitous throughout state-based Americanization policies and progressive social welfare in general. The labor camp and housing inspection programs developed by the CCIH and the NYBII were based upon the belief that immigrant workers and tenants could not—or should not—organize themselves in order to improve their working and living conditions. Complaint resolution programs operated under the assumption that immigrants could not negotiate the American legal system or other institutions by themselves to resolve their problems, and that immigrant institutions, such as national societies or immigrant churches, were inadequate or inappropriate resources for protecting the foreign-born. Home teaching presumed to instruct immigrant women cooking, childcare, and housekeeping.

Yet it is not paternalistic or condescending to insist on equality before the law; to object to discrimination on the basis of race, nationality, religion, or gender; or to give individuals access to tools they might need to pursue their ambitions and defend their interests and property.

To some extent, Americanizers' assumptions about the helplessness of newcomers in American society were correct: Non-English-speaking immigrants faced daily obstacles and disadvantages that made it more difficult for them to achieve their goals for coming to the United States. Americanizers were also right to draw critical attention to the hostility, callousness, and general indifference with which Americans often treated the foreign-born. The metaphor Kellor, Grace Abbott, and the California commissioners used of immigrants as guests in the collective home of Americans represented the liberal cosmopolitanism of progressivism at its best. The progressive message that immigrants should be treated as guests, not servants, until they decided to either leave or "marry" (literally or figuratively) into the American family was a positive value in immigrant social welfare that has been largely ignored or dismissed by scholars of the Americanization movement. Speaking out against discrimination and prejudice and urging social equality and harmony, progressive Americanizers envisioned the United States as the product of the interaction and blending of many cultures and peoples for the benefit of all.

Yet Americanization was politically and ideologically flexible enough to include the worst elements of progressive reform. Marian K. Clark's advocacy of eugenics and her and the Massachusetts Division of Immigration and Americanization's tolerance of the racial underpinnings of immigration restriction undermined the optimism progressive Americanizers brought to the movement, and caused the foreign-born to view Americanization as intolerant, coercive, and fundamentally anti-immigrant. The California Commission of Immigration and Housing's ultimate endorsement of the restriction of immigration from Mexico was a bitter finale for Americanization's most progressive branch.

A superficial glance at the Americanization policy movement in the 1910s and 1920s shows that Americanization as a form of social welfare for immigrants failed largely for political reasons. Americanization activists and bureaucrats lacked the power and resources to accomplish their goals. But a lack of political power was not the only reason for the failure of Americanization policies.

By putting forth a unitary model of American citizenship and national identity that emphasized values and behavior, progressives alienated their immigrant constituents, who objected to interference in their cultures. Coming from strong nation-states, immigrants adopted a pluralistic view of citizenship in which individuals were free to define Americanism for themselves; the chief requirements of citizenship under this pluralistic model were simply to obey the law as determined by the Constitution and foreswear political loyalty to another government.

Furthermore, by arguing that American citizenship should be broadly defined by a set of moral values and behaviors, progressive Americanizers made themselves vulnerable to attacks by both immigrants and conservatives, who questioned why progressives should be the ones to determine who was "a good American" and who was not. Progressives' answer, on the basis of their expertise, was weak. Conservatives, who could reach back to the founding of America to defend their definition of American national identity as Anglo-Saxon Protestant, were more successful in the policy arena with the passage of immigration restriction.

Immigrant indifference and resistance to Americanization programs certainly did not help progressive activists who sought larger budgets and greater authority. But conservative attacks on progressives' methods and goals were even more damaging. Americanization as a policy movement failed primarily because conservatives were successful in cutting off funding to immigrant social welfare agencies, ironically, by attacking progressives' ideas and policies as "un-American." Immigration restrictionists and eugenicists were able to convince a large majority of the American public that immigration, immigrants, and progressive Americanization were dangers to the nation. Rejecting progressive Americanization, Americans adopted an alternative, static model of American citizenship that was based upon "national origins" and traditional nineteenth-century theories about the role of government in the economy.

The efforts of progressives to remake the immigrant working class into middle-class Americans were also largely unsuccessful. But Americanization as a form of social welfare did provide some opportunities for the few immigrants who interacted with state Americanization agencies. Americanization policies improved living and working conditions for working-class residents by establishing higher sanitary and safety standards, and they contributed significantly to the development of adult education programs. These were valuable and necessary reforms, but they were weakened by progressives' insistence on attaching them to American citizenship and national identity.

Today, the federal government grapples with border control and the questions of "how many?" and "from where?" while providing immigrants interested in citizenship with information about naturalization as it did in the 1920s. Meanwhile, states and communities have begun to deal with the consequences of federal immigration policy by reconnecting citizenship to social welfare. But while progressives provided government assistance to immigrants *because* they were aliens, now Americans seek to expel undocumented immigrants by denying them social welfare benefits.

Whether for the purpose of integration or exclusion, linking social welfare to citizenship is a dangerous game, as progressive Americanizers learned in the 1920s. Successful social welfare policy requires a stronger foundation than the vague and contested ideas of "Americanism" and "good citizenship."

NOTES

Introduction

1. My definition of assimilation comes from Kazal, "Revisiting Assimilation," p. 438.
2. For instance, Fitzgerald, *The Face of the Nation*; King, *Making Americans*; Tichenor, *Dividing Lines*; and Zolberg, *A Nation by Design*.
3. Higham, *Strangers in the Land*; Korman, *Industrialization, Immigrants and Americanizers*; Barrett, "Americanization from the Bottom Up"; González, *Labor and Community*; Sánchez, "'Go After the Women'"; King, *Making Americans*, particularly chapter 4: "Americanization and U.S. Identity"; and Van Nuys, *Americanizing the West*.
4. McClymer, "The Federal Government and the Americanization Movement"; Mink, *The Wages of Motherhood*; and Gullett, "Women Progressives and the Politics of Americanization in California."
5. Good historiographical descriptions can be found in Higham, "Current Trends in the Study of Ethnicity in the United States" and Gjerde, "New Growth on Old Vines." See also, Gerstle, "Liberty, Coercion, and the Making of Americans"; Hollinger, "National Solidarity at the End of the Twentieth Century"; Higham, "Multiculturalism and Universalism," and *Send These to Me*, chapters 9 and 10; Gleason, *Speaking of Diversity*, chapter 3; and "American Identity and Americanization" in *Harvard Encyclopedia of American Ethnic Groups*.
6. Gerstle, "Liberty, Coercion, and the Making of Americans," and *American Crucible*.
7. Kelley, "The Idea of Policy History."
8. March and Olsen, "The New Institutionalism"; Skocpol, *Protecting Soldiers and Mothers*.
9. U.S. Census Bureau, *Thirteenth Census* (1910), pp. 185–264.
10. U.S. Census Bureau, *Thirteenth Census* (1910), "Population—New York," pp. 213–224.
11. U.S. Census Bureau, *Thirteenth Census* (1910), "Statistics for California," pp. 567–568; U.S. Census Bureau, *Fourteenth Census* (1920), "Statistics for California," p. 25.
12. U.S. Census Bureau, *Thirteenth Census* (1910), "Population—Massachusetts," pp. 851–896.
13. U.S. Census Bureau, *Thirteenth Census* (1910), "Population—Illinois," pp. 568–648.
14. A good historiography is Hays and Sklar, "The Progressive Movement."
15. The scholars who have most influenced my thinking about this period of U.S.

history are Rodgers, "In Search of Progressivism"; McCormick, *The Party Period and Public Policy*; Kloppenberg, *Uncertain Victory*; Eisenach, *The Lost Promise of Progressivism*; Furner and Supple, eds., *The State and Economic Knowledge*; and Furner and Lacey, eds., *The State and Social Investigation*.

16. In this important respect, I disagree with McGerr's emphasis on income and occupation in defining "middle class," McGerr, *A Fierce Discontent*, chapter 2.

17. For example, Beckert, "Propertied of a Different Kind," p. 292, argues that progressives were "bourgeois." Walkowitz, *Working with Class*, emphasizes the interrelationship between gender, race, religion, and class identities and the "language of class." Blumin, *The Emergence of the Middle Class*, especially chapter 1, points to work, consumption, residential location, voluntary association, and family organization as the key "categories of experience"; I would add education.

18. The link among class, values, and culture in the Progressive Era is explored in Coben, *Rebelling Against Victorianism*, p. 4, p. 31. Also see Moskowitz, *Standard of Living*, pp. 2–3, and Baritz, *The Good Life*.

19. Wyman, *Round-Trip to America*; and Ewen, *Immigrant Women in the Land of Dollars*.

20. Mohl, "Cultural Assimilation Versus Cultural Pluralism"; Barrett, "Americanization from the Bottom Up"; and Kessner, *The Golden Door*.

21. Eisenach, *The Lost Promise of Progressivism*. Many of the progressive Americanizers in this story knew each other and participated in the larger progressive network.

22. Boris, "Reconstructing the 'Family'"; and Eisenach, *Lost Promise*, pp. 25–29, pp. 77–81, pp. 87–91.

23. Furner, "The Republican Tradition and the New Liberalism." Yellowitz, *Labor and the Progressive Movement in New York State*, introduction, distinguishes between types of progressives.

24. Furner and Lacey, ed., *The State and Social Investigation in Britain and the United States*; Bulmer, Bales, and Sklar, eds., *The Social Survey in Historical Perspective*; and Eisenach, *The Lost Promise of Progressivism*.

25. Nehls, "A Grand and Glorious Feeling"; Morgan, *Women and Patriotism in Jim Crow America*; McConnell, "Reading the Flag"; and O'Leary, *To Die For*.

26. McGerr, *A Fierce Discontent*, p. 15.

27. Gordon, *Assimilation in American Life*; Morgan, *Women and Patriotism*.

28. Coben, *Rebelling Against Victorianism*, p. 4.

29. Gerstle, *American Crucible*, chapter 2.

30. The most prominent role played by African Americans in Americanization was the participation of Booker T. Washington in the July 4, 1915, Americanization Day observations. Progressives' failure to confront racial discrimination is well documented; for example, see McGerr, *A Fierce Discontent*, chapter 6.

31. Bogardus, *Essentials of Americanization*, also included Appalachian whites as needing Americanization.

32. King, *Making Americans*, argues that the Americanization movement was racially discriminatory in excluding African Americans, Asian Americans, and American Indians, yet he also finds Americanization culturally chauvinistic and coercive; so

it is unclear how non-European immigrants and blacks could have benefited from the movement if it was as offensive as King describes it.

33. Gleason, *Speaking of Diversity*; and Kazal, "Revisiting Assimilation."

34. Gerstle, "Liberty, Coercion, and the Making of Americans"; Kazal, "Revisiting Assimilation"; Wacker, "Assimilation and Cultural Pluralism in American Social Thought"; and Matthews, "The Revolt against Americanism." By 1930 Parkian theories of assimilation, ethnic conflict, and identity were dominant in sociology. For example, please see Drachsler, *Democracy and Assimilation*; Brown, *Immigration*; and Smith, *Americans in the Making*.

35. Jacobson, *Whiteness of a Different Color*.

36. Gerstle, *American Crucible*, calls this "civic nationalism," while Hollinger, *Postethnic America*, uses the phrase "community of consent."

37. Kevles, *In the Name of Eugenics*.

38. Hollinger, *Postethnic America*.

39. Skocpol, *Protecting Soldiers and Mothers*.

Chapter 1. The Start of a Movement: The New York Bureau of Industries and Immigration, 1908–1914

1. Wesser, *Charles Evans Hughes*, chapter 13.

2. Maxwell, "Frances Kellor in the Progressive Era," pp. 166–171. The temporary commissioners were Jewish attorney and state Republican leader Louis Marshall (chair); Labor Department official Philip V. Danahy; Inter-Municipal Committee on Research and Women's Municipal League research director Frances A. Kellor (secretary); former state assembly member Charles W. Larmon of Salem (Washington County); National Civic Federation leader Marcus M. Marks; Republican Party activist James B. Reynolds; Society for the Protection of Italian Immigrants attorney Gino C. Speranza; Henry Street Settlement head resident Lillian D. Wald; and Judge Edward B. Whitney, former assistant attorney general under President Grover Cleveland.

3. Commissioner Whitney issued a minority report opposing the creation of a new agency. Commission of Immigration of the State of New York, 1909 report; "Urges State Care for Aliens," *New York Times*, April 6, 1909, p. 18; "Call for a State Industrial Bureau," *New York Times*, May 24, 1909, p. 6; and "Marshall Suggests New Department," *New York Times*, January 2, 1910, p. 8.

4. Kellor created the New York–New Jersey Committee of the North American Civic League for Immigrants to lobby for the creation of a permanent bureau after the temporary commission disbanded. See Hartmann, *The Movement to Americanize the Immigrant*, pp. 56–63; Maxwell, "Frances Kellor in the Progressive Era," pp. 177–184; "League to Protect Aliens from Fraud," *New York Times*, January 10, 1910, p. 8; and "Protect the Immigrants," *New York Times*, April 2, 1910, p. 2.

5. Fitzpatrick, *Endless Crusade*, p. 145, p. 154, p. 148. Higham, *Strangers in the Land*, p. 239, calls her "a crisp, authoritative young lady with an instinct for order and organization."

6. Eisenach, *The Lost Promise of Progressivism*, pp. 25–31, pp. 77–80, pp. 87–91, discusses social control as a fundamental component of progressivism; and McCly-

mer, *War and Welfare*, pp. 110–113, also discusses social control in relation to Kellor's work.

7. Maxwell, "Frances Kellor in the Progressive Era," pp. 63–68, notes that Kellor's mother was a single parent who took in laundry, one of the hardest and lowest paid forms of work for women. Although Kellor attended the University of Chicago from 1898–1903, she left Chicago without her PhD.

8. Maxwell, "Frances Kellor in the Progressive Era," pp. 100–124; and Fitzpatrick, *Endless Crusade*, pp. 58–66, p. 133, p. 139.

9. In 1902–1905 Kellor lived alternately at Hull-House when she was in Chicago and the New York College Settlement on Rivington Street. In 1908, after living with the Dreier family in Brooklyn, Kellor and Mary Dreier moved into an apartment in Manhattan, where the two women lived together for nearly fifty years, until Kellor's death in 1952. See Maxwell, "Frances Kellor in the Progressive Era," chapters 5 and 6.

10. Kellor was a strong supporter of both men, working first on Roosevelt's Progressive Bull Moose campaign and then for Hughes in his presidential bid in 1916. See Maxwell, "Frances Kellor in the Progressive Era," pp. 139–166; and M. Wood, "Mapping a National Campaign Strategy."

11. New York Department of Efficiency and Economy and the New York Bureau of Municipal Research, *State of New York: A Description of its Organization and Functions* (1915); and NYBII, *First Annual Report* (1912), pp. 26–27. In addition to the Immigration Bureau, the Labor Department contained bureaus of mercantile inspection, legal affairs, statistics and employment, and their branch offices in cities such as Albany and Buffalo.

12. NYBII, *First Annual Report* (1912), pp. 16–17.

13. Ibid., pp. 23–25, and appendix 2, "Finances." Woerishoffer's grandparents edited a German newspaper, the *New Yorker Staats-Zeitung*; her father, Charles Frederick Woerishoffer, was a Wall Street banker. Upon her premature death on September 11, 1911, Woerishoffer left $750,000 to Bryn Mawr College to establish a graduate department of social work and social research.

14. McClymer, *War and Welfare*; Fitzpatrick, *Endless Crusade*, chapter 6.

15. Rodgers argued that progressivism had three discourses: society (meaning anti-individualism), anti-monopoly (meaning equality of opportunity), and efficiency; see "In Search of Progressivism." Kellor fits Gerstle's definition of a "civic nationalist": She was deeply influenced by Roosevelt's New Nationalism, but she had more tolerant racial views than he, Gerstle, *American Crucible*.

16. NYBII, *First Annual Report* (1912), p. 13.

17. Wyman, *Round-Trip to America*, pp. 32–36.

18. NYBII, *First Annual Report* (1912), pp. 14–15.

19. Fitzpatrick, *Endless Crusade*, p. 136, p. 141; and Wesser, *Charles Evans Hughes*, chapter 13.

20. NYBII, *First Annual Report* (1912), section 3, and Pittenger, "A World of Difference," pp. 26–65, give good examples of the research methods used by Kellor and the bureau; Bulmer, Bales, and Sklar, eds., *The Social Survey in Historical Perspective*.

21. NYBII, *First Annual Report* (1912), pp. 23–26.

22. In 1907 Kellor received a salary of $900 per year as the director of the Inter-

Municipal Committee on Research. See Maxwell, "Frances Kellor in the Progressive Era," p. 147, p. 183, footnote 1. Also see McClymer, *War and Welfare*, pp. 110–122, for a discussion of Kellor's habit of blending public and private work throughout her career.

23. NACL New York–New Jersey Committee report (December 1909–March 1911), p. 38.

24. NYBII, *First Annual Report* (1912), pp. 28–30; NYBII, *Third Annual Report* (1914), pp. 65–66.

25. NYBII, *First Annual Report* (1912), pp. 123–133; ibid., appendix 7, "Complaints of Aliens in Transit," pp. 150–155; and NYBII, *Third Annual Report* (1914), p. 8, pp. 15–32, details the complaints for 1913.

26. NYBII, *First Annual Report* (1912), pp. 42–62. The NACL's New York–New Jersey Committee considered it a major victory when it persuaded New York City officials to increase the number of police at the Battery from one officer to three; see NACL New York–New Jersey Committee report (December 1909–March, 1911), p. 13.

27. NYBII, *First Annual Report* (1912), p. 53.

28. NYBII, *First Annual Report* (1912), pp. 52–53, p. 55, notes the lack of municipal interest in regulating cab drivers and teamsters; NYBII, *Third Annual Report* (1914), pp. 37–39.

29. NYBII, *First Annual Report*, p. 49.

30. Runners frequently solicited tickets from travelers to get them stamped and then charged a fee for the service. NYBII, *First Annual Report* (1912), appendix 2, "Steamship Ticket Laws," appendix 3, "Soliciting Steamship Tickets," and pp. 143–144, give the texts of the laws.

31. NYBII, *First Annual Report* (1912), pp. 53–55, appendix 5, "Licensing of Immigrant Lodging Places," and appendix 6, "Rules and Regulations for Immigrant Lodging Places," pp. 145–150, for the new law regarding the licensing of immigrant lodging places.

32. NYBII, *First Annual Report* (1912), p. 55.

33. U.S. Census Bureau, *Thirteenth Census* (1910), "Population—New York," table 2, pp. 238–242.

34. Glazier, *Dispersing the Ghetto*; Kessner, *The Golden Door*, p. 39.

35. NYBII, *First Annual Report* (1912), pp. 33–34. The NACL's distribution committee included representatives from the federal division of information, an office within the Bureau of Naturalization, and the New York Department of Agriculture.

36. NYBII, *First Annual Report* (1912), pp. 39–42, for labor distribution, pp. 93–98, for real estate fraud, pp. 62–75, for labor camps and colonies, and pp. 128–133, summary of complaints. Also please see NYBII, *Second Annual Report* (1913), pp. 28–29, for land investments.

37. Kellor visited more than 730 employment offices in New York, Boston, Philadelphia, and Chicago in 1902 and 1903 for her book, *Out of Work*. See Breen, *Labor Market Politics and the Great War*, pp. 3–7, on the movement for public employment offices.

38. NYBII, *First Annual Report* (1912), appendix 19, "Law Creating the Bureau of Industries and Immigration," section 155, pp. 176–177.

39. New York Department of Efficiency and Economy and the New York Bureau of Municipal Research, *Government of the State of New York: A Description of its Organization and Functions*, pp. 227–247, including chart; and NYBII, *First Annual Report* (1912), p. 62.

40. NYBII, *First Annual Report* (1912), pp. 62–72; *Second Annual Report* (1913), pp. 19–23; and *Third Annual Report* (1914), pp. 48–52, p. 75, diagram 5

41. NYBII, *First Annual Report* (1912), pp. 64–67; and Peck, *Reinventing Free Labor*.

42. NYBII, *First Annual Report* (1912), pp. 67–69.

43. Ibid., p. 64.

44. Ibid., pp. 73–75.

45. Ibid., pp. 74–75.

46. NYBII, *Second Annual Report* (1913), pp. 8–12.

47. NYBII, *First Annual Report* (1912), p. 104.

48. Jones, "From Social to Financial Capital."

49. The United States suffered ninety bank suspensions in 1907 and 153 in 1908 as a result of the 1907 Panic, U.S. Census Bureau, *Historical Statistics of the United States, 1789–1945*, Chart Series N 135–140, p. 273.

50. NYBII, *First Annual Report* (1912), pp. 82–93; and "Immigrants Sent $275,000,000 Abroad in One Year," *New York Times*, October 2, 1910, p. SM7.

51. NYBII, *First Annual Report* (1912), pp. 85–87; NYBII, *Second Annual Report* (1913), pp. 14–16.

52. NYBII, *First Annual Report* (1912), pp. 105–118. Although Fitzpatrick, *Endless Crusade*, p. 144, points to the education program as an example of Kellor's enthusiasm for coercion, she misses the more important point that the education project was a complete failure and quickly abandoned after one year.

53. NYBII, *First Annual Report* (1912), appendices 1–15, pp. 143–169, also diagram 9, legislation bureau chart.

54. NYBII, *First Annual Report* (1912), p. 36, notes resistance to state enforcement of the law regulating employment agencies, particularly by New York City; and NYBII, *Second Annual Report* (1913), pp. 3–4, notes collaboration between the NYBII and the New York City Bureau of Licenses against licensed cab drivers and porters.

55. Kellor and Mayper, "Recommendations for a Federal Bureau of Distribution"; and NYBII, *Second Annual Report* (1913), p. 6.

56. NYBII, *Second Annual Report* (1913), pp. 11–12; and NYBII, *Third Annual Report* (1914), p. 53, notes legal challenges to the bureau's definition of the immigrant lodging house licensing law.

57. NYBII, *First Annual Report* (1912), p. 4; and NYBII, *Second Annual Report* (1913), preface "Officers," pp. 1–2. The bureau frequently used temporary employees hired for one-time investigations so total staff numbers are difficult to track, but these numbers are those reported by the bureau. NYBII, *Third Annual Report* (1914), pp. 5–6, notes that although the staff had increased from fourteen to twenty-three in 1912–1913, Kellor personally employed at her own expense at least six people—a secretary, statistician, file clerk, and two stenographers—who left the bureau when Kellor resigned in early 1913. The $14,800 estimate is based upon the 1915 *Department*

of Efficiency and Economy State Budget Report, p. 202, p. 217, which granted $3,000 for the special investigator, $2,800 for counsel, and $9,000 for six agents—the staff Kellor had in 1912.

58. NYBII, *Second Annual Report* (1913), pp. 8–12 for lodging house program; pp. 19–24 for labor camp inspection program; NYBII, *Third Annual Report* (1914), pp. 48–52 for changes in labor camp inspection program; and ibid., pp. 66–69 for education program.

59. NYBII, *Third Annual Report* (1914), p. 45.

60. Ibid., p. 8, table.

61. McClymer, "Gender and the 'American Way of Life,'" pp. 3–21; Mink, *The Wages of Motherhood*; and Sánchez, "'Go After the Women.'"

62. The Progressive Party's Progressive Service was a research group devoted to investigation and social policy advocacy. Fitzpatrick, *Endless Crusade*, pp. 146–149, notes Kellor's work for the Progressive Party; and Costin, *Two Sisters for Social Justice*, pp. 48–49, notes Grace and Edith Abbott's attendance at the 1912 convention. In 1908 Kellor had met with Grace Abbott and other IPL organizers in Chicago to discuss possible collaborative work. In 1910 there had been talk of the IPL joining the NACL, González, "Immigrants in Our Midst," pp. 267–268.

63. Maxwell, "Frances Kellor in the Progressive Era," p. 203, and chapter 7; and Davis, "The Social Workers and the Progressive Party."

64. Mayper, the son of Jewish immigrants from Lithuania, worked with Kellor for many years: He was chief secretary of the NACL New York–New Jersey Committee in 1913–1915; wrote "Americanization in National Defense" (1917) for the Chamber of Commerce's Immigration Committee, a group Kellor was active in; and was executive secretary of Kellor's Inter-Racial Council in the early 1920s. He died in 1967.

Chapter 2. The California Plan: The Commission of Immigration and Housing, 1913–1917

1. Lower, *A Bloc of One*; and Olin, *California's Prodigal Sons*.

2. Parker was fired in the fall of 1914 and replaced by the attorney George L. Bell, who retained his position as counsel. Regarding Parker's firing, see Parker to Lubin, October 3, 1914; telegrams from Parker to Lubin, October 5, 1914, and October 6, 1914, and Parker to Lubin, October 12, 1914, in file Carleton Hubbell Parker, 1879–1918, 46 letters, 1913–1914, box 3; and letters to Lubin, M–Z, Lubin to Parker, September 30, 1914, and Lubin to Cornelia Stratton Parker (Parker's wife), October 10, 1914, file outgoing letters, 1914, June–December, box 4, letters written by Lubin, 1915–1932, Lubin Papers.

3. The California legislature sat every two years in this period, so appropriations were made biennially. California controller, *Biennial Report for the Sixty-fourth Fiscal Year, ending June 30, 1913, and the Sixty-fifth Fiscal Year, ending June 30, 1914*, p. 196. The CCIH received $60,000 for 1915–1917, state controller, *Biennial Report for the Sixty-sixth Fiscal Year, ending June 30, 1915, and the Sixty-seventh Fiscal Year, ending June 30, 1916*, p. 58.

4. CCIH meeting minutes, May 21, 1915; note "that the Commission is not allowed

to employ aliens, but that at this present time there are no people being employed by the Commission to conflict with this law." On labor's concerns, please see Wood, "The California State Commission of Immigration and Housing," pp. 99–100; Felton to Lubin, January 16, 1913, file Katherine C. Felton, 12 letters 1912–1913, box 2, letters Br–L, Lubin Papers. As the chief lobbyist for the CFL, Scharrenberg had led the lobbying effort against the CCIH; and in retaliation, Johnson appointed him to the commission, Paul Scharrenberg, "Reminiscences."

5. Scharrenberg opposed Asian immigration; McBride possibly opposed Asian immigration as well. In a December 6, 1919, letter to Carol Aronovici, McBride wrote: "The question asked in regard to Chinese labor and Japanese immigration was asked by a man who is interested in importing or trying to get the Government to import Chinese laborers. He was, of course, more than disappointed at your reply. Personally, I agree with your position, though I think it is a question to be avoided." The message was enclosed in letter from McBride to Lubin. File James Harvey McBride, 16 letters, 1915–19, box 3, letters to Lubin, M–Z, Lubin Papers. Lubin's, Gibson's, and Hanna's positions on Asian immigration are unknown, but they opposed restriction in general.

6. CCIH, *First Annual Report* (1915), p. 5, introduction; White, "The Growth and Future of State Boards and Commissions," pp. 222–239; and Beard, "Commissions in American Government," pp. 350–354.

7. CCIH, *First Annual Report* (1915), pp. 7–9. An amendment to the 1915 Labor Camp Sanitation Act gave the CCIH authority to enforce the law. Another 1921 amendment gave CCIH inspectors specific power to enter labor camps and other private property and to make arrests, CCIH, *Annual Report* (1923), pp. 26–27; Wood, "The California State Commission of Immigration and Housing," p. 132.

8. CCIH meeting minutes, July 29, 1914; Lubin to R. Justin Miller memo, October 27, 1920, included in CCIH meeting minutes, November 5, 1920.

9. Olin, "European Immigrant and Oriental Alien," p. 305; Wood, "The California State Commission of Immigration and Housing," p. 82.

10. "Reminiscences" of Mrs. Simon J. Lubin, file Lubin family, carton 1, Lubin Papers; *California Blue Book* 1913–1915, p. 492; "S. J. Lubin, Civic Leader, Expires Here," *San Francisco Chronicle*, April 16, 1936, p. 5; "Friends Gather to Pay Homage to Simon Lubin," *San Francisco Chronicle*, April 17, 1936, p. 4; Olin, *California's Prodigal Sons*, pp. 76–77; and Wood, "The California State Commission of Immigration and Housing," pp. 82–89.

11. "Reminiscences" of Mrs. Simon J. Lubin contradict the arguments made by Issel, "'Citizens Outside the Government,'" and Daniel, *Bitter Harvest*, who both contended that Lubin opposed unions. Based upon Lubin's longtime friendship and collaboration with Scharrenberg, I do not believe Issel and Daniel are correct on this point.

12. In an August 23, 1912, letter to Dr. David Blaustein of Columbia University's School of Philanthropy, Lubin wrote: "I came in contact with people who should have been interested in immigration, and with more who sincerely thought that they were interested. I came to the conclusion that they were all on the wrong track, especially our Jewish friends in San Francisco. After many interviews, I decided that the great

work of organization should be undertaken by the State," file outgoing letters, 1912, August–October, box 4, letters written by Lubin, 1912–1914, Lubin Papers.

13. Gibson was a founding member of the Los Angeles Woman's Club and the Friday Morning Club; chair of the Southern California Cause and Cure of War Committee; director of the League of Nations Nonpartisan Association; a leader in the English Speaking Union and the Council of International Relations; founder of the League of Women Voters in California; one of the original trustees of the Haynes Foundation; a leader in the American Indian National Defense Association; and director of Los Angeles County's Health and Tuberculosis Association, *California Blue Book* (1915), p. 492; Raftery, "Los Angeles Clubwomen and Progressive Reform"; Gullett, *Becoming Citizens*, p. 33; "Hugh Gibson's Mother Dead At L.A. Home," *San Francisco Chronicle*, September 12, 1930, p. 5; and "Mrs. Frank A. Gibson Dies," *Los Angeles Times*, September 12, 1930, sec. 11, p. 1.

14. Gosney and Popenoe, *Sterilization for Human Betterment* (1931) lists McBride as an advisor, although he had died in 1928. McBride never advocated eugenics in relation to immigration in his commission work.

15. *Who Was Who in America*, p. 796.

16. Gribble, "Church, State, and the American Immigrant"; "A Rough Road to San Francisco"; and *Catholicism and the San Francisco Labor Movement*, chapter 6.

17. Paul Scharrenberg, "Reminiscences," "California Joint Immigration Committee," "Immigration," subject files, carton 1, Scharrenberg Papers. Burki (now Mason), "Paul Scharrenberg: White Shirt Sailor," argues that Scharrenberg's anti-Asian attitudes were rooted in racial prejudice, not in economic reality, chapter 4.

18. Testimony of J. B. Dale of the American Federation of Labor in the final report of the U.S. Commission on Industrial Relations, pp. 4972–4979; Daniel, *Bitter Harvest*, pp. 77–81; and Knight, *Industrial Relations in the San Francisco Bay Area*, p. 275. Note that Scharrenberg, Sailors Union president Andrew Furuseth, and Building Trades Union leader Olaf Tveitmoe were unsuccessful in efforts to organize migrant laborers in 1910–1915.

19. "Labor Pioneer, Rites for Paul Scharrenberg," *San Francisco Chronicle*, October 29, 1969, p. A49; Burki (now Mason), "Paul Scharrenberg: White Shirt Sailor," p. 35; and Nelson, "J. Vance Thompson: The Industrial Workers of the World and the Mood of Syndicalism." A "white shirt sailor" was one who no longer went to sea but worked at a white-collar job, such as union newspaper editor.

20. Lubin, speech to the YMCA at the First Annual Lincoln's Birthday International Musical and Folk Festival, 1913, file Simon J. Lubin, articles and addresses, etc., carton 1, Lubin Papers.

21. Lubin to J. E. Langdon of the *Sacramento Bee*, June 29, 1914, file outgoing letters 1914, June–December, box 4, letters from Lubin, 1912–1914, Lubin Papers.

22. Olin, "European Immigrant and Oriental Alien."

23. CCIH, *Report on Unemployment* (December 9, 1914); and Parker, Wheatland hop fields report (1914).

24. A poster advertisement for work at the Durst Ranch said that the Dursts owned 735 acres, file CCIH, Wheatland hops field riot investigation, carton 1, Lubin Papers.

The Dursts' stationery claimed 639 acres, letters from Ralph Durst to Lubin, file R.H. Durst, 3 letters, 1914, box 2, letters Br–L, Lubin Papers.

25. Parker, *Wheatland*, p. 174.

26. Parker, *Wheatland*; and Bell, "The Wheatland Hop-Fields' Riot," *Outlook* (May 16, 1914), 118–123. Two IWW organizers, Richard "Blackie" Ford and Herman D. Suhr, were charged with the murder of Yuba County District Attorney Edward Manwell. On the basis of questionable evidence, they were convicted and sentenced to life imprisonment in early 1914. They were paroled by Gov. C.C. Young in 1926.

27. Vaught, *Cultivating California*, blames the IWW for the violence and notes that the Durst operation was competing against a new mechanical picker that had been introduced by their competitor, E. Clemens Horst, in 1910; that the hops ripened two weeks early, catching the growers unprepared; and that a large number of urban workers was thrown out of work by economic recession. However, Vaught times this downturn six months too early; the economy began to slow down in the winter of 1913–1914 *after* the Wheatland riot. Van Nuys, *Americanizing the West*, pp. 78–79, has a more even-handed assessment of Wheatland.

28. Johnson to Lubin, January 28, 1914, March 17, 1914, March 27, 1914, file Hiram Warren Johnson, 27 letters, 1912–1919, box 2, letters Br–L, Lubin Papers.

29. Gordon, *Employment Expansion and Population Growth*, p. 33; Nash, *State Government and Economic Development*, chapter 15; McWilliams, *Ill Fares the Land*; and Vaught, *Cultivating California*, pp. 43–44.

30. McWilliams is credited with the term "factories in the field" in his classic *Factories in the Field*, but attorney Austin Lewis spoke of "the hop field as an open-air factory and not as, typically, an agricultural pursuit," in his testimony before the U.S. Commission on Industrial Relations, report, p. 5000. Gordon, *Employment Expansion and Population Growth*, and McEntire, *The Labor Force in California*, note the corporate nature of California agriculture.

31. California Board of Control, *Biannual Report*, 1913–1915; and Anderson, *California State Government*, p. 142.

32. John P. McLaughlin to Robert Newton Lynch, September 20, 1912, file California, Bureau of Labor Statistics, 2 letters, 1912–1915, box 2, letters Br–Lubin Papers. The letter notes McLaughlin's opposition to municipal employment bureaus. Felton to Lubin, November 16, 1912, file Katherine C. Felton, 12 letters, 1912–1913, box 2, letters Br–L, Lubin Papers. Felton expressed concern that the Bureau of Labor Statistics was dominated by the San Francisco Union Labor party and thus biased in labor matters.

33. CCIH, *Report on Unemployment* (December 9, 1914); *Report on Relief of the Destitute Unemployed* (June 25, 1915); Johnson to Lubin, January 28, 1914, file Hiram Warren Johnson, 27 letters, 1912–1919, box 2, letters Br–L, Lubin Papers; Parker, *Wheatland*; and Parker, *The Casual Laborer*. Scharrenberg's rejection of Parker's analysis is in Scharrenberg, *Wheatland Hop-fields Riot Investigation: Minority Report*. Several letters between Harris Weinstock (Lubin's uncle), Parker, and Lubin detail the relationship between the CCIH and the federal Commission on Industrial Relations (of which Weinstock was a member): Parker to Weinstock, January 10, 1914, January 21, 1914, and January 26, 1914; Lubin to Parker, February 9, 1914, February 13, 1914; Parker to Weinstock, March 9, 1914, and March 27, 1914; Lubin to Weinstock, April 1,

1914; Parker to Lubin, February 10, 1914, March 27, 1914, April 2, 1914; Lubin to Weinstock, April 5, 1914, May 2, 1914; and Lubin to Gibson, January 12, 1914, file outgoing letters, 1914, January–March, box 4, outgoing letters, 1012–1014, Lubin Papers.

34. CCIH, *First Annual Report* (1915), pp. 19–51, details the commission's first year of camp inspection work in 1914.

35. Johnson to Lubin, March 28, 1914, file Hiram Warren Johnson, 27 letters, 1912–19, box 2, letters Br–L; Parker to Johnson, May 11, 1914, file outgoing letters, 1914, April–May, box 4; Bell to Lubin, April 28, 1914, May 6, 1914, June 24, 1914, file Bell, George Lewis, 1888–1958, 57 letters, 1913–1915, box 1, letters to Lubin, miscellany, A–Bq, box 2, letters Br–L: file R.H. Durst, 3 letters, 1914, Lubin Papers; and CCIH, *First Annual Report* (1915), p. 19.

36. CCIH *Advisory Pamphlet on Camp Sanitation and Housing* (July 1914), p. 1.

37. Parker, Wheatland, p. 197.

38. Lubin to Ralph Durst, June 11, 1914, June 27, 1914, file outgoing letters, 1914, June–December, box 4, letters written by Lubin, 1912–1914, Lubin Papers.

39. CCIH, *Advisory Pamphlet on Camp Sanitation* (July 1914), p. 7; CCIH, *Report on Unemployment* (December 9, 1914), p. 18.

40. Sánchez, "'Go After the Women,'" and González, *Labor and Community*, chapter 5, argue that the commission's activities served the purposes and interests of white employers, especially large agricultural growers, by working to change the undesirable aspects of their Mexican workers through Americanization.

41. CCIH, *First Annual Report* (1923), p. 45, chart "Labor Camp Statistics"; and CCIH, *Second Annual Report* (1916), p. 334, lists the staff as of January 2, 1916.

42. Bell to Lubin, June 29, 1915, file Bell, George Lewis, 1888–1958, 63 letters, 1916–1923, box 1, letters to Lubin, miscellany, A–Bq, Lubin Papers.

43. CCIH, *Second Annual Report* (1916), pp. 10–12. Moskowitz, *Standard of Living*, chapter 2, discusses the emphasis on personal hygiene, regular bathing, and the installation of bathtubs and showers in private homes in the Progressive Era.

44. CCIH executive officer report, March 1, 1917–June 27, 1917, p. 6, notes that farmworkers made 161 complaints about camp conditions in the month of May; whereas the CCIH *Second Annual Report* (1916), p. 117a, table 11, "Complaints by Month (1915)," showed 139–491 complaints per month.

45. Daniel, *Bitter Harvest*, pp. 76–81, pp. 91–102, argues that the CCIH opposed the organization of farmworkers. Please see reports of John Vance Thompson to Lubin about the belief that the AWO was an IWW union, in four files labeled IWW Investigation, carton 1, Lubin Papers.

46. Parker to Lubin, July 7, 1914, and undated marked "sat. aft," in file Carleton Hubbell Parker, 1879–1918, 46 letters, 1913–1914, box 3, letters to Lubin, M–Z, Lubin Papers, for quote. Also see Lubin to Parker, February 2, 1914, in file outgoing letters, 1914, January–March, and Lubin to Austin Lewis, July 2, 1914, file outgoing letters 1914, June–December, box 4, letters written by Lubin, 1912–1914, and files in carton 1, Lubin Papers.

47. Frank Cunningham to Lubin in undated, subfolder Cunningham, F.J., file miscellany A–H, box 1, letters to Lubin, miscellany, A–Bq; letters in file J. Vance Thompson, 5 letters, 1915–1919, box 3, letters to Lubin, M–Z, Lubin Papers; *San Pedro Pilot*,

July 16, 1923, clipping, in file 1 "IWW," subject files, carton 1, Scharrenberg Papers; and Burki, "Paul Scharrenberg," chapter 5.

Chapter 3. An Unhealthy Relationship: Eugenics and Americanization in New York, 1914–1917

1. Hartmann, *The Movement to Americanize the Immigrant*, pp. 71–87.
2. I have been unable to find anything of significance about Clark's background. The U.S. Census of 1910 lists a Marian K. Clark, born about 1873, thirty—seven-years old, widowed, with both parents born in Ireland, and living in Manhattan's Ward 12. The New York City directory for 1916–1917, vol. A–Esha, lists Clark and a Robert B. Clark living at 749 West End Avenue on Manhattan's Upper West Side, but Robert was not listed with Marian in any other year from 1917 to 1923; and after 1925, Marian was not listed, nor is she listed in *Who's Who In America* or *Who's Who in New York*. A letter to the editor entitled "Nixon Called Reformer," identifies Clark as living in Rosyln, N.Y., a village on Long Island, *New York Times*, September 28, 1952, p. E8.
3. Scholars' emphasis on immigration (versus immigrant) policy means they miss the influence of eugenics and immigration restriction politics at the state and local levels. For example, please see Fitzgerald, *Face of the Nation*; King, *Making Americans*; and Jacobson, *Whiteness of a Different Color*.
4. Kline, *Building a Better Race*, pp. 11–13.
5. Dikötter, "Race Culture: Perspectives on the History of Eugenics," pp. 467–478.
6. Note the dominance of Mendelian eugenics in the United States over neo-Lamarckian influences in Kevles, *In the Name of Eugenics*; Stern, *Eugenic Nation*, p. 16; and Kline, *Building a Better Race*, pp. 20–25. Dikötter, "Race Culture," p. 473, notes the ideological flexibility of eugenics to include both Mendelian and Lamarckian theories, depending on the problem being addressed. Alcoholism, for instance, was most commonly described in Lamarckian terms, while Down syndrome was seen as an example of Mendelian genetics.
7. Woods, "Assimilation: A Double-Edged Sword," *Americans in Process*.
8. Gerstle, *American Crucible*, focuses on groups perceived as unfit for citizenship for reasons of history and culture as well as race, particularly Asians, African Americans, and others deemed nonwhite. NYBII, *Fourth Annual Report* (1915), pp. 276–280, lists the cases of fifteen aliens who were admitted under bond but were deemed "feeble-minded" by unidentified officials. The fact that none of these individuals was institutionalized at the time was regarded by Clark as a greater social threat than the cost of institutionalization, presumably because of the chance of their reproducing.
9. Kellor, *Straight America*, pp. 14–15, lists Kellor's chief expectations of immigrants: Learning English and naturalizing—provided that adequate educational opportunities were provided and the naturalization process made easier.
10. NYBII, *Fifth Annual Report* (1916), p. 1.
11. Kellor, *Out of Work*.
12. NYBII, *Fourth Annual Report* (1915), pp. 275–276.
13. Kellor, *Straight America*, p. 82.
14. NYBII, *Fifth Annual Report* (1916), p. 2.

15. NYBII, *Fourth Annual Report* (1915), pp. 276–280, reports that Williams was commissioner at Ellis Island in 1902–1905 and 1909–1914; Watchorn was commissioner in 1905–1909; and Howe was commissioner in 1915–1921.

16. Frederic C. Howe, *The Confessions of a Reformer*, chapters 25 and 28, discuss Howe's policies at Ellis Island and his views about immigration and immigrants.

17. Clark to Davenport, November 24, 1914, in Davenport Papers.

18. NYBII, *Fourth Annual Report* (1915), pp. 279–280; NYBII, *Fifth Annual Report* (1916), pp. 23–28. In 1914 the head tax was $4; by 1915 the Bureau of Immigration had a surplus of $9 million in head tax revenues, which went directly into the U.S. Treasury.

19. NYBII, *Fifth Annual Report* (1916), pp. 2–3.

20. Kellor, *Straight America*, p. 66, emphasis in original. Kellor's views about African, Caribbean, or Asian immigrants are unclear from her writings.

21. Clark to Davenport, November 24, 1914, p. 2: "I have long been in favor of drastic legislation on the subject of sterilization, but while this has been attempted, you are of course aware of its present status. On the other hand, it would appear to me that the immediate future would offer a most excellent opportunity for deportation, especially of alien criminals," Davenport Papers.

22. NYBII, *Fourth Annual Report* (1915), p. 243.

23. Ibid., pp. 286–287.

24. NYBII, *Fifth Annual Report* (1916), pp. 6–8, pp. 11–14; NYBII, *Sixth Annual Report* (1917), p. 13.

25. For instance, the bureau was unable to get the city to approve a 1915 ordinance that would have regulated public porters at rail terminals, NYBII, *Fifth Annual Report* (1916), pp. 11–14.

26. NYBII, *Fourth Annual Report* (1915), pp. 244–247. Kellor had first identified this problem but had been unable to stop it, NYBII, *First Annual Report* (1912), pp. 46–47.

27. NYBII, *Fifth Annual Report* (1916), pp. 6–8; and NYBII *Fourth Annual Report* (1915), pp. 250–251, italics in original, describes the problem of overcharging for baggage handling.

28. NYBII, *Fourth Annual Report* (1915), pp. 255–256.

29. NYBII, *Fifth Annual Report* (1916), pp. 11–14.

30. NYBII, *Fourth Annual Report* (1915), pp. 280–283; NYBII, *Third Annual Report* (1914), pp. 44–47.

31. NYBII, *Fourth Annual Report* (1915), pp. 286–289.

32. Ibid., pp. 283–284. NYBII, *Fifth Annual Report* (1916), pp. 32–37, summarizes the bureau's inspection work.

33. NYBII, *Fourth Annual Report* (1915), pp. 270–273, pp. 292–298, and NYBII, *Fifth Annual Report* (1916), pp. 20–22, pp. 32–37, are summaries of inspections. Statistics for 1916 are unavailable because budget cuts delayed inspections until after the bureau had reported its activities for the year.

34. "Immigration Progress," *The Immigrants in America Review* (March 1915), p. 89.

35. NYBII, *Fourth Annual Report* (1915), pp. 263–267. Clark was very aware of the publicity that the CCIH was receiving at the time for its camp sanitation program.

36. "The Immigrant and the 'Quack,'" *The Immigrants in America Review*, (June 1915), pp. 8–9; NYBII, *Fifth Annual Report* (1916), pp. 14–19; and NYBII, *Sixth Annual Report* (1917), pp. 8–9. Clark first reported the problem in NYBII, *Fourth Annual Report* (1915), pp. 256–260. Auerbach had been an investigator for the Massachusetts Immigration Commission in 1913 before coming to New York.

37. "Arrests Open War on Bogus Lawyers," *New York Times*, October 19, 1915, p. 8; "Seven Men Held as Bogus Lawyers," *New York Times*, October 20, 1915, p. 8; and NYBII, *Sixth Annual Report* (1917), pp. 9–12.

38. NYBII, *Sixth Annual Report* (1917), pp. 12–13.

39. Yellowitz, *Labor and the Progressive Movement in New York State*, pp. 118–119.

40. New York Department of Efficiency and Economy, *Budget Report*, p. 202, p. 217.

41. Italian-born Caesar B. F. Barra represented New York County's Third District in 1916–1917 before taking over Al Smith's Second District in 1918; Lithuanian-born Samuel Dickstein represented the Tenth District in 1919–1922; and German-born Robert F. Wagner was a state senator in 1909–1918. The assembly also had several Jewish and Catholic members. See Political Graveyard Web site, http://politicalgraveyard.com; accessed October 25, 2006. See foreign-born politicians cross-indexed with New York Assembly and Senate members.

42. Among those Clark enlisted was eugenics leader Charles B. Davenport of the Cold Springs Harbor Laboratory on Long Island, correspondence between Clark and Davenport, February 3, 1916, February 24, 1916, May 16, 1916, and May 18, 1916, in Davenport Papers.

43. NYBII, *Sixth Annual Report* (1917), pp. 16–22.

44. New York Department of Education, *Elementary Education* (1917), pp. 83–91.

45. "Record of Progress," *The Immigrants in America Review* (September 1915), pp. 102–103.

46. Ibid., p. 100, p. 101; "Record of Progress," *The Immigrants in America Review* (July 1916), p. 71.

47. "Record of Progress," *The Immigrants in America Review* (April 1916), p. 84; "Record of Progress," *The Immigrants in America Review* (July 1916), p. 71.

48. "Immigration Progress," *The Immigrants in America Review* (March 1915), p. 88.

Chapter 4. Americanizing the Home: Housing Reform and the California Home Teacher Act of 1915

1. Housing commissioner Arthur Fleming rarely attended meetings, leaving the housing division directionless until Fleming was removed and McBride joined the commission in February 1915.

2. Schleef was one of the first people hired by the commission in late 1913, and she worked for the CCIH until July 1919. She was originally from London, England, UC–Berkeley yearbook Blue & Gold, vol. 39, p. 102. CCIH, *Annual Report* (1923), p. 2, lists four inspectors, including Schleef's replacement Elise Harlan; a director; and a stenographer in the housing division.

3. CCIH, *First Annual Report* (1915), pp. 71–94.

4. Ibid., pp. 92–95, notes Los Angeles' and San Diego's housing programs; CCIH, *Second Annual Report* (1916), pp. 197–244, notes many cities' lack of enforcement of state and local housing codes.

5. CCIH, *First Annual Report* (1915), p. 71, and on p. 96: "Cities seem reluctant to take up their own problems, and local health officers, who are usually practicing physicians, are underpaid and too busy to attend to their official duties. Moreover, there is always a strong local and political influence brought to bear upon such officials to curb their activities when the property of influential owners is affected." CCIH, *Second Annual Report* (1916), pp. 201–202, notes cities' resentment of perceived state interference.

6. Lubin to the commission, June 19, 1923, on the approaching tenth anniversary of the establishment of the CCIH, in CCIH Executive Officer's Reports, 1922–24, p. 6.

7. CCIH, *Annual Report* (1919), p. 11.

8. Lubin speech, address at Pacific Coast Immigration Congress, April 14–15 in San Francisco, in Blanpied, compiler, "A Humanitarian Study of the Coming Immigration Program on the Pacific Coast."

9. McBride to Lubin April 7, 1919, in file James Harvey McBride, 16 letters, 1915–19, box 3, letters to Lubin, M–Z, Lubin Papers. CCIH, *Report on Large Landholdings in Southern California* (1919) most clearly expresses the CCIH's belief in the yeoman farmer ideal.

10. CCIH, *An A-B-C of Housing* (1915), printed in the CCIH, *Second Annual Report* (1916), p. 281, argues that in their plans, cities should allow room for "detached one family houses, with lawn and room for rear garden."

11. McBride, "The Life and Health of Our Girls in Relation to Their Future," and "The Physician and Human Conservation."

12. CCIH: *An A-B-C of Housing*, p. 284.

13. For example, CCIH, *Second Annual Report*, pp. 262–265, about Los Angeles' Chinatown.

14. CCIH, *An A-B-C of Housing*, p. 285, proposes the idea of citizens' committees, which should have "a physician, a lawyer, an architect, a clergyman, a representative of labor, a business man; be made up of natives and foreigners, men and women," to inspect neighborhoods to ensure compliance.

15. CCIH, *An A-B-C of Housing* (1915), pp. 283–289. Raftery, "Los Angeles Clubwomen and Progressive Reform," pp. 158–164. Edson and Gibson were friends from Los Angeles' Friday Morning Club, an important woman's club active in social reform.

16. CCIH, *Second Annual Report* (1916), p. 265.

17. Philpott, *The Slum and the Ghetto*; Weiss, *The Rise of the Community Builders*.

18. Gibson to Lubin, February 3, 1915, in file Mary Simons Gibson, 98 letters, 1913–1920, box 2, letters Br–L, Lubin Papers. Gibson complained of Schleef in regards to her lobbying: "Miss Schleef makes no impression, except of youth and inexperience, and so does absolute harm to the bill."

19. CCIH, *Second Annual Report* (1916), pp. 206–207, notes the difficulty Schleef had in locating property owners.

20. Ibid., p. 209, pp. 231–232.

21. Ibid., p. 198, notes that in 1915 the commission was able to get a statewide housing bill covering all dwellings, not just tenements, introduced into the state legislature, but "the opposition was so strong that it was impossible even to get the bill out of committee."

22. CCIH, *Draft of Proposed Tenement House Law* (1916), explanatory forward, p. 3. Please also see CCIH meeting minutes August 27, 1915, January 14, 1916, and March 10, 1916.

23. CCIH, *State Housing Manual* (October 1917).

24. CCIH, *Second Annual Report* (1916), p. 202.

25. CCIH, *Draft of Proposed Tenement House Law* (1916), p. 3; and Burnett, *The Tenement House Act and the Hotel and Lodging House Act of California*, p. 23.

26. Commission housing literature is filled with discussions of opposition to its proposed legislative regulations.

27. The Home Teacher Act, No. 1617b in the political code, 1915, taken from the CCIH, *Annual Report* (1916), p. 150.

28. McClymer, "Gender and the 'American Way of Life'"; Gullett, "Women Progressives and the Politics of Americanization in California"; Mink, *The Wages of Motherhood*; Raftery, "Los Angeles Clubwomen and Progressive Reform."

29. Herman, "Neighbors on the Golden Mountain," pp. 359–362, notes progressive reforms in education. Hyatt to Bartlett, December 13, 1912, enclosed in Bartlett to Lubin letter of December 18, 1912. It notes Hyatt's reluctance to assume leadership for a state immigration policy in file Bartlett, Dana Webster, 1860–, 51 letters, 1912–1913, box 1, letters to Lubin, miscellany, A–Bq, Lubin Papers.

30. Gibson to Lubin, December 12, 1913, file Mary Simons Gibson, 98 letters, 1913–1920, box 2, letters Br–L, Lubin Papers.

31. CCIH, immigration education leaflet no. 3, "The State and the Immigrant," reprinted in the *Second Annual Report* (1916), pp. 131–132, directly attributes the "immigrant gifts" idea to the settlement house movement. Gibson's attitudes toward segregation are noted in a July 14, 1919, letter from Gibson to Lubin, file Mary Simons Gibson, 98 letters, 1913–1920, box 2, letters Br–L, Lubin Papers.

32. D. Wood, "Immigrant Mothers, Female Reformers, and Women Teachers," p. 32, pp. 36–37.

33. Gullett, "Women Progressives and the Politics of Americanization in California, 1915–1920."

34. DuBois, "Harriot Stanton Blatch and the Transformation of Class Relations among Woman Suffragists." Also please see Scott, *Natural Allies*, and Blair, *The Clubwoman as Feminist*. Gibson, a peace activist, also left the Republican Party because of its refusal to support the Treaty of Versailles. Also see Raftery, "Los Angeles Clubwomen and Progressive Reform," p. 157.

35. Muncy, *Creating a Female Dominion in American Reform*; Mink, *The Wages of Motherhood*; and Morgan, *Women and Patriotism in Jim Crow America*, pp. 84–90.

36. CCIH meeting minutes, May 27, 1914, and February 12, 1915; CCIH, *First Annual Report* (1915), pp. 99–100.

37. Berrol, "Ethnicity and American Children," in *American Childhood*, and Ewen,

Immigrant Women in the Land of Dollars, discuss immigrant and first-generation children's feelings of alienation from their parents. Odem, "City Mothers and Delinquent Daughters," p. 183, notes that 41 percent of girls arrested for delinquency in Los Angeles were either immigrants or the daughters of immigrants. Rothman, *Conscience and Convenience*, chapter 6, notes progressive efforts against juvenile delinquency. See also CCIH, "What Our Neglect of the Immigrant Costs: The Result of a Study in Los Angeles," chart in immigrant education leaflets no. 1, pp. 123–125, and no. 2, p. 127, both reprinted in CCIH, *Second Annual Report* (1916).

38. Ewen, *Immigrant Women in the Land of Dollars*, pp. 72–73.

39. CCIH, *Heroes of Freedom* (1919), p. 8, p. 19 (bibliography).

40. CCIH, *Heroes of Freedom* (1919); CCIH, immigrant education leaflet no. 3 reprinted in CCIH, *Second Annual Report* (1916), p. 131.

41. "Mary S. Gibson Explains Why Progressive Women Should Uplift Immigrant Women," *Major Problems in California History*, p. 207.

42. CCIH/General Federation of Women's Clubs, "A Suggested Program for Americanization" (1919), p. 14.

43. Chase, address to a joint session of the National Congress of Mothers and the Parent-Teachers Association, Oakland, California, 1915, reprinted in the CCIH *Second Annual Report* (1916), p. 154.

44. Herman, "Neighbors on the Golden Mountain," p. 378.

45. Richardson, a Bryn Mawr graduate, also managed the Los Angeles office and served briefly as executive director in 1919. She left the CCIH in late 1919 to become assistant superintendent of immigrant education, a position she held until 1929. She married Los Angeles attorney H. Clifford Allen in 1927 and died in Pennsylvania at the age of 78, obituary, Allen, Ethel Richardson, *Pasadena Star-News*, January 24, 1966, p. 22.

46. Herman, "Neighbors on the Golden Mountain," pp. 378–380; CCIH, *Report on an Experiment Made in Los Angeles in the Summer of 1917 for the Americanization of Foreign Women* (1917).

47. CCIH, *Second Annual Report* (1916), p. 118–120; "What Our Neglect of the Immigrant Costs: The Results of a Study in Los Angeles," p. 124, chart.

48. D. Wood, "Immigrant Mothers, Female Reformers, and Women Teachers," p. 56, on Chase, who was hired by the Los Angeles School District as a regular teacher in late 1916; and executive officer report, December 1, 1916–January 26, 1917. One-third of the neighborhood was Japanese, and "the remaining one-sixth comprise Italians, Arabians, Syrians, Poles, Spaniards and Negroes," CCIH, *Second Annual Report* (1916), p. 139.

49. Chase, address to a joint session of the National Congress of Mothers and the Parent-Teachers Association, Oakland, California, 1915, reprinted in the CCIH, *Second Annual Report* (1916), p. 155; D. Wood, "Immigrant Mothers," pp. 129–134, discusses the tensions among home teachers, social workers, and home economists.

50. Chase, "Report of Home Teacher," CCIH, *Second Annual Report* (1916), pp. 139–146; Chase, "Home Teacher Report," in CCIH, *Report on An Experiment Made in Los Angeles in the Summer of 1917 for the Americanization of Foreign Women* (1917), pp. 20–21; and Herman, "Neighbors on the Golden Mountain," pp. 381–384.

51. Chase, "Report of Home Teacher," pp. 139–146, and "Working Plans for the Home Teacher," *The Home Teacher: The Act with a Working Plan and Forty Lessons in English* (1915), pp. 153–158.

52. CCIH meeting minutes, December 1, 1916.

53. CCIH meeting minutes, August 27, 1915. Hyatt described unassimilated foreigners as a "menace," and the public school as a camel, overloaded with the "hampering smothering, impossible weight" of teaching immigrants, written in "Bulletin Addressed to County Superintendents of Schools in California," p. 32, and "A New Profession," pp. 36–37, both in CCIH, *A Discussion of Methods of Teaching English to Adult Foreigners* (1918). Herman, "Neighbors on the Golden Mountain," p. 361, notes Hyatt's work on behalf of kindergartens, the establishment of junior high schools, and the introduction and improvement of physical, vocational, agricultural, and home economics education in California schools.

54. CCIH, *Report on An Experiment Made in Los Angeles in the Summer of 1917 for the Americanization of Foreign Women* (1917). *A Discussion of Methods of Teaching English to Adult Foreigners, with a Report on Los Angeles County*, pp. 13–14, says that fifty normal school students participated in the 1917 summer experiment. Also see, CCIH executive officer report, for March 1, 1917–June 27, 1917, p. 11.

55. CCIH meeting minutes, August 29, 1917; CCIH, *The Home Teacher: The Act with a Working Plan and Forty Lessons in English* (1915); *Methods of Teaching English*; and *Primer for Foreign-speaking Women* (1918), parts 1 and 2. *The Home Teacher* was reprinted in the 1916 *Second Annual Report*.

56. CCIH, *Second Annual Report* (1916), p. 155–158.

57. CCIH, *Primer for Foreign-speaking Women* (1918), part 2, introduction.

58. Schneider and Schneider, *American Women in the Progressive Era*, p. 41, notes: "The 'New Nutritionists' were calculating caloric and protein needs much too high (as high as 7,000 calories a day for a 70-kilo man at hard labor), preaching the wisdom of ingesting lots of fat, advising people to eat more white flour, denigrating most fruits and vegetables, dismissing tomatoes as without food value, advocating the use of condensed milk only, and boiling vegetables to a fare-the-well." McClymer, "Gender and the 'American Way of Life,'" p. 12, and Mink, *The Wages of Motherhood*, pp. 89–95, are particularly critical of Americanizers' focus on food as a measure of assimilation.

59. CCIH, *Primer for Foreign-speaking Women*, (1918), parts 1 and 2.

60. Muncy, *Creating a Female Dominion*, pp. 112–113.

61. CCIH, *Primer for Foreign-speaking Women*, part 2, "Patriotic Lessons," pp. 31–39.

62. CCIH, *The Home Teacher*, pp. 160–195, lists the English lessons, and p. 186, contains quotes. Please see also *Primer for Foreign-speaking Women*, (1918), parts 1 and 2.

63. CCIH, *The Home Teacher*, p. 151, and *Primer for Foreign-speaking Women*, part 2, p. 9.

64. CCIH, *The Home Teacher*, p. 151; *Primer for Foreign-speaking Women*, part 2, p. 9; CCIH, *Methods of Teaching English*.

65. D. Wood, "Immigrant Mothers, Female Reformers, and Women Teachers," chapter 5, notes the gradual professionalization of the home teacher within California's education system.

66. Gibson, "Department of Education," *The Clubwoman* (July 1918), pp. 21–23; and Krysto, "They Also Serve," *The Clubwoman* (December 1918), p. 24. D. Wood, "Immigrant Mothers, Female Reformers, and Woman Teachers," p. 79, notes that Los Angeles School District employed 63 home teachers in 1918.

67. Lubin to Gibson, June 19, 1919, in file Mary Simons Gibson, 98 letters, 1913–1920, box 2, letters Br–L, Lubin Papers.

68. D. Wood, "Immigrant Mothers," pp. 127–129, notes that California did not begin offering a specialized credential in the teaching of citizenship to adults until 1925.

69. Muncy, *Creating a Female Dominion in American Reform*, chapter 4. In "The Functions of Organized Charity in the Progressive Era," p. 662, Kusmer discusses "friendly visitors" who sought to transfer their superior moral values to the poor. Mink, in *The Wages of Motherhood*, and Gordon, in *Pitied But Not Entitled*, tie mothers' pensions to Americanization campaigns by urban maternalist reformers. CCIH, *Second Annual Report* (1916), p. 153, refers to Indian schools.

70. Mink, *The Wages of Motherhood*, only briefly discusses home teaching on pp. 94–95; and Rothman, *Woman's Proper Place*, pp. 101–103, and Raftery, *Land of Fair Promise*, discuss the kindergarten.

71. Chase was willing to advise charity workers to deny aid to Mexican families who did not send their children to school and participate in immigrant education programs, CCIH, *Second Annual Report* (1916), p. 143.

72. For example, Sánchez, "'Go After the Women'"; Schwartz Seller, "The Education of the Immigrant Woman"; McClymer, "Gender and the 'American Way of Life'"; Gullett, "Women Progressives and the Politics of Americanization in California"; and Pascoe, *Relations of Rescue*, p. 122. Although González considers home teaching to be largely ineffective, he also finds Mexican women receptive to the home teachers' instructions on sanitation, hygiene, and especially English, *Labor and Community*, pp. 123–124.

73. For example, please see CCIH, *Report on An Experiment Made in Los Angeles in the Summer of 1917 for the Americanization of Foreign Women* (1917), pp. 7–10.

74. CCIH, *Second Annual Report* (1916), p. 158.

75. CCIH, *Methods of Teaching English*, (1918), pp. 14–17.

76. Chase, "Working Plans for the Home Teacher," in *A Manual for Home Teachers* (1916), p. 157, says specifically: "The Home Teacher must recognize and appeal to the dramatic spirit of a play folk."

Chapter 5. Wartime Americanization in the States: New York, California, and Massachusetts 1917–1918

1. Higham, *Strangers in the Land*, chapter 9; Gerstle, *American Crucible*; and King, *Making Americans*.

2. Eisenach, *The Lost Promise of Progressivism*, pp. 243–248; Schaffer, *America In the Great War*, chapters 2 and 4; Kennedy, *Over Here*; Skocpol, Munson, Karch, and Camp, "Patriotic Partnerships"; and Skocpol, *Diminished Democracy*, pp. 60–67.

3. Higham, *Strangers in the Land*, p. 211.

4. Eisenach, *The Lost Promise of Progressivism*, pp. 122–129, on Wilson's philosophy

of nationalism. Kennedy, *Over Here*, chapter 2, discusses the Democratic Party's resistance to the business-government cooperation needed for war.

5. Schaffer, *America in the Great War*, chapter 2; Higham, *Strangers in the Land*, pp. 204–212.

6. McClymer, "The Federal Government and the Americanization Movement," pp. 233–252.

7. U.S. Commissioner of Education, *Annual Report* (1917); U.S. Commissioner of Naturalization, *Annual Report* (1918).

8. Kennedy, *Over Here*, p. 169. The United States drafted 4.7 million men, but only about half went overseas.

9. Breen, *Uncle Sam at Home*; McClymer, *War and Welfare*.

10. Breen, *Uncle Sam at Home*, p. 7, pp. 54–55. The Massachusetts council had access to $2 million in state funds; and 251 out of 295 communities were represented by town councils.

11. Breen, *Uncle Sam at Home*, p. 53.

12. One of the first things Stotesbury did was to create a Division of Aliens, headed by Frances A. Kellor, who immediately sought to claim the leadership of New York's Americanization policy.

13. Johnson so disliked and distrusted Stephens that after he was elected senator in November 1916, he refused to vacate the governor's office until his senatorial swearing-in required him to go to Washington, Lower, *A Bloc of One*, pp. 89–91. DeWitt, *Images of Alien and Radical Violence in California Politics*, pp. 7–14, argues that Stephens attempted to use the defense council to build a base of political support separate from Johnson. Breen, *Uncle Sam at Home*, p. 100, says that as a result, California was the least effectively organized state in the country by spring 1918.

14. California Board of Control, *Biannual Report*, 1917–1919, p. 10, p. 32; California Controller, *Biennial Report* (1917–1918), p. 62, p. 155, p. 198.

15. Vaughn, *Democracy, Nationalism, and the Committee on Public Information*, chapter 3.

16. In this I disagree with Gerstle, who argues that the CPI propaganda about American democracy highlighted the inconsistencies and contradictions between the message and the reality, *American Crucible*, pp. 89–91.

17. Vaughn, *Democracy, Nationalism, and the Committee on Public Information*, chapters 3 and 4.

18. Higham, *Strangers in the Land*, pp. 196–197.

19. CCIH, *Annual Report* (1919), pp. 14–16; CCIH, executive officer report, from March 1, 1917, to June 27, 1917, pp. 13–15; NYBII, *Seventh Annual Report* (1918), p. 10; and MBI, *First Annual Report* (1919), pp. 13–18.

20. Massachusetts Department of Education advisory board minutes, July 27, 1917, September 5, 1917, and November 20, 1917, in Department of Education Papers.

21. MBI, *First Annual Report* (1919), pp. 10–11; Massachusetts Department of Education advisory board minutes, December 26, 1917.

22. MBI, *Second Annual Report* (1920), pp. 19–20, pp. 43–46. The appendix lists the bureau's local correspondents and advisory committees in 1919. Fifty-one local correspondents are listed, but the bureau says on p. 19 that "about 60" had been re-

cruited. The names are almost all English, Scottish, or Irish, which suggests that the correspondents were native-born.

23. Kellor to foreign press editors, May 22, 1917, in New York Council of Defense Papers; MBI, *First Annual Report* (1919), pp. 30-31.

24. McClymer, "The Federal Government and the Americanization Movement."

25. Schaffer, *America in the Great War*, p. 65.

26. CCIH executive officer report, March 1, 1917–June 27, 1917, pp. 3–6.

27. DeWitt, *Alien and Radical*, pp. 10–11; Breen, *Uncle Sam at Home*, p. 106. CCIH meeting minutes of October 25, 1917, November 14, 1917, and November 15, 1917, reflect ongoing discussions about the importation of workers from Mexico.

28. CCIH executive officer report, March 1, 1917–June 27, 1917, p. 4.

29. Breen, *Uncle Sam at Home*, p. 106.

30. CCIH executive officer report, July 17, 1918, p. 3.

31. CCIH acting executive officer report, December 4, 1918, p. 2.

32. California War Council, "California in the War," (addresses San Francisco, March 5–6, 1918); and California Historical Survey Commission, "California in the War."

33. DeWitt, *Images of Alien and Radical Violence in California Politics*, p. 9; and Breen, *Uncle Sam at Home*, p. 100.

34. Townsend, *Running the Gauntlet*; and DeWitt, *Alien and Radical Violence*. Kennedy, in *Over Here*, p. 266, lists strike figures. Some of the more notorious incidents in July 1917 were the lynching of IWW organizer Frank Little in Montana, the deportation of more than 1,200 suspected IWW members by the Bisbee, Arizona, sheriff, and the abandonment of radical labor organizers in the California desert by Jerome, Arizona, mineowners.

35. Telegrams, many written in a simple code, file Bell, George Lewis, 1888–1958, 63 letters, 1916–1923, folder 2, box 1, letters to Lubin, miscellany, A–Bq, Lubin Papers.

36. Bell to Lubin, June 19, 1917, in file Bell, George Lewis, 1888–1958, 63 letters, 1916–1923, folder 2, box 1, letters to Lubin, miscellany, A–Bq, Lubin Papers. Commission investigator John Vance Thompson, a naturalized Englishman and a member of the Seamen's Union, claimed credit for proposing the idea of internment. Please see "Suggestions, May 13, 1918," file IWW investigation, folder 1, carton 1, Lubin Papers.

37. File IWW investigation, folder 3, carton 1, Lubin Papers; Townsend, *Running the Gauntlet*; and DeWitt, *Alien and Radical Violence*.

38. Preston, *Aliens and Dissenters*, pp. 99–103; Wilson's secretary, J. P. Tumulty, to Lubin, April 1, 1918, May 6, 1918, in file Woodrow Wilson, 2 letters, 1918, box 3, letters to Lubin, miscellany, A–Bq, Lubin Papers.

39. Preston, *Aliens and Dissenters*, chapters 4 and 5.

40. Bell to Lubin, "night letter," August 27, 1917, and Bell to Supreme Court Justice J. Harry Covington, September 1, 1917, both in file Bell, George Lewis, 1888–1958, 63 letters, 1916–1923, folder 2, box 1, letters to Lubin, miscellany, A–Bq, Lubin Papers.

41. DeWitt, *Alien and Radical Violence*, p. 10, pp. 18–20.

42. As early as December 1915 the CCIH refused to distribute the "America First" poster designed by Kellor's Americanization Committee and the U.S. Bureau of Education, CCIH meeting minutes, December 10, 1915. Paul Scharrenberg and most

members of the California Labor Federation opposed the United States' entry into the war and viewed it as a conspiracy of capitalism against labor. Burki, "Paul Scharrenberg: White Shirt Sailor," pp.112–116; and Lower, *A Bloc of One*, chapter 3, notes Johnson's opposition to the United States' entry into the war.

43. Bell, "Americanization as a Necessity to National Defense" (1917), p. 18, notes the role of labor unions in fostering assimilation. The CCIH's monitoring of the IWW during the war quickly lost touch with reality as investigator Thompson accused Scharrenberg of IWW membership and espionage for Germany, accusations Lubin never took seriously. Please see Nelson, "J. Vance Thompson, the Industrial Workers of the World and the Mood of Syndicalism," and Thompson's reports to Lubin in file IWW investigation, folders 1–4, carton 1, Lubin Papers.

44. Once in charge, Sayer abolished Kellor's Division of Aliens, and transferred its functions to the new Industrial Division. Kellor left the BRM by late July 1917 to head the Division of Immigrant Education in the federal Bureau of Education, where she had more influence over federal Americanization policy, in "Activities of the Industrial Division, State Defense Council," thirteen-page document, undated, unsigned, New York Council of Defense Papers. The federal government also took over the New York Bureau of Employment and a public-private jobs clearinghouse, though the New York legislature continued to pay for the office.

45. New York Industrial Commission, *Annual Report* (1918), pp. 24–27. The *Governor's Tentative Appropriation Act for 1917–1918*, pp. 571–572, notes that the bureau's proposed appropriation was $21,660 for twenty-one employees, seventeen in Manhattan and three in Buffalo. In the *Governor's Tentative Appropriation Act for 1918–1919*, pp. 592–593, the Immigration Bureau would receive $27,380. That same year the Bureau of Employment received $53,279 and the Bureau of Inspections $373,271.

46. NYBII, *Seventh Annual Report* (1918), pp. 5–7.

47. New York Industrial Commission, *Annual Report* (1919), pp. 206–209, requests $100,000 for the NYBII to promote factory schools; New York Department of Education, *Annual Report* (1926), pp. 114–115.

48. Hartmann, *The Movement to Americanize the Immigrant*, p. 179.

49. New York Department of Education, *Annual Report* (1926), pp. 114–116, gives a figure of $12,000 for teacher training, but the U.S. Commissioner of Education, *Annual Report* (1918), p. 45, says that the amount was $20,000. I am taking the $12,000 figure as accurate because the source is the state agency that received the funds.

50. Edwards, *Patriots in Pinstripe*, p. 105.

51. "Americanization Plan to Engage the Nation," *New York Times*, September 17, 1917, p. 4; "Making Good Citizens of the Foreign Born," *New York Times*, October 28, 1917, p. SM5.

52. MBI, *First Annual Report* (1919), pp. 34–38; Massachusetts Division of University Extension, *Fourth Annual Report* (1919), pp. 5–8. The March 28, 1918, minutes of the advisory board to the Massachusetts Board of Education note Towne's hiring.

53. CCIH, *Americanization: The California Program* (January and November 1918); CCIH meeting minutes, April 21, 1918, and October 30, 1918.

54. U.S. Bureau of Education, Americanization conference (1919); Hartmann, *The Movement to Americanize the Immigrant*, chapters 7 and 8; McClymer, *War and Wel-*

fare, chapter 5; and McClymer, "The Federal Government and the Americanization Movement."

55. U.S. Commission of Education *Annual Report* (1917), pp. 61–62.

56. U.S. Commission of Education *Annual Report* (1918), pp. 146–140; Edwards, *Patriots in Pinstripe*, pp. 106–109.

57. O'Leary, *To Die For*, pp. 232–234.

58. California Board of Education, *Third Biennial Report* (1916–1918), pp. 13–14; CCIH, *Our Soldiers and the English Language, A San Francisco Enterprise* (March 1918); and CCIH, *Annual Report* (1919), pp. 45–46.

59. CCIH meeting minutes, May 6, 1918; and Breen, *Uncle Sam at Home*, chapter 9.

60. CCIH, *Americanization: California's Answer* (June 1, 1920), p. 3.

61. CCIH meeting minutes, May 6, 1918; and acting executive officer reports, October 30, 1918, pp. 7–9, and December 4, 1918, p. 3.

62. CCIH meeting minutes, April 20, 1918, and April 24, 1918; acting executive officer report, October 30, 1918, pp. 8–9; CCIH, *Americanization: The California Program* (1919), pp. 8–15.

63. CCIH, *Americanization: The California Program* (1919), pp. 11–12.

64. CCIH, *Americanization: The California Program* (1919).

65. Ibid., p. 5.

66. Ibid., p.7.

67. CCIH, executive officer report, July 17, 1918. These contradictions reflected the problems in the national community organization movement. See U.S. Commissioner of Education *Annual Report* (1919), pp. 36–42.

68. CCIH, acting executive officer report, October 30, 1918, pp. 8–9, lists the county chairs.

69. CCIH, *Americanization: The California Program* (1919), p. 8.

70. CCIH, acting executive officer report, October 30, 1918, pp. 7–8.

71. CCIH, *The Spirit of the Nation* (March 1918), and *Americanization: Suggestions for Speakers* (1919).

72. CCIH, *The Spirit of the Nation* (March 1918), p. 1.

73. Torpey, "Passports and the Development of Immigration Controls in the North Atlantic World During the Long Nineteenth Century."

74. MBI, *First Annual Report* (1919), pp. 7–8; and Hartmann, *The Movement to Americanize the Immigrant*, p. 178.

75. MBI, *First Annual Report* (1919), pp. 7–8.

76. Ibid., p. 16.

77. MBI, *Second Annual Report* (1920), p. 6.

78. Ibid., p. 7.

79. MBI, *First Annual Report* (1919), p. 34.

80. Ibid., p. 11, says: "Resumption of immigration on a large scale may be anticipated after the signing of the peace treaties unless Congress passes some additional restrictive measures—a subject deserving most careful and statesmanlike consideration."

81. U.S. Bureau of Naturalization, *Annual Report* (1919), p. 35.

82. O'Leary, *To Die For*, p. 232 for quote, pp. 176–186 on the schoolhouse flag movement, pp. 232–236 for wartime flag protection movement; Schaffer, *America in*

the Great War, pp. 21–23, on vigilantism involving the flag; and Morgan, *Women and Patriotism in Jim Crow America*, pp. 82–83, on the DAR.

Chapter 6. Cosmopolitanism Cut Short:
The Illinois Immigrants Commission, 1919–1921

1. Finegold, *Experts and Politicians*, p. 15.
2. Morton, *Justice and Humanity,* and Merriner, *Grafters and Goo Goos*, both note Chicago and Illinois progressives' failure to make the leap from private institutions to political power and office.
3. Pegram, *Partisans and Progressives*.
4. Hartmann, *The Movement to Americanize the Immigrant*, pp. 216–237.
5. Buroker, "From Voluntary Association to Welfare State"; IPL, *Sixth Annual Report* (1915); and Edith Abbott, "Protecting Immigrant Arrivals," pp. 110–111, in folder 6, box 90, Grace and Edith Abbott Papers.
6. Lissak, "Liberal Progressives and 'New Immigrants,'" pp. 79–103; Lissak, *Pluralism and Progressives*; Mink, *The Wages of Motherhood*; and Muncy, *Creating a Female Dominion in American Reform*. Buroker, "From Voluntary Association to Welfare State," p. 649, argues: "A leader of the League was thus likely to be a Protestant, well-educated, middle-class, native-stock American."
7. Lissak is correct, however, that progressives believed "the members of the lower classes were ill-equipped for leadership. They lacked the middle-class value system which enabled its members to look beyond their personal, narrow and selfish interests to the good of the whole society," in "Liberal Progressives and 'New Immigrants,'" p. 101.
8. Rosenwald to Breckinridge, January 24, 1918, in folder 53a, box 5, Immigrants' Protective League, correspondence and reports, 1910–November 1918, IPL Papers. Rosenwald wrote: "The fact that there have been few immigrants during the past four or five years would, I think, naturally tend toward lack of interest on the part of contributors."
9. González, "Immigrants in Our Midst," p. 367.
10. Senate Bill 343, carried by Chicago Republican Morton Hull, passed June 11, 1919, in *Blue Book of the State of Illinois* (1919–1920), p. 302.
11. Morton, *Justice and Humanity*.
12. IIC meeting notes, March 19, 1920, in Immigrants' Protective League, supplement II, folder 58, box 4, Illinois Immigrants Commission, early years, March 1920–November 1922, IPL Papers.
13. Laws of Illinois, 1919, section 82, appendix, p. 202, box 4, folder 47, the Illinois Immigrants Commission, September 1919–November 1936, IPL Papers.
14. Philpott, *The Slum and the Ghetto*.
15. Untitled, undated document found in folder 47, box 4, the Illinois Immigrants Commission, September 1919–November 1936, IPL Papers.
16. IIC meeting minutes, March 19, 1920, supplement II, folder 58, box 4, Illinois Immigrants Commission, early years, March 1920–November 1922, IPL Papers. Also

Breckinridge to Tiffany Blake, June 11, 1919, and October 6, 1919, and Breckinridge to Mrs. Dunlap Smith, November 14, 1919, folder 53b, box 5, Immigrants' Protective League, correspondence and reports, January 1919–December 1924, IPL Papers.

17. IIC meeting minutes, May 8, 1920, Immigrants' Protective League, supplement 2, folder 58 box 4, Illinois Immigrants Commission, early years, March 1920–November 1922, IPL Papers. First names for some of these individuals are not available; Gaiczunas is also spelled "Graiczunas" in the document.

18. "State Convention—Illinois League of Women Voters Session of Education Committee November 16, 1926," in folder 47, box 4, the Illinois Immigrants Commission, September 1919–November 1936, IPL Papers.

19. González, "Immigrants in Our Midst," p. 372.

20. Buroker, "From Voluntary Association to Welfare State," p. 656.

21. Laws of Illinois, 1919, note the appropriation. "Memorandum as to Appropriations of other Commissions, Boards or Bureaus charged with duties similar to those of the Illinois Commission," in Immigrants' Protective League, supplement 2, folder 58, box 4, Illinois Immigrants Commission, early years, March 1920–November 1922, IPL Papers.

22. Edith Abbott, "New Horizons, Massachusetts Immigration Commission, 1913–1914," part 3, folder 11, box 91, Edith and Grace Abbott Papers; Costin, *Two Sisters for Social Justice*; González, "Immigrants in Our Midst," pp. 75–100. Abbott was also an alumna of the College Settlement on Rivington Street in New York City. Abbott's thoughts about World War I and its impact on Chicago's immigrant communities can be found in *The Immigrant and the War, being the Ninth Annual Report of the Immigrants' Protective League, for the Year ending December 31, 1917*, folder 60a, box 4,Immigrants' Protective League, annual reports 2, 1917–1954, 1958, IPL Papers.

23. Abbott testified against a proposed literacy test in 1912, in untitled document, dated December 2, 1949, (handwritten), folder 6, box 90, Edith and Grace Abbott Papers.

24. Grace Abbott, "True Americanization," *Americanization* (November 1, 1918), p. 4.

25. M. Gordon, *Assimilation in American Life*, called this "cultural assimilation," which he defined as a shallow form of assimilation in which the alien adapts to a new cultural context without increasing social interaction with the dominant group in such ways as would encourage intermarriage. Also see Lissak, *Pluralism & Progressives*, chapter 2.

26. Mohl, "Cultural Assimilation versus Cultural Pluralism"; Wacker, "Assimilation and Cultural Pluralism in American Social Thought"; Matthews, "The Revolt against Americanism"; and Higham, *Send These to Me*, chapter 9.

27. Grace Abbott, "The Immigrant as a Problem in Community Planning."

28. Massachusetts Commission on Immigration, 1914 report, p. 37.

29. González, "Immigrants in Our Midst," chapter 3; Massachusetts Commission on Immigration, 1914 report, pp. 47–51, pp. 18–19 (recommendations), pp. 226–227; and "An Act Concerning State Free Employment Offices."

30. For example, Grace Abbott, "A Study of the Greeks of Chicago."

31. IPL, *Seventh Annual Report*, p. 15, in folder 59a, box 4, supplement 2, Immigrants' Protective League, annual reports 1, 1909–1916, IPL Papers.

32. Grace Abbott's testimony before Congress, 1912, p. 6, in folder 6, box 90, "Protecting Immigrant Arrivals," sub-sub-series 4, the Hull-House Years, 1908–1914, Grace and Edith Abbott Papers.

33. González, "Immigrants in Our Midst," pp. 220–231, notes Abbott's ideas about immigrants' role in urban politics and good citizenship.

34. IPL, *Annual Report* (1909–1910), p. 25, folder 59a, box 4, supplement 2, Immigrants' Protective League annual reports 1, 1909–1916, IPL Papers.

35. IPL, *Annual Report* (1909–1910), p. 21, in box 4, folder 59a, supplement 2, Immigrants' Protective League, annual reports 1, 1909–1916, IPL Papers.

36. "The Children of Immigrants and Child Labor," p. 5, in folder 9, box 90, Edith and Grace Abbott Papers.

37. Ibid., pp. 4–8.

38. Grace Abbott, "True Americanization," *Americanization* (November 1, 1918), p. 4.

39. Massachusetts Commission on Immigration, 1914 report, p. 15.

40. A person reading Abbott's papers and the records of the IPL could easily forget that the Red Scare even occurred in 1919–1920. Murray, *Red Scare*, p. 116, notes the presence of the U.S. Army in Chicago on July 4, 1919. Chicago was also the headquarters of the Industrial Workers of the World, which was prosecuted by the federal government in 1917–1918 for criminal conspiracy to obstruct the war effort. See Preston, *Aliens and Dissenters*, chapter 4 and chapter 5.

41. IIC executive secretary, *Quarterly Report* (January, February, and March 1920), pp. 6–7, in Immigrants' Protective League, supplement 2, folder 58, box 4, Illinois Immigrants Commission, early years, March 1920–November 1922, IPL Papers. Muncy, *Creating a Female Dominion in American Reform*, p. 129, notes attacks on Abbott as an alleged Bolshevik for her work with the United States Children's Bureau, attacks Abbott did not take seriously.

42. González, "Immigrants in Our Midst," pp. 100–104.

43. For example, IIC, March 19, 1920, "Memorandum as to work to be immediately undertaken by the Immigrants Commission," IPL Papers.

44. IIC meeting minutes, March 19, 1920, and March 19, 1920, in "Memorandum as to work to be immediately undertaken by the Immigrants Commission," IPL Papers.

45. IIC meeting minutes, June 18, 1920, and IIC executive secretary, *Second Quarterly Report* (April, May, and June 1920), in Immigrants' Protective League, supplement 2, folder 58, box 4, Illinois Immigrants Commission, early years, March 1920–November 1922, IPL Papers. IIC executive secretary's quarterly reports for 1920 list the number of inquiries each quarter.

46. IIC executive secretary, *Third Quarterly Report* (July, August, and September 1920), *Fourth Quarterly Report* (October, November, and December 1920), and *First Quarterly Report* (January, February, and March 1921); Immigrants' Protective League, supplement 2, folder 58, box 4, Illinois Immigrants Commission, early years, March 1920–November 1922, IPL Papers.

47. IIC executive secretary, *Second Quarterly Report* (April, May, and June 1920), Immigrants' Protective League, supplement 2, folder 58, box 4, Illinois Immigrants Commission, early years, March 1920–November 1922, IPL Papers.

48. The *Social Survey in Historical Perspective*, Bulmer, Bales, and Sklar, eds.; Fitzpatrick, *Endless Crusade*.

49. Abbott, *The Educational Needs of Immigrants in Illinois* (1920), pp. 18–19; Massachusetts Commission on Immigration, 1914 report, p. 195.

50. Abbott, *The Educational Needs of Immigrants in Illinois* (1920), pp. 5–6.

51. Abbott, *The Educational Needs of Immigrants in Illinois* (1920), pp. 3–4.

52. Abbott, "Education of Foreigners in American Citizenship" (1909), p. 377.

53. IIC annual budget, adopted October 18, 1920, Immigrants' Protective League, supplement 2, folder 58, box 4, Illinois Immigrants Commission, early years, March 1920–November 1922, IPL Papers.

54. An appropriation of $53,670 was requested, IIC annual budget adopted October 18, 1920; and IIC meeting minutes October 18, 1920, in Immigrants' Protective League, supplement 2, folder 58, box 4, Illinois Immigrants Commission, early years, March 1920–November 1922, IPL Papers.

55. Costin, *Two Sisters for Social Justice*, p. 120. Also see, "The Illinois State Immigrants Commission," 3, folder 10, box 91, Edith and Grace Abbott Papers. Pegram, in *Partisans and Progressives*, p. 205, notes: "In Small's hands, the clear channels of executive authority developed by Lowden became arteries for a vast patronage network. Small cast aside civil service restrictions, removing unwanted personnel on the transparent grounds of 'incompetency.'"

56. IPL president Ernst Freund "to the members and friends of the Immigrants' Protective League," December 12, 1921; Ernst speech, November 16, 1926, to the state convention of the Illinois League of Women Voters; and resolution from Chicago Women's Club, December 1929, and the Illinois Immigrants Commission, April 8, 19299–all in folder 47, box 4, Illinois Immigrants Commission, September 1919–November 1936, IPL Papers. Also see Buroker, "From Voluntary Association to Welfare State," p. 659.

Chapter 7. Schooling the Immigrant: Americanization and Adult Education, 1919–1929

1. Van Nuys, *Americanizing the West*, p. 179.

2. Hartmann, *The Movement to Americanize the Immigrant*, pp. 225–233.

3. U.S. Commissioner of Naturalization, *Annual Report* (1918), pp. 29–33; Hartmann, *The Movement to Americanize the Immigrant*, pp. 235–236.

4. For example, please see U.S. Commissioner of Education, *Annual Report* (1919), pp. 42–46. Kennedy, *Over Here*, pp. 187–189, notes that Army tests revealed that the median number of years of education for enlisted men was 6.9 for native whites, 2.6 for black southerners, and 4.7 for immigrants. Fewer than 18 percent of native white draftees had attended high school. Tichenor discusses southern support for restriction in *Dividing Lines*, pp. 119–121.

5. New York Department of Education, *Annual Report* (1926), p. 115, for quote; "Regents Disclose Americanization Plan," *New York Times*, January 31, 1919, p. 11; and "New York State Americanization Activities," *Americanization* (August 1, 1919), p. 8.

6. Pfannestiel, *Rethinking the Red Scare*, pp. 97–133.

7. New York Department of Education, *Annual Report* (1923), pp. 204–205. In 1921 only twenty-eight communities had no evening schools, and forty offered only English language instruction.

8. New York Department of Education, *Annual Report* (1923), p. 208; New York Department of Education, *Annual Report* (1924), p. 115.

9. "$400,000 for Junior High," *New York Times*, July 16, 1920, p. 10; "1921 School Budget Cut to $78,000,000," *New York Times*, October 29, 1920, p. 9; and "One Official Is Called City's Biggest Problem," *New York Times*, November 21, 1920, p. 4.

10. New York Department of Education, *Annual Report* (1924), pp. 117–118.

11. New York Department of Education, *Annual Report* (1924), chart, p. 118, and *Annual Report* (1925), p. 219.

12. New York Department of Education, *Annual Report* (1926), pp. 219–220.

13. U.S. Commissioner of Naturalization, *Annual Report* (1920), p. 44, table B. McClymer, "The Americanization Movement and the Education of the Foreign-Born Adult," pp. 102–103, warns against trusting the Bureau of Naturalization's use of statistics in reporting on participation in its programs.

14. Massachusetts Division of University Extension, *The Federal-State Program for Immigrant Education* (January 1919), p. 4.

15. Massachusetts Division of University Extension, *The Problem of Immigrant Education in Massachusetts* (July 1919), p. 6.

16. Ibid., p. 7.

17. Ibid., p. 8.

18. U.S. Commissioner of Naturalization, *Annual Report* (1920), p. 81. Mahoney replaced Charles F. Towne.

19. Massachusetts Division of University Extension, *Ninth Annual Report* (March 1924), pp. 4–11.

20. Massachusetts Division of University Extension, *Fifth Annual Report* (March 1920), pp. 6–7.

21. Massachusetts Division of University Extension, *A Survey of Adult Alien Education in Massachusetts* (November 1927), p. 16.

22. Massachusetts Division of University Extension, *The Massachusetts Problem of Immigrant Education in 1921–1922* (November 1922), p. 4.

23. Massachusetts Division of University Extension, *Fifth Annual Report* (March 1920), p. 30; *Seventh Annual Report* (March 1922), p. 28; and *Ninth Annual Report* (March 1924), p. 16.

24. U.S. Census Bureau, *Fourteenth Census* (1920), table 4, p. 20, for Massachusetts; table 4, p. 30 for New York.

25. U.S. Census Bureau, *Fourteenth Census* (1920), "Statistics for California," table 20, p. 48.

26. Whipple, "Americanization in Industry" (1919). Brandes, *American Welfare Capitalism*, and Brody, *Workers in Industrial America*, debate the motivations behind corporate welfare. See also Korman, *Industrialization, Immigrants and Americanizers* and "Americanization at the Factory Gate."

27. New York Department of Education, *Annual Report* (1926), pp. 115–116.

28. New York Department of Education, *Annual Report* (1923), pp. 214–215.

29. New York Department of Education, *Annual Report* (1924), p. 122. Students enrolled in industrial education classes were not classified by citizenship or nationality, see chart, p. 111.

30. New York Department of Education, *Annual Report* (1924), pp. 130-132.

31. Massachusetts Division of University Extension, *Sixth Annual Report* (March 1921), p. 3.

32. MIB, *Second Annual Report* (1920), pp. 30-31.

33. "Massachusetts Discusses Plant Americanization Plans," *Americanization* (July 1, 1919), p. 5; "Industrial Conference Experts Meet in Massachusetts," *Americanization* (August 1, 1919), p. 7; and Hartmann, *The Movement to Americanize the Immigrant*, p. 241.

34. Herlihy replaced Mahoney in 1922 as supervisor of adult alien education, a position he held until 1928, Massachusetts Division of University Extension, *Seventh Annual Report* (March 1922), p. 2. He also sat on the Division of Immigration and Americanization's advisory board in 1927-1928.

35. Massachusetts Division of University Extension, *Sixth Annual Report* (March 1921), p. 3, quote p. 13.

36. Massachusetts Division of University Extension, *A Survey of Adult Alien Education in Massachusetts* (November 1927), p. 14.

37. "New York City Plans for Alien Mothers," *Americanization* (October 1, 1919), p. 7; and "Visiting Teachers," *New York Times*, May 23, 1920, p. XX6.

38. "Education of Foreign-Born Women in New York State," *Americanization* (September 1, 1919), pp. 1-3.

39. New York Department of Education, *Annual Report* (1924), p. 120.

40. U.S. Commissioner of Naturalization, *Annual Report* (1923), p. 18.

41. New York Department of Education: *Annual Report* (1923), p. 312; *Annual Report* (1924), p. 122; and *Annual Report* (1924), p. 120.

42. New York Department of Education, *Annual Report* (1924), p. 123.

43. Massachusetts Division of University Extension, *A Survey of Adult Alien Education in Massachusetts* (November 1927), pp. 6-7.

44. Muncy, *Creating a Female Dominion in American Reform*, p. 115, discusses "Little Mothers" clubs; "Fight Bolshevism the Country Over," *New York Times*, July 27, 1919, p. 14; and Edwards, *Patriots in Pinstripe*, pp. 104-109.

45. McConnell, "Reading the Flag."

46. "All Pupils to Sign Pledge of Loyalty," *New York Times*, December 15, 1919, p. 17.

47. Morgan, *Women and Patriotism in Jim Crow America*, pp. 136-137, notes the DAR's withdrawal from the Women's Joint Congressional Committee and the National Council of Women in 1923 and its opposition to the renewal of the Sheppard-Towner Maternity and Infancy Act in 1929, all progressive groups and programs that the DAR had once supported. Nehls, "A Grand and Glorious Feeling," p. 199, notes the American Legion's support for immigration restriction.

48. Gibson, "Schools for the Whole Family," *Survey Graphic* (June 1, 1926), p. 303; Woo-Sam, "Domesticating the Immigrant," pp. 148-149.

49. New York Department of Education, *Annual Report* (1924), pp. 124-127. This

law had the effect of pulling immigrant youths out of evening schools and into part-time day schools, thus causing evening school enrollment figures to drop.

50. University of the State of New York, *Immigrant Education* (1921); and Butler, *State Americanization* (1920), pp. 12–15. New York Department of Education, *Annual Report* (1923), pp. 207–208, notes Hill's background and discusses the program.

51. Goldberger, *Teaching English to the Foreign Born: A Teacher's Handbook* (1920).

52. Massachusetts Division of University Extension, *Americanization: One Language—One People* (July 1919), p. 8, notes Towne's involvement; and *Americanization* (January 1920) was probably taught by Mahoney, who led an Americanization course at Harvard University's summer school in 1919 and was a supervisor of Americanization.

53. CCIH executive officer report, July 25, 1919, p. 7. Wood agreed only after the CCIH consented to pay Baughman's $2,400 salary.

54. CCIH executive officer reports, September 23, 1919, pp. 1–2; October 24, 1919, p. 4; December 12, 1919, p. 5; and January 28, 1920, p. 4. Gibson to Lubin, two letters dated September 15, 1919, in file Mary Simons Gibson, 98 letters, 1913–1920, box 2, letters Br-L, Lubin Papers; Richardson, California Superintendent of Public Instruction, *Biannual Report*, 1922–1924.

55. CCIH executive officer report, December 12, 1919, p. 5. Gibson to Lubin with clipping attached, November 14, 1919, file Mary Simons Gibson, 98 letters, 1913–1920, box 2, letters Br-L, Lubin Papers. Gibson wrote Lubin several times in October 1919 describing the negotiations among herself, Richardson, and Wood.

56. California Board of Education, *Fifth Biennial Report*, 1920–1922 (1923), p. 34 and Richardson's section of the report is pp. 36–45; D. Wood, "Immigrant Mothers, Female Reformers, and Women Teachers," p. 72, pp. 137–140.

57. Richardson, California Superintendent of Public Instruction, *Biannual Report*, 1922–1924, p. 49; CCIH executive officer report, July 11, 1921, p. 6, notes Richardson's resignation from the CCIH. CCIH, *Annual Report* (1923), p. 95, notes that the CCIH paid Richardson's salary the first year she was assistant superintendent.

58. Krysto, "They Also Serve," *The Clubwoman* (December 1918), p. 24; Raftery, *Land of Fair Promise*, p. 79. D. Wood, "Immigrant Mothers, Female Reformers, and Woman Teachers," p. 79, notes that the Los Angeles School District employed sixty-three home teachers in 19259. CCIH, *Annual Report* (1923), pp. 95–97; Pond, "Education and Americanization of Adult Immigrants in California" (1920), pp. 59–60, notes number and location of evening schools in 1920.

60. California Board of Education, *Fifth Biennial Report* (1923–1925), pp. 37–39; CCIH executive officer reports, June 18, 1920, pp. 7–9, and October 18, 1920, exhibits 7 and 8 (reports from Richardson and Collier, respectively).

61. McClymer, "The Americanization Movement and the Education of the Foreign-Born Adult"; Mink, *The Wages of Motherhood*.

62. CCIH, *Heroes of Freedom* (1919).

63. Ibid., p. 5.

64. Ibid., p. 12.

65. Ibid., p. 13.

66. CCIH, *Americanization: The California Program* (1919), p. 5.

67. Massachusetts Division of University Extension, *A Teacher's Handbook* (May 1919), p. 4.

68. Ibid., p. 5.

69. Massachusetts Division of University Extension, *Civics for Naturalization* (July 1919), pp. 7–10.

70. Massachusetts Division of University Extension, *Americanization* (January 1920), pp. 6–7, pp. 9–10. Mahoney is assumed to be the author because he was supervisor of immigrant education at the time.

71. McClymer, "The Americanization Movement and the Education of the Foreign-Born Adult," p. 109.

72. Massachusetts Division of University Extension, *Americanization* (January 1920), p. 7.

73. Ibid., p. 10.

74. Massachusetts Division of University Extension, *Thirty Lessons in Naturalization and Citizenship* (November 1921), p. 19.

75. Ibid., p. 28.

76. Ibid., p. 18, p. 20, p. 26, p. 29, p. 31.

77. Ibid., p. 69.

78. CCIH executive officer report, October 18, 1920, see exhibit 7 for Richardson's work. D. Wood, "Immigrant Mothers, Female Reformers, and Women Teachers," pp. 127–129, notes that such a certificate was not adopted until 1925.

79. Pond, "Education and Americanization of Adult Immigrants in California," pp. 69–76, notes cities with immigrant education programs and their interaction with other organizations, particularly in the areas of citizenship education and naturalization preparation.

80. California Board of Education, *Fifth Biennial Report* (1923–1925), p. 25.

81. D. Wood, "Immigrant Mothers," pp. 149–151.

82. New York Department of Education, *Annual Report* (1924), pp. 125–126.

83. New York Department of Education, annual reports, 1924–1929, vol. 2, statistics show attendance in different types of classes offered.

84. New York Department of Education, *Annual Report* (1924), p. 125.

85. Ibid., p. 115.

86. Ibid., p. 130.

87. Crawford, "The New York State Literacy Test," *The American Political Science Review* (May, 1923), pp. 260–263. The New York voter literacy test was struck down in Cardona v. Power (1966) as a violation of the 1965 Voting Rights Act.

88. McGerr, *The Decline of Popular Politics*, examines the decline in voter turnout during the Progressive Era.

89. New York Department of Education, *Annual Report* (1929), p. 137.

90. New York Department of Education annual reports: 1926, p. 222, table 35; 1929, p. 137, table 35; and 1930 p. 154, table 53.

91. Massachusetts Division of University Extension annual reports: tenth (March 1925), p. 13; fourteenth (March 1929), pp. 6–7; and sixteenth (March 1931), pp. 5–6.

Chapter 8. Americanization versus Restriction: Immigrant Social Welfare Policy in New York, California, and Massachusetts, 1919–1929

1. McClymer, "The Federal Government and the Americanization Movement," pp. 233–252, and "The Americanization Movement and the Education of the Foreign-born Adult"; Higham, *Strangers in the Land*; and Mink, *The Wages of Motherhood*. I side with those historians who see progressivism continuing into the 1920s, such as Putnam, "The Persistence of Progressivism in the 1920s" and Muncy, *Creating a Female Dominion in American Reform*.

2. King, *Making Americans*; Fitzgerald, *The Face of the Nation*; and Tichenor, *Dividing Lines*—all discuss the role of eugenics in shaping federal immigration policy in the 1920s. Only King discusses Americanization, but he combines it with eugenics as one of two efforts to define American identity in racial terms.

3. MBI, *Second Annual Report* (1920), p. 24.

4. Ibid.

5. Ibid., p. 6.

6. MBI, *First Annual Report* (1919); Massachusetts Commission on Immigration, 1914 report.

7. MBI, *Second Annual Report* (1920), pp. 11–12. The fact that the bureau considered the reorganization legislation poorly and hastily written indicates that it had little to no hand in its drafting and was unable to influence the direction of the reorganization.

8. Massachusetts legislature, appropriations for commonwealth agencies in 1920–1929.

9. MBI, *Second Annual Report* (1920), pp. 45–46. MDIA *Annual Report* (1921) notes Thayer as director of Immigration and Americanization.

10. Besides D'Allesandro, the advisory committee included Francis W. Tully of Brookline; Stanislaus Mieczkowski of Worcester; Mary A. Barr of Boston; Henry P. Kendall of Walpole; and Abraham E. Pinanski of Boston. This panel sat as a group until 1924, with Barr and Pinanski serving until 1929. Advisory board members are not identified in the annual reports of 1923, 1924, 1925, and 1926.

11. Murray, *Red Scare*, pp. 234–235, writes that New York also had a "red flag" law. Both measures banned the display of red banners believed to be a stimulus to anarchism or anti-government activity.

12. Gibson to Christina Krysto, November 13, 1919, and Gibson to Lubin, November 19, 1919, in file Mary Simons Gibson, 98 letters, 1913–1920, box 2, Br–L. November 24, 1919, letter from Lubin to Gibson, in file outgoing letters, 1919 July–December, box 5, letters written by Lubin, 1915–1932, Lubin Papers.

13. Lubin, Krysto, "The Strength of America the Melting Pot," series in *Survey*: part 1, "Cracks in the Melting Pot," December 20, 1919; part 2, "The Conception of Nationality," January 3, 1920; part 3, "The Significance of Modern Migration," January 24, 1920; part 4, "Will Immigration Be Curtailed?" February 7, 1920; and part 5, "The Menace of Americanization," February 21, 1920.

14. Lubin, Krysto, "The Menace of Americanization," p. 612.

15. Layton, "The Better America Federation"; Sitton, "John Randolph Haynes and the Left Wing of California Progressivism," pp. 27–28. In an August 2, 1920, letter to BAF president H.M. Haldemann, Lubin wrote of Scharrenberg: "I further know,

that among the so-called radical element of labor unions, Mr. Scharrenberg is rather looked upon as a reactionary, the very opposite of a radical," in file outgoing letters 1920, box 5, letters written by Lubin, 1915–1932, Lubin Papers.

16. Pfaffenstiel, *Rethinking the Red Scare*.

17. The NYBII went unmentioned in the thousands of pages of the Lusk Committee report; please see the last two volumes of the New York Joint Legislative Committee Investigating Seditious Activities, *Revolutionary Radicalism* (1920).

18. NYBII, *Annual Report* (1920).

19. Ibid., p. 230.

20. Ibid., pp. 231–232.

21. Ibid., p. 237, p. 234.

22. Stern, *Eugenic Nation*, p. 16; and Kline, *Building a Better Race*, pp. 20–25.

23. NYBII, *Annual Report* (1920), p. 232.

24. Ibid.

25. New York Industrial Commission, *Annual Report* (1921), p. 195.

26. Ibid., p. 207. In 1919 Clark reported no inspections, and in 1920 she only listed investigations and client interactions by number, with no breakdown for activity.

27. New York Industrial Commission, *Annual Report* (1922); New York Department of Labor, bulletins, March 1921, p. 1, and June 1921, p. 171.

28. New York Industrial Commission, *Annual Report* (1922), p. 7, hints at progressives' concerns, which echoed those expressed in the 1910s; Yellowitz, *Labor and the Progressive Movement in New York State*, pp. 118–119.

29. New York Department of Labor, "Governor's Recommendations," *Bulletin* (January 1921), p. 65.

30. New York Department of Labor, *Bulletin* (July–August 1921), pp. 176–177; see also New York Industrial Commission *Annual Report* (1922), p. 65, for a list of Division of Aliens staff and their salaries.

31. Garis, *Immigration Restriction*, pp. 142–143; Daniels, *Guarding the Golden Door*, p. 49. Also, see Department of Homeland Security, Bureau of Immigration and Citizenship, Quota Law of May 19, 1921, (42 Statutes-at-Large 45), and Act of May 11, 1922, (42 Statutes-at-Large 540).

32. MDIA, *Annual Report* (1922), pp. 13–17.

33. New York Industrial Commission, *Annual Report* (1923), pp. 138–139.

34. MDIA, *Annual Report* (1921), p. 10.

35. MDIA, *Annual Report* (1922), pp. 13–14.

36. MDIA, *Annual Report* (1923), p. 12, pp. 17–19.

37. MDIA, *Annual Report* (1924), p. 7.

38. CCIH, *Annual Report* (1923), pp. 58–59, table "Causes of Complaints," January 1, 1922–November 1, 1922, and "Disposition of Complaints," January 1, 1922–November 1, 1922.

39. CCIH, *Annual Report* (1924), p. 12, table, "Causes of Complaints," January 1, 1924–January 1, 1925.

40. Housing Institute minutes, first and second sessions, 1922–1923 in California Department of Industrial Relations files; CCIH, *Annual Report* (1923), pp. 75–86; and CCIH executive officer reports, January 28, 1920, p. 3, May 14, 1920, p. 7, and June 18, 1920, pp. 4–7.

41. CCIH executive officer report, June 16, 1923, including a Housing Department report, November 1, 1922–to June 1, 1923, pp. 1–3. The bill was introduced by State Senator Inman as Senate Bill No. 52, but State Senator Lester Burnett introduced an identical measure as Senate Bill No. 29 which was passed and signed by Richardson.

42. California Budget Board, recommendations and estimated revenues, July 1, 1923–June 30, 1925, p. 9.

43. Wood, "The California State Commission of Immigration and Housing," pp. 133–134.

44. California Budget Board, *Biannual Report*, 1921–1923, p. 19.

45. "Scharrenberg's Loss Felt in I.W.W. Trouble," *Sacramento Bee*, April 26, 1923. See also "Statement given to the press by the governor on the day he dismissed Scharrenberg, April 19, 1923," in file Dismissal of Paul Scharrenberg, carton 1, Lubin Papers.

46. California State Federation of Labor May 3, 1923, in file proposals, programs, reports, minutes, carton 1, Lubin Papers.

47. "Lubin Breaks With Governor," *San Francisco Examiner*, April 26, 1923, p. 1; dismissal of Paul Scharrenberg, carton 1, Lubin Papers; Wood, "The California State Commission of Immigration and Housing," pp. 135–137. Lubin's statement was published in the *Bee*, April 25, 1923.

48. "Lubin Ousted by Governor," *San Francisco Examiner*, October 16, 1923, p. 1. An October 17, 1923, *Sacramento Union* article suggested that McBride also faced removal because he allegedly was out of the country for two years, which was not true.

49. After Gibson left the commission in 1922, she became active with projects advocated by her late husband and joined John Randolph Haynes in his work with California's Indians, serving as one of the original trustees of the Haynes Foundation and acting as a leader in the American Indian National Defense Association. She also continued to be active in peace work, serving as the chair of the Southern California Cause and Cure of War Committee and director of the League of Nations Nonpartisan Association and raising money for the University of California International House, a facility designed to promote world understanding by bringing foreign and American students together.

50. *San Francisco Chronicle*, "Funeral Rite for Ocheltree Set for Tomorrow," August 6, 1936, p. 13; and Wood, "The California State Commission of Immigration and Housing," p. 114, footnote 17.

51. Putnam, "The Persistence of Progressivism in the 1920s," pp. 399–400.

52. New York Industrial Commission, *Annual Report* (1922), pp. 194–195.

53. New York Industrial Commission, *Annual Report* (1923), pp. 138–139. The Division of Aliens' budget was $12,757 in 1923 and $11,779 in 1924. See annual budgets for the New York Industrial Commission, 1924, p. 26, and 1925, p. 29.

54. New York Industrial Commission, *Annual Report* (1924), p. 134.

55. New York Joint Legislative Committee on the Exploitation of Immigrants report, pp. 15–16.

56. Ibid., p. 68, p. 72, p. 78.

57. *New York Industrial Commission Annual Report* (1926), pp. 452–465, and *Annual Report* (1927), pp. 401–405.

58. New York Industrial Commission, *Annual Report* (1927), p. 392.

59. New York Industrial Commission, *Annual Report* (1928), pp. 216–219.

60. New York Industrial Commission, *Annual Report* (1930), p. 27; New York Industrial Commission, *Annual Report* (1931), p. 46.

61. Smith appointed Perkins to the Industrial Commission first in 1918 and again in 1922, and made her chair of the Industrial Board in 1926. Please also see Buenker, *Urban Liberalism and Progressive Reform*.

62. Immigration statistics found at: http://teacher.scholastic.com/activities/immigration (accessed December 4, 2008); and MDIA, *Annual Report* (1924), p. 6.

63. Daniels, *Guarding the Golden Door*, pp. 51–53; Garis, *Immigration Restriction*, chapter 7, p. 183, for quote.

64. MDIA, *Annual Report* (1927), pp. 4–5.

65. Daniels, *Guarding the Golden Door*, p. 53.

66. CCIH, *Annual Report* (1927), pp. 9–10.

67. U.S. Census Bureau, *Thirteenth Census* (1910), "Statistics for California," table 5, p. 587; *Fourteenth Census* (1920), "Statistics for California," table 6, p. 25.

68. CCIH, *Annual Report* (1927), p. 8.

69. Lubin, Krysto, "Nation Building," pp. 692–693.

70. Americanization Conference proceedings, exchanges between Bell and Louis Nusbaum, associate superintendent of schools, in Philadelphia, May 12–15, 1919, pp. 341–343.

71. CCIH, *Annual Report* (1921), p. 9.

72. MDIA, annual reports: 1924, for citizenship work, pp. 2–3; 1923, for investigations of immigrant banks, p. 10; and 1921, for investigations into investment fraud pp. 15–17.

73. Tichenor, *Dividing Lines*, pp. 144–145, and chapter 6.

Conclusion

1. Hartmann's *The Movement to Americanize the Immigrant*, originally written in 1948, is a valuable narrative of Americanization activities and programs, but provides little analysis or interpretation, which McClymer does in such work as "The Federal Government and the Americanization Movement" and "Gender and the 'American Way of Life.'" Carlson's "Americanization as an Early Twentieth-Century Adult Education Movement" and *The Quest for Conformity* preceded McClymer's initial work but do not consider policy aspects of Americanization as thoughtfully as McClymer. Gullett's "Women Progressives and the Politics of Americanization in California" and Sánchez's "'Go After the Women'" also discuss Americanization as primarily an education movement; both focus on the programs of the California Commission of Immigration and Housing.

2. Gerstle, *American Crucible*; and King, *Making Americans*.

3. Cornford, *Workers and Dissent in the Redwood Empire*; González, *Labor and Community*; and Van Nuys, *Americanizing the West*.

4. Gerstle, *American Crucible*.

BIBLIOGRAPHY

Abbott, Edith and Grace. Papers. Special Collections Research Center, Regenstein Library, University of Chicago.

Abbott, Grace. "Education of Foreigners in American Citizenship." Proceedings of the Buffalo Conference for Good City Government and the Sixteenth Annual Meeting of the National Municipal League, 1909.

———. "The Immigrant as a Problem in Community Planning." Proceedings of the Twelfth Annual Meeting of the American Sociological Society, Philadelphia, December 27–29, 1917. Vol. 12, *Social Control*. Chicago: University of Chicago Press, 1917.

———. "A Study of the Greeks of Chicago." *American Journal of Sociology* 15, October 1909: 379–393.

Abramson, Harold J. "Assimilation and Pluralism." In *Harvard Encyclopedia of American Ethnic Groups*. Edited by Stephan Thernstrom. Cambridge, Mass.: Belknap Press of Harvard University Press, 1980. 150–160.

Aleinikoff, Thomas Alexander, David A. Martin and Hiroshi Motomura eds. *Immigration and Citizenship: Process and Policy*. 5th ed. St. Paul: Thomson West, 2003.

"Americanization in Industries." Proceedings of a national conference, Atlantic House, Nantasket Beach, Mass., June 22–24, 1919.

Anderson, Dewey. *California State Government*. Stanford, Calif.: Stanford University Press, 1942.

Baritz, Loren. *The Good Life: The Meaning of Success for the American Middle Class*. New York: Alfred A. Knopf, 1989.

Barrett, James R. "Americanization from the Bottom Up: Immigration and the Remaking of the Working Class in the United States, 1880–1930." *Journal of American History* 79, December 1992: 996–1020.

Beard, Charles. "Commissions in American Government." *Cyclopedia of American Government*. Vol. 1, *Abattoirs-Finality*. Edited by Andrew C. McLaughlin and Albert Bushnell Hart, 350–354. New York: D. Appleton, 1914.

Beckert, Sven. "Propertied of a Different Kind: Bourgeoisie and Lower Middle Class in the Nineteenth-Century United States." In *The Middling Sorts: Explorations in the History of the American Middle Class*. Edited by Burton J. Bledstein and Robert D. Johnston. New York: Routledge, 2001.

Bell, George L. "The Wheatland Hop-fields' Riot." *Outlook*, May 16, 1914: 118–123.

———. "Americanization as a Necessity to National Defense." Speech at the convention of the California Federation of Women's Clubs, Pasadena, Calif. Reprinted in *Clubwoman*, April 1917: 16–19.

Berrol, Selma. "Ethnicity and American Children." In *American Childhood*. Edited by Joseph M. Hawes and N. Ray Hines. Westport, Conn.: Greenwood, 1985.

Blair, Karen J. *The Clubwoman as Feminist: True Womanhood Redefined, 1868–1914*. New York: Holmes & Meier, 1980.

Blanpied, Charles W. "A Humanitarian Study of the Coming Immigration Program on the Pacific Coast." Address in San Francisco April 14–15, 1913. Young Men's Christian Association archives, Bancroft Library, University of California–Berkeley.

Blumin, Stuart M. *The Emergence of the Middle Class: Social Experience in the American City, 1760–1900*. Cambridge: Cambridge University Press, 1989.

Bogardus, Emory S. *Essentials of Americanization*. Los Angeles: University of Southern California Press, 1919.

Bogen, Elizabeth. *Immigration in New York*. Westport, Conn.: Praeger, 1987.

Boris, Eileen. "Reconstructing the 'Family': Women, Progressive Reform, and the Problem of Social Control." Chap. 6 in *Gender, Class, Race, and Reform in the Progressive Era*. Edited by Noralee Frankel and Nancy S. Dye. Lexington: University Press of Kentucky, 1991.

Brandes, Stuart D. *American Welfare Capitalism, 1880–1940*. Chicago: University of Chicago Press, 1976.

Breen, William J. *Uncle Sam at Home: Civilian Mobilization, Wartime Federalism, and the Council of National Defense, 1917–1919*. Westport, Conn.: Greenwood, 1984.

———. *Labor Market Politics and the Great War: The Department of Labor, the States, and the First U.S. Employment Service, 1907–1933*. Kent, Ohio: Kent State University Press, 1997.

Brody, David. "The Rise and Decline of Welfare Capitalism." Chap. 2 in *Workers in Industrial America: Essays on the Twentieth Century Struggle*. Oxford: Oxford University Press, 1980.

Brown, Lawrence Guy. *Immigration: Cultural Conflicts and Social Adjustments*. New York: Longmans, Green, 1933.

Brownlee, W. Elliot. "Historiography and Bibliography." In *Federal Taxation in America: A Short History*. Cambridge: Cambridge University Press and the Woodrow Wilson Center Press 1996.

Bryn Mawr College Class of 1907, comps. *Carola Woerishoffer, Her Life and Work*. Bryn Mawr, Penn.: Bryn Mawr College, 1912. Reprinted Manchester, N.H.: Ayer, 1974.

Bulmer, Martin. "The Decline of the Social Survey Movement and the Rise of American Empirical Sociology." In *The Social Survey in Historical Perspective, 1880–1940*. Edited by Martin Bulmer, Kevin Bales, and Kathryn Kish Sklar. Cambridge: Cambridge University Press, 1991.

Burki (Mason), Mary Ann. "Paul Scharrenberg: White Shirt Sailor." Ph.D. diss., Rochester, N.Y.: University of Rochester, 1971.

Buroker, Robert L. "From Voluntary Association to Welfare State: The Illinois Immigrants' Protective League, 1908–1926." *Journal of American History* 58, December 1971: 643–661.

California Blue Book or State Roster, 1913–1915. Sacramento: California State Printing Office, 1915.

California Board of Control. Annual reports, 1913–1919. Sacramento: California State Printing Office.

California Board of Education. Biennial reports, 1914–1924 Sacramento: California State Printing Office.

———. Legislative bulletin on education proposals, prepared by the commissioner of secondary schools, March 1, 1915. Sacramento: California State Printing Office, 1915.

California Budget Board. Annual reports, 1921–1929. Sacramento: California State Printing Office. (Please note: In 1919 the State Board of Control and the State Controller combined to form the Budget Board.)

California Commission of Immigration and Housing. *Report on Wheatland Hop Fields Riot*. Submitted by Carleton H. Parker. Sacramento: California State Printing Office, 1913.

———. *Advisory Pamphlet on Camp Sanitation and Housing*. 1914.

———. *Report on Unemployment to Gov. Hiram W. Johnson*. Sacramento: California State Printing Office, 1914.

———. *Report on Relief of Destitute Unemployed, 1914–1915*. Sacramento: California State Printing Office, 1915.

———. Minutes of meetings and reports of attorney and executive officers, 1916–24. Department of Industrial Relations, California State Archives, Sacramento.

———. Annual reports, 1915, 1916, 1919, 1923, 1925, 1927, Sacramento: California State Printing Office.

———. *Primer for Foreign-speaking Women*. Parts 1 and 2, Sacramento: California State Printing Office, 1918.

———. *Our Soldiers and the English Language: A San Francisco Enterprise*. Sacramento: California State Printing Office, 1918.

———. *The Spirit of the Nation*. Copyrighted W. L. & Co. 1918.

———. *A Discussion of Methods of Teaching English to Adult Foreigners, with a Report on Los Angeles County*. Sacramento: California State Printing Office, 1918.

———. *Heroes of Freedom*. Sacramento: California State Printing Office, 1919.

———. *A Report on Large Landholdings in Southern California, With Recommendations*. Sacramento: California State Printing Office. 1919.

———. *A Manual for Home Teachers*. Sacramento: California State Printing Office, 1919.

———. *Americanization: The California Program*. Sacramento: California State Printing Office. 1918.

———. *Americanization: Suggestions for Speakers*. Sacramento: California State Printing Office. 1919.

———. *Americanization: California's Answer*. Sacramento: California State Printing Office. 1920.

———. Bulletin of information for immigrants, 1920.

———. Bulletin summarizing immigration and Americanization work. September and November 1920.

California Controller. Biennial reports, 1910–1924. Sacramento: California State Printing Office.

California Council of Defense. "California in the War: Addresses Delivered at State War Council," San Francisco, March 5–6, 1918. Sacramento: California State Printing Office, 1918.

California Department of Education. *Blue Bulletin*, 1915–1920. Sacramento: California State Printing Office.

———. California Community Exchange. *Bulletin*, 1914–1931. Stanford University, Cubberley Library. California State Printing Office.

California Federation of Women's Clubs. Special Collections and Archives, University Library, University of California–Santa Cruz.

California Governor William D. Stephens. *Addresses, Proclamations and Patriotic Messages*. Issued by the California Historical Survey Commission. Sacramento: California State Printing Office, 1917.

———. *California in the War: Addresses, Proclamations and Patriotic Messages*. Issued by the California Historical Survey Commission. Sacramento: California State Printing Office, 1917.

California Legislature. *Senate Journal*. Forty-First Session, Monday, January 4–Sunday, May 9, 1915. Sacramento: California State Printing Office, 1915.

Carlson, Robert A. "Americanization as an Early Twentieth-Century Adult Education Movement." In *Americanization, Social Control, and Philanthropy*. Edited by George E. Pozzetta. New York: Garland Publishing Inc., 1991. Reprint of *History of Education Quarterly* 10, Winter 1970: 440–464.

———. *The Quest for Conformity: Americanization through Education*. New York: Wiley, 1975.

Chambers, Clarke A. *Seedtime of Reform: American Social Service and Social Action, 1918–1933*. Minneapolis: University of Minnesota Press, 1963.

Chambers II, John Whiteclay. *The Tyranny of Change: America in the Progressive Era, 1900–1917*. New York: St. Martin's, 1980.

Coben, Stanley. "Postwar Upheaval: The Red Scare." In *The Impact of World War I*. Edited by Arthur S. Link. New York: Harper & Row, 1969.

———. *Rebelling Against Victorianism: The Impetus for Cultural Change in 1920s America*. Oxford: Oxford University Press, 1991.

Cohen, Ronald D. "Child-Saving and Progressivism, 1885–1915." In *American Childhood*. Edited by Joseph M. Hawes and N. Ray Hines. Westport, Conn.: Greenwood, 1985.

Cole, William I. *Immigrant Races in Massachusetts: The Greeks*. Boston: Massachusetts Bureau of Immigration, 1919.

Cooper, John Milton. *The Warrior and the Priest: Woodrow Wilson and Theodore Roosevelt*. Cambridge, Mass.: Belknap Press of Harvard University Press, 1983.

Cornford, Daniel A. *Workers and Dissent in the Redwood Empire*. Philadelphia: Temple University Press, 1987.

Costin, Lela B. *Two Sisters for Social Justice: A Biography of Grace and Edith Abbott*. Urbana and Chicago: University of Illinois Press, 1983.

Crawford, F. G. "The New York State Literacy Test." *American Political Science Review* 17, May 1923: 260–263.

Crawford, James. *Bilingual Education: History, Politics, Theory and Practice.* 3rd edition. Los Angeles: Bilingual Education Services, 1995.
Cremin, Lawrence A. *The Transformation of the School: Progressivism in American Education, 1876–1957.* New York: Alfred A. Knopf, 1961.
Cuff, Robert D. "War Mobilization, Institutional Learning and State Building in the United States, 1917–1941." In *The State and Social Investigation in Britain and the United States.* Edited by Michael J. Lacey and Mary O. Furner. Cambridge: International Center for Scholars and Cambridge University Press, 1993.
Daniel, Cletus E. *Bitter Harvest: A History of California Farmworkers, 1870–1941.* Ithaca, N.Y.: Cornell University Press, 1981.
Daniels, Roger. *Guarding the Golden Door: American Immigration Policy and Immigrants Since 1882.* New York: Hill and Wang, 2004.
Davenport, Charles B. Papers. American Philosophical Society Manuscripts Department. Philadelphia.
Davis, Allen F. "The Social Workers and the Progressive Party, 1912–1916." *American Historical Review* 69, April 1964: 671–688.
———. *Spearheads for Reform: The Social Settlements and the Progressive Movement, 1890–1914.* Oxford: Oxford University Press, 1967.
DeWitt, Howard A. *Images of Alien and Radical Violence in California Politics, 1917–1930: A Survey.* San Francisco: R and E Research Associates, 1975.
Dikötter, Frank. "Race Culture: Perspectives on the History of Eugenics." *American Historical Review* 102, April 1998: 467–478.
Drachsler, Julius. *Democracy and Assimilation: The Blending of Immigrant Heritages in America.* New York: Macmillan, 1920.
Dubofsky, Melvyn. *We Shall Be All: A History of the Industrial Workers of the World.* Chicago: Quadrangle Books, 1969.
Edwards, John Carver. *Patriots in Pinstripe: Men of the National Security League.* Washington, D.C.: University Press of America, 1982.
Eisenach, Eldon J. *The Lost Promise of Progressivism.* Lawrence: University Press of Kansas, 1994.
Ewen, Elizabeth. *Immigrant Women in the Land of Dollars: Life and Culture on the Lower East Side, 1890–1925.* New York: Monthly Review Press, 1985.
Fairfield, John D. "The Scientific Management of Urban Space: Professional City Planning and the Legacy of Progressive Reform." *Journal of Urban History* 20, February 1994: 179–204.
Fass, Paula S. *Outside In: Minorities and the Transformation of American Education.* Oxford: Oxford University Press, 1989.
Finegold, Kenneth. *Experts and Politicians: Reform Challenges to Machine Politics in New York, Cleveland, and Chicago.* Princeton, N.J.: Princeton University Press, 1995.
Fitzgerald, Keith. *The Face of the Nation: Immigration, the State and the National Identity.* Stanford, Calif.: Stanford University Press, 1996.
Fitzpatrick, Ellen. *Endless Crusade: Women Social Scientists and Progressive Reform.* Oxford: Oxford University Press, 1990.

Fuchs, Lawrence H. "Immigration Reform in 1911 and 1981: The Role of Select Commissions." *Journal of American Ethnic History* 3, Fall 1983: 58–89.

Furner, Mary O. "Knowing Capitalism: Public Investigation and the Labor Question in the Long Progressive Era." In *The State and Economic Knowledge: The American and British Experiences*. Edited by Mary O. Furner and Barry Supple. Cambridge: Cambridge University Press and Woodrow Wilson International Center for Scholars, 1990.

———. "The Republican Tradition and the New Liberalism: Social Investigation, State Building, and Social Learning in the Gilded Age." In *The State and Social Investigation in Britain and the United States*. Edited by Michael J. Lacey and Mary O. Furner. Cambridge: Cambridge University Press and International Center for Scholars, 1993.

Garis, Roy L. *Immigration Restriction: A Study of Opposition to and Regulation of Immigration into the United States*. New York: Macmillan, 1927.

Garraty, John A. and Mark C. Carnes, eds. *American National Biography*. Oxford: Oxford University Press, 1999.

Gerstle, Gary. *American Crucible: Race and Nation in the Twentieth Century*. Princeton, N.J.: Princeton University Press, 2001.

———. "Liberty, Coercion, and the Making of Americans." *Journal of American History* 84, September 1997: 524–558.

Gibson, Mary S. "Mary S. Gibson Explains Why Progressive Women Should Uplift Immigrant Women 1914." In *Major Problems in California History, Documents and Essays*. Edited by Sucheng Chan, Spencer C. Olin. Chap. 8, "California Progressives: The Ambiguities of Political and Moral Reform." Boston: Houghton Mifflin, 1997. Originally published as "The Immigrant Woman." *California Outlook* 19, May 9, 1914: 6–7.

———. *A Record of Twenty-five Years: California Federation of Women's Clubs, 1900–1925*. Vol. 1. Bancroft Library, University of California–Berkeley.

———. "A Suggested Program for Americanization," presented by the California Commission of Immigration, 1920.

———. "Schools for the Whole Family." *Survey Graphic* 56, June 1, 1926: 300–303.

Gjerde, Jon. "New Growth on Old Vines: The State of the Field: The Social History of Immigration to and Ethnicity in the United States." *Journal of American Ethnic History* 18, Summer 1999: 40–65.

Glazier, Jack. *Dispersing the Ghetto: The Relocation of Jewish Americans across America*. Ithaca, N.Y.: Cornell University Press, 1998.

Gleason, Phillip. *Speaking of Diversity: Language and Ethnicity in Twentieth-Century America*. Baltimore: Johns Hopkins University Press, 1992.

———. "American Identity and Americanization." In *Harvard Encyclopedia of American Ethnic Groups*. Edited by Stephan Thernstrom, 31–58. Cambridge, Mass.: Belknap Press of Harvard University Press, 1980.

González, Gilbert. *Labor and Community: Mexican Citrus Worker Villages in a Southern California County, 1900–1950*. Urbana and Chicago: University of Illinois Press, 1994.

Gonzalez, Suronda. "Immigrants in Our Midst: Grace Abbott, the Immigrants' Protective League of Chicago, and the New American Citizenship, 1908–1924." Ph.D. diss., State University of New York Binghamton, 2004.

Gordon, Linda. *Pitied But Not Entitled: Single Mothers and the History of Welfare* Cambridge, Mass.: Harvard University Press, 1994.

Gordon, Margaret S. *Employment Expansion and Population Growth: The California Experience, 1900–1950.* Berkeley and Los Angeles: University of California Press, Institute of Industrial Relations, 1954.

Gordon, Milton. *Assimilation in American Life: The Role of Race, Religion, and National Origins.* New York: Oxford University Press, 1964.

Gosney, E.S., and Paul Popenoe. *Sterilization for Human Betterment: A Summary of Results of 6,000 Operations in California, 1900–1929.* New York: Macmillan, 1931.

Gribble, Richard. *Catholicism and the San Francisco Labor Movement, 1896–1921.* San Francisco: Mellen Research University Press, 1993.

———. "Church, State, and the American Immigrant: The Multiple Contributions of Archbishop Edward J. Hanna." *U.S. Catholic Historian* 16, Fall 1998: 1–18.

———. "A Rough Road to San Francisco: The Case of Edward Hanna, 1907–1915." *Southern California Quarterly* 78, no. 3: 225–242.

Gullett, Gayle. *Becoming Citizens: The Emergence and Development of the California Women's Movement, 1880–1911.* Urbana: University of Illinois, 2000.

———. "Women Progressives and the Politics of Americanization in California, 1915–1920." *Pacific Historical Review* 64, February 1995: 71–94.

Hanna, Archbishop Edward J. Papers. Archdiocese of San Francisco Archives, St. Patrick's Seminary, Menlo Park, Calif.

Hardy, Gayle J. *American Women Civil Rights Activists: Biobibliographies of 68 Leaders, 1825–1992.* See especially profiles of Emily Greene Balch and Lillian D. Wald. Jefferson, N.C., and London: McFarland, 1993.

Hartmann, Edward George. *The Movement to Americanize the Immigrant.* New York: AMS Press, 1967. First published by Columbia University Press, New York, 1948.

Hawley, Ellis W. *The Great War and the Search for a Modern Order: A History of the American People and Their Institutions, 1917–1933.* New York: St. Martin's, 1992.

Hays, Samuel P., and Kathryn Kish Sklar. "The Progressive Movement: Elitist or Democratic?" In *Interpretations of American History, Patterns and Perspectives.* Vol. 2, chap. 6, *From Reconstruction.* Edited by Frances G. Couvares, Martha Saxton, Gerald N. Grob, and George Athan Billias. 7th ed. New York: Free Press, 2000.

Herman, David George. "Neighbors on the Golden Mountain, the Americanization of Immigrants in California: Public Instruction as an Agency of Ethnic Assimilation, 1850–1933." Ph.D. diss., University of California–Berkeley, 1981.

Higham, John. *Send These to Me: Immigrants in Urban America.* Baltimore: Johns Hopkins University Press, 1984.

———. *Strangers in the Land: Patterns of American Nativism, 1860–1925.* 4th ed. New Brunswick, N.J.: Rutgers University Press, 1994.

———. "Current Trends in the Study of Ethnicity in the United States," *Journal of American Ethnic History* 2, Fall 1982: 5–15.

Hollinger, David A. "National Solidarity at the End of the Twentieth Century: Reflections on the United States and Liberal Nationalism." *Journal of American History* 84, September 1997: 559–569.

———. *Postethnic America: Beyond Multiculturalism.* New York: Basic Books, 2000.

Howard, Robert P. *Mostly Good and Competent Men: Illinois Governors, 1818–1988.* Springfield: Sangamon State University and Illinois State Historical Society, 1988.

Howe, Frederic C. *The Confessions of a Reformer.* Kent, Ohio: Kent State University Press, 1988. First published in 1925 by Charles Scribner's Sons.

Illinois Blue Book, 1919–1920. Edited by Louis L. Emmerson. Springfield: Illinois State Journal Company, 1919.

Illinois Immigrants Commission. *Educational Needs of Immigrants in Illinois.* Springfield: Danville Print Company, 1920.

———. *The Immigrant and the Coal-Mining Communities in Illinois.* Springfield: Illinois Immigrants Commission, 1920.

Immigrants in America Review. Vol. 1, March, June, September 1915 and January 1916; Vol. 2 April and July 1916. New York: Committee for Immigrants in America.

Issel, William. "'Citizens Outside the Government': Business and Urban Policy in San Francisco and Los Angeles, 1890–1932." *Pacific Historical Review* 57, May 1988: 117–145.

Jacobson, Matthew Frye. *Whiteness of a Different Color: European Immigrants and the Alchemy of Race.* Cambridge, Mass.: Harvard University Press, 1998.

Johnson, Hiram W. Papers. Bancroft Library, UC–Berkeley.

Jones, Alethia. "From Private to Neighborhood Banks: European Immigrants in Chicago, 1890–1929." Chap. 3 in "From Social to Financial Capital: Immigrant Access to Banking Institutions." Ph.D. diss., Yale University, 2004.

Katz, Michael B. *Reconstructing American Education.* Cambridge, Mass.: Harvard University Press, 1987.

Kazal, Russell A. "Revisiting Assimilation: The Rise, Fall, and Reappraisal of a Concept in American Ethnic History." *American Historical Review* 100, April 1995: 437–471.

Kelley, Robert. "The Idea of Policy History." *Public Historian* 10, Winter 1988.

Kellor, Frances A. "The Immigrant Woman." *Atlantic Monthly,* September 1907: 401–407.

———. "The Protection of Immigrant Women." *Atlantic Monthly,* February 1908: 246–255.

———. "Who Is Responsible for the Immigrant?" *Outlook,* April 25, 1914: 912–917.

———. *Immigrants in America: Program for a Domestic Policy.* New York: The Committee for Immigrants in America, n.d. [1915?].

———. *Out of Work: A Study of Unemployment.* New York and London: G. P. Putnam's Sons and Knickerbocker Press, 1915. First published in 1904 as *Out of Work: A Study of Employment Agencies* by G. P. Putnam's Sons.

———. *Straight America: A Call to National Service.* New York: Macmillan, 1916.

———. "Americanization of Women: A Discussion of an Emergency Created by Granting the Vote to Women in New York State." Lecture at a course sponsored by the New York State Woman's Suffrage Party, New York, January 17, 1918.

———. "Neighborhood Americanization: A Discussion of the Alien in a New Country and of the Native American in His Home Country." Address at a Colony Club course on citizenship, New York, February 8, 1918.

———. *Immigration and the Future*. New York: George H. Doran, 1920.

———. "What Is Americanization?" In *Immigration and Americanization: Selected Readings*. Compiled and edited by Philip Davis, 623–628. Boston: Ginn and Company, 1920. First published in 1919 in *Yale Review*.

Kellor, Frances A., and Joseph Mayper. "Recommendations for a Federal Bureau of Distribution." In *New York: North American Civic League for Immigrants, Committee on Legislation*, 1913.

Kennedy, David M. *Over Here: The First World War and American Society*. Oxford: Oxford University Press, 1980.

Kessner, Thomas. *The Golden Door: Italian and Jewish Mobility in New York City, 1880–1915*. New York: Oxford University Press, 1977.

Kevles, Daniel J. *In the Name of Eugenics: Genetics and the Uses of Human Heredity*. New York: Knopf, 1985.

King, Desmond. *Making Americans: Immigration, Race, and the Origins of the Diverse Democracy*. Cambridge, Mass.: Harvard University Press, 2000.

Kline, Wendy. *Building a Better Race: Gender, Sexuality, and Eugenics from the Turn of the Century to the Baby Boom*. Berkeley and Los Angeles: University of California Press, 2001.

Kloppenberg, James. *Uncertain Victory: Social Democracy and Progressivism in European and American Thought*. Oxford: Oxford University Press, 1986.

Knight, Robert Edward Lee. *Industrial Relations in the San Francisco Bay Area, 1900–1918*. Berkeley and Los Angeles: University of California Press, 1960.

Kolchin, Peter. "Whiteness Studies: The New History of Race in America." *Journal of American History* 89, June 2002: 1–41.

Korman, Gerd. *Industrialization, Immigrants and Americanizers: The View from Milwaukee, 1866–1921*. Madison: Wisconsin Historical Society, 1967.

Kusmer, Kenneth L. "The Functions of Organized Charity in the Progressive Era: Chicago as a Case Study." *Journal of American History* 60, December 1973.

LaVally, Rebecca. *Californians Together: Defining the State's Role in Immigration*. Sacramento: California Senate Office of Research, 1993.

Layton, Edwin. "The Better America Federation: A Case Study of Superpatriotism." *Pacific Historical Review* 30, May 1961: 137–147.

Lissak, Rivka. "Liberal Progressives and 'New Immigrants': The Immigrants' Protective League of Chicago, 1908–1919." Vol. 14, *Americanization, Social Control, and Philanthropy*. Edited by George E. Pozzetta. New York: Garland, 1991.

———. *Pluralism & Progressives: Hull-House and the New Immigrants, 1890–1919*. Chicago: University of Chicago Press, 1989.

Lower, Richard Coke. *A Bloc of One: The Political Career of Hiram W. Johnson*. Stanford, Cslif.: Stanford University Press, 1993.

Lubin, Simon J. Papers. Bancroft Library, UC–Berkeley.

Lubin, Simon J., and Christina Krysto. "The Strength of America: Cracks in the Melting Pot," *Survey*, December 20, 1919; January 20 and January 24, 1920; and February 7 and February 21, 1920.

Lubin, Mrs. Simon J. "Reminiscences," interview with Corrine L. Gilb, March 11, 1954. Oral History Project, Bancroft Library, University of California–Berkeley.

Lubove, Roy. *The Professional Altruist: The Emergence of Social Work as a Career, 1880–1930.* Cambridge, Mass.: Harvard University Press, 1965.

Mason, Mary Ann. "Neither Friends Nor Foes: Organized Labor and the California Progressives." In *California Progressivism Revisited.* Edited by William Deverell and Tom Sitton, 57–71. Berkeley and Los Angeles: University of California Press, 1994.

Massachusetts Commission on Immigration, Bureau of Immigration, and Division of Immigration and Americanization. Annual reports, 1919–1929. Boston: Wright & Potter.

Massachusetts Commission on Immigration. *Report on the Problem of Immigration in Massachusetts.* Boston: Wright & Potter, 1914.

Massachusetts Commonwealth. Budgets 1918–1930. Archives State Library of Massachusetts, Boston.

Massachusetts Department of Education, Bureau of Immigration Papers. Massachusetts Archives, University of Massachusetts, Boston.

Massachusetts Department of Education, Division of University Extension. Annual reports, 1918–1931. Boston: Commonwealth of Massachusetts.

———. *The Federal-State Program for Immigrant Education.* Bulletin 4, no. 1, January 1919.

———. *A Teacher's Handbook to Accompany Standard Lessons In English for American Citizenship: A Comprehensive-Direct Method of Teaching English.* Bulletin 4, no. 3, May 1919.

———. *The Problem of Immigrant Education in Massachusetts.* Bulletin 4, no. 4, July 1919.

———. "Americanization: One Language—One People," "Methods of Teaching English to Immigrants," and "Organization and Supervision of Americanization Work." Courses taught in cooperation with the State Normal School at Hyannis, Mass.. Bulletin 6, no. 4-B, July 1919.

———. *Civics for Naturalization.* Bulletin 4, no. 4-A, July 1919; and 6, no. 3, May 1921.

———. *Adult Immigrant Education in Massachusetts, 1920–1921.* Bulletin 6, no. 4, July 1921.

———. *Thirty Lessons in Naturalization and Citizenship: An Outline for Teachers of Adult Immigrants.* Bulletin 6, no. 6, November 1921.

———. *Announcement of Course in the Project Method of Teaching Citizenship in the First Six Grades.* Bulletin 6, no. 1A, January 1922.

———. *The Massachusetts Problem of Immigrant Education in 1921–22.* Bulletin 7, no. 6, November 1922.

———. *A Survey of Adult Alien Education in Massachusetts.* Bulletin 12, no. 6B, November 1927.

Massachusetts Statutes. Appropriation acts covering commonwealth agencies, including the Division of Immigration and Americanization, 1918–1930.

Matthews, F. H. "The Revolt against Americanism: Cultural Pluralism and Cultural Relativism as an Ideology of Liberation." In *Assimilation, Acculturation, and Social Mobility.* Edited by George E. Pozzetta. New York: Garland, 1991.

Maxwell, William Joseph. "Frances Kellor in the Progressive Era: A Case Study in the Professionalization of Reform." Ed.D. diss., Columbia University, New York, 1968.

McBride, James Harvey. "The Life and Health of Our Girls in Relation to Their Future." Address to the American Academy of Medicine, Washington, D.C., May 11, 1903. Reprinted in the *Bulletin of the American Academy of Medicine* 6, no. 8, 3–17.

———. "The Physician and Human Conservation." Chicago: American Medical Association, 1919: 1–11. Reprinted from the *Archives of Neurology and Psychiatry* 2, August 1919: 149–157.

McClymer, John F. "The Americanization Movement and the Education of the Foreign-born Adult, 1914–25." In *American Education and the European Immigrant*. Edited by Bernard J. Weiss. Urbana: University of Illinois Press, 1982.

———. "The Federal Government and the Americanization Movement, 1915–1924." In *Americanization, Social Control, and Philanthropy*. Edited by George E. Pozzetta. New York: Garland, 1991. First published Spring 1978 in *Prologue*: 23–41.

———. "Gender and the 'American Way of Life': Women in the Americanization Movement." *Journal of American Ethnic History* 10, Spring 1991: 3–21.

———. *War and Welfare: Social Engineering in America, 1890–1925*. Westport, Conn.: Greenwood, 1980.

McConnell, Stuart. "Reading the Flag: A Reconsideration of the Patriotic Cults of the 1890s." Chap. 6 in *Bonds of Affection: Americans Define Their Patriotism*. Edited by John Bodnar. Princeton, N.J.: Princeton University Press, 1996.

McCormick, Richard L. *The Party Period and Public Policy*. Oxford: Oxford University Press, 1986.

McEntire, Davis. *The Labor Force in California: A Study of Characteristics and Trends in Labor Force Employment, and Occupations in California, 1900–1950*. Berkeley and Los Angeles: University of California Press, 1952.

McGerr, Michael E. *The Decline of Popular Politics: The American North, 1865–1928*. Oxford: Oxford University Press, 1986.

———. *A Fierce Discontent: The Rise and Fall of the Progressive Movement in America, 1870–1920*. New York: Free Press, 2003.

McWilliams, Carey. *Factories in the Field: The Story of Migratory Farm Labor in California*. North Haven, Conn.: Archon Books, 1969. First published in 1935 by Peregrine Smith Books.

———. *Ill Fares the Land: Migrants and Migratory Labor in the United States*. New York: Barnes & Noble, 1941.

Merriner, James L. *Grafters and Goo Goos: Corruption and Reform in Chicago, 1833–2003*. Carbondale: Southern Illinois University Press, 2004.

Mink, Gwendolyn. *The Wages of Motherhood: Inequality in the Welfare State, 1917–1932*. Ithaca, N.Y.: Cornell University Press, 1995.

Mohl, Raymond A. "Cultural Assimilation versus Cultural Pluralism." In *Assimilation, Acculturation, and Social Mobility*. Edited by George E. Pozzetta. New York: Garland, 1991.

Morgan, Francesca. *Women and Patriotism in Jim Crow America*. Chapel Hill: University of North Carolina Press, 2005.

Morton, Richard Allen. *Justice and Humanity: Edward F. Dunne, Illinois Progressive.* Carbondale: Southern Illinois University Press, 1997.

Moskowitz, Marina. *Standard of Living: The Measure of the Middle Class in Modern America.* Baltimore: Johns Hopkins University Press, 2004.

Muncy, Robyn. *Creating a Female Dominion in American Reform, 1890–1935.* Oxford: Oxford University Press, 1991.

Nasaw, David. *Schooled to Order: A Social History of Public Schooling in the United States.* Oxford: Oxford University Press, 1979.

Nash, Gerald. *State Government and Economic Development: A History of Administrative Policies in California, 1849–1922.* Berkeley: Institute of Governmental Studies, University of California–Berkeley, 1964.

Nehls, Christopher Courtney. "A Grand and Glorious Feeling: The American Legion and American Nationalism between the World Wars." Ph.D. diss., University of Virginia, 2007.

Neils Conzen, Kathleen. "German-Americans and the Invention of Ethnicity." In *America and the Germans: An Assessment of a Three Hundred-Year History.* Vol. 1, *Immigration, Language, Ethnicity.* Edited by Frank Trommler and Joseph McVeigh, 131–147. Philadelphia: University of Pennsylvania Press, 1985.

Nelson, Bruce. "J. Vance Thompson: the Industrial Workers of the World and the Mood of Syndicalism." *Labor's Heritage* 2, no. 4, 1990: 44–65.

New York Bureau of Municipal Research. *The History of Appropriations in the Legislative Session of 1916, New York State.* New York: n.p., 1916.

———. *The New York Legislative Budget and Financial Measures for 1918.* New York, n.p., 1918.

New York Commission of Immigration. Report. Albany, N.Y.: J.B. Lyon, 1909.

New York Council of Defense. Papers. New York Archives, Albany, N.Y..

New York Department of Efficiency and Economy. Appropriation request to the governor on March 16, 1914, for the fiscal year beginning October 1, 1914. Albany, N.Y.: J. B. Lyon, 1914.

———. Appropriation request to the state legislature on January 21, 1915. Albany, N.Y.: J. B. Lyon , 1915.

New York Department of Efficiency and Economy and Bureau of Municipal Research. *Government of the State of New York: A Description of Its Organization and Functions.* New York: New York State Constitutional Convention Commission, 1915.

New York Department of Labor and Bureau of Industries and Immigration. Annual reports, 1912–1917; and Industrial Commission Annual reports, 1918–1930. Albany, N.Y.: State Department of Labor.

New York Education Department. Annual reports, 1913–1924. Albany, N.Y.: University of the State of New York.

———. *Community Organization and Program for Americanization Work.* Albany, N.Y.: University of the State of New York, 1919.

———. *Immigrant Education: Summer Courses for Evening and Extension School Teachers and Supervisors in the State of New York, Season 1921.* Albany, N.Y.: University of the State of New York, 1921.

New York Governor. Tentative budget proposals, 1916–1917, 1917–1918, 1918–1919, Albany, N.Y.: J. B. Lyon.
New York Joint Legislative Committee Investigating Seditious Activities. *Revolutionary Radicalism: Its History, Purpose and Tactics.* Albany, N.Y.: J. B. Lyon, 1920.
New York Joint Legislative Committee on the Exploitation of Immigrants. Legislative document no. 76. Albany, N.Y.: J. B. Lyon, 1924.
New York–New Jersey Committee of the North American Civic League for Immigrants. Publications covering December 1909– February 1913. New York: n.p., n.d.
New York Reconstruction Commission. *Americanization: Report of the Committee on Education.* May 14, 1919. Albany, N.Y.: J. B. Lyon, 1919.
North American Civic League for Immigrants. Annual reports, 1908–1918. Boston.
———. *Messages for Newcomers to the United States.* Boston: n.p., 1910.
Odem, Mary. "City Mothers and Delinquent Daughters, Female Juvenile Justice Reform in Early Twentieth-Century Los Angeles." In *California Progressivism Revisited.* Edited by William Deverell and Tom Sitton, 175–199. Berkeley and Los Angeles: University of California Press, 1994.
O'Leary, Cecilia Elizabeth. *To Die For: The Paradox of American Patriotism.* Princeton, NJ: Princeton University Press, 1999.
Olin, Spencer C. *California's Prodigal Sons: Hiram Johnson and the Progressives, 1911–1917.* Berkeley and Los Angeles: University of California Press, 1968.
———. "European Immigrant and Oriental Alien: Acceptance and Rejection by the California Legislature of 1913." *Pacific Historical Review* 33, August 1966: 303–315.
Parker, Carleton H. *The Casual Laborer and Other Essays.* New York: Harcourt, Brace, and Howe, 1920.
Pascoe, Peggy. *Relations of Rescue: The Search for Female Moral Authority in the American West, 1874–1939.* Oxford: Oxford University Press, 1990.
Peck, Gunther. *Reinventing Free Labor: Padrones and Immigrant Workers in the North American West, 1880–1930.* Cambridge: Cambridge University Press, 2000.
Pengram, Thomas R. *Partisans and Progressives: Private Interest and Public Policy in Illinois, 1870–1922.* Urbana and Chicago: University of Illinois Press, 1992.
Perkins, Dexter. *Charles Evans Hughes and American Democratic Statesmanship.* Edited by Oscar Handlin. Boston: Little, Brown, 1956.
Pfannestiel, Todd J. *Rethinking the Red Scare: The Lusk Committee and New York's Crusade against Radicalism, 1919–1923.* New York: Routledge, 2003.
Philpott, Thomas Lee. *The Slum and the Ghetto: Neighborhood Deterioration and Middle-Class Reform, Chicago, 1880–1930.* Oxford: Oxford University Press, 1978.
Pittenger, Mark. "A World of Difference: Constructing the 'Underclass' in Progressive America." *American Quarterly* 49, March 1997: 26–65.
Pond, Elsie Ada. "Education and Americanization of Adult Immigrants in California." Master's thesis, Stanford University, 1920.
Preston Jr., William. *Aliens and Dissenters: Federal Suppression of Radicals, 1903–1933.* 2nd ed. Urbana and Chicago: University of Illinois Press, 1994.
Raftery, Judith. *Land of Fair Promise: Politics and Reform in Los Angeles Schools, 1885–1941.* Stanford, Calif.: Stanford University Press, 1992.
———. "Los Angeles Clubwomen and Progressive Reform." In *California Progressiv-*

ism Revisited. Edited by William Deverell and Tom Sitton, 144–174. Berkeley and Los Angeles: University of California Press, 1994.

Richardson, Ethel. "Doing the Thing That Couldn't Be Done." *Survey Graphic* 57, June 1, 1926.

———. *The Immigrant Child in the Public Schools*. Superintendent of Public Instruction report. Sacramento: California State Printing Office, 1922.

Rodgers, Daniel T. "In Search of Progressivism." *Reviews in American History* 10, December 1982: 113–132.

Roediger, David R. *Towards the Abolition of Whiteness: Essays on Race, Politics, and Working Class History*. London: Verso, 1994.

———. *Working Toward Whiteness: How America's Immigrants Became White, The Strange Journey from Ellis Island to the Suburbs*. New York: Basic Books, 2005.

Rothman, Shelia. *Woman's Proper Place: A History of Changing Ideals and Practices*. New York: Basic Books, 1987.

Sánchez, George. "'Go After the Women': Americanization and the Mexican Immigrant Woman, 1915–1929." In *Unequal Sisters: A Multicultural Reader in United States Women's History*. Edited by Ellen Carol DuBois and Vicki Ruiz. New York: Routledge, 1991.

Schaffer, Ronald. *America in the Great War: The Rise of the War Welfare State*. Oxford: Oxford University Press, 1991.

Scharrenberg, Paul. Papers. Bancroft Library, UC–Berkeley.

———. "Reminiscences." Interview with Corrine L. Gilb, May–August 1954. Oral history project. Bancroft Library, University of California–Berkeley.

———. *Wheatland Hop-fields Riot Investigation: Minority Report*. Austin Lewis Papers. Bancroft Library, University of California–Berkeley.

Schneider, Dorothy, and Carl J. Schneider. *American Women in the Progressive Era, 1900–1920*. New York: Facts on File, 1993.

Scott, Anne Firor. *Natural Allies: Women's Associations in American History*. Urbana and Chicago: University of Illinois Press, 1991.

Sharlip, William, and Albert A. Owens. *Adult Immigrant Education: Its Scope, Content, and Methods*. New York: Macmillan, 1925.

Sklar, Kathryn Kish. "Hull-House Maps and Papers: Social Science as Women's Work in the 1890s." In *The Social Survey in Historical Perspective, 1880–1940*. Edited by Martin Bulmer, Kevin Bales, and Kathryn Kish Sklar. Cambridge: Cambridge University Press, 1991.

Skocpol, Theda. *Diminished Democracy: From Membership to Management in American Civic Life*. Norman: University of Oklahoma, 2003.

———. *Protecting Soldiers and Mothers: The Political Origins of Social Policy in the United States*. Boston: Belknap Press of Harvard University Press, 1992.

Skocpol, Theda, Ziad Munson, Andrew Karch, and Bayliss Camp. "Patriotic Partnerships: Why Great Wars Nourished American Civic Volunteerism." Chap. 6 in *Shaped by War and Trade: International Influences on American Political Development*. Edited by Ira Katznelson and Martin Shefter. Princeton, N.J.: Princeton University Press, 2002.

Smith, William Carlson. *Americans in the Making: The Natural History of the Assimilation of Immigrants*. New York: D. Appleton-Century, 1939.

Sobel, Robert and John Raimo, eds. *Biographical Directory of the Governors of the United States, 1789–1978*. Westport, Conn.: Meckler Books, 1978.

Stern, Alexandra Minna. *Eugenic Nation: Faults and Frontiers of Better Breeding in Modern America*. Berkeley and Los Angeles: University of California Press, 2005.

Tichenor, Daniel J. *Dividing Lines: the Politics of Immigration Control in America*. Princeton, N.J.: Princeton University Press, 2002.

Torpey, John. "Passports and the Development of Immigration Controls in the North Atlantic World During the Long Nineteenth Century." Chap. 5 in *Migration Control in the North Atlantic World: The Evolution of State Practices in Europe and the United States from the French Revolution to the Inter-War Period*. Edited by Andreas Fahrmeir, Olivier Faron, and Patrick Weil. New York: Berghahn Books, 2003.

Townsend, John Clendenin. *Running the Gauntlet: Cultural Sources of Violence Against the I.W.W.* New York: Garland, 1986.

Trautwein, Mary Cunliffe. "A History of the Development of Schools for Foreign-born Adults in Los Angeles." Master's thesis, Los Angeles: University of Southern California, 1928.

Tyack, David B., ed. *Turning Points in American Educational History*. Waltham, Mass.: Blaisdell Publishing, division of Ginn and Company, 1967.

U.S. Bureau of Education. *Americanization*. September 15, 1918–November 1, 1919. Washington, D.C.: Government Printing Office.

———. "Education of the Immigrant," abstracts of papers read at a conference sponsored by the New York-New Jersey Committee of the North American Civic League for Immigrants. *Bulletin*, no. 51, 1913, Washington, D.C.: Government Printing Office, 1913.

———. *Public Facilities for Educating the Alien*. Prepared for the Division of Immigrant Education by Frederic Ernest Farrington. *Bulletin*, no. 18, 1916. Washington, D.C.: Government Printing Office, 1916.

———. *Proceedings of the Americanization Conference*, Washington, D.C. May 12–15, 1919. Washington, D.C.: Government Printing Office, 1919.

———. Annual reports. 1913–1914 and 1916–1930). Washington, D.C.: Government Printing Office.

———. *State Americanization: The Part of the State in the Education and Assimilation of the Immigrant*. Prepared for the Division of Immigrant Education by Fred Clayton Butler. *Bulletin*, no. 77, 1919. Washington, D.C.: Government Printing Office, 1920.

———. *Teaching English to the Foreign Born: A Teacher's Handbook*. Prepared for Division of Immigrant Education by Henry H. Goldberger. *Bulletin*, no. 80, 1919. Washington, D.C.: Government Printing Office, 1920.

———. *Training Teachers for Americanization: A Course of Study for Normal Schools and Teachers' Institutes*. Prepared for the Division of Immigrant Education by John J. Mahoney. *Bulletin*, no. 12. Washington, D.C.: Government Printing Office, 1920.

U.S. Bureau of Immigration and Citizenship. Quota Law of May 19, 1921, and Act of May 11, 1922.

U.S. Bureau of Naturalization. Annual reports, 1914–1929. Washington, D.C.: Government Printing Office.

———. *Syllabus of the Naturalization Law: An Aid to Public-School Teachers in the Instruction of Aliens in the Requirements of the Naturalization Law*. Washington, D.C.: Government Printing Office, 1916.

———. *Syllabus of the Naturalization Law: For Use of Those Cooperating with the Division of Citizenship Training in Assisting Aliens Desiring Citizenship*. Washington, D.C.: Government Printing Office, 1916.

———. *Proceedings of the First Citizenship Convention: Held at Washington, D.C., July 10–15, 1916*. Washington, D.C.: Government Printing Office, 1917.

———. *Suggestions for Americanization Work Among Foreign-born Women*. Washington, D.C.: Government Printing Office, 1921.

———. Preliminary teacher's manual to accompany Part 1 of the federal citizenship textbook, *English for American Citizenship*. Washington, D.C.: Government Printing Office, 1921.

———. *Suggestions for Securing and Holding Attendance of Foreign-born Adults Upon Public-School English and Citizenship Classes*. Washington, D.C.: Government Printing Office, 1922.

———. *Work of the Public Schools with the Bureau of Naturalization in the Preparation for Citizenship Responsibilities of the Candidate for Naturalization*. Washington, D.C.: Government Printing Office, 1917–1920.

U.S. Census Bureau. *Historical Statistics of the United States, 1789–1945*. Washington, D.C.: Government Printing Office, 1949.

———. *Thirteenth United States Census* (1910). Washington, D.C.: Government Printing Office, 1913.

———. *Fourteenth United States Census* (1920). Washington, D.C.: Government Printing Office, 1924.

U.S. Commission on Immigration Reform. *Becoming an American: Immigration and Immigrant Policy*. Report to Congress, 1997. Washington, D.C.: Government Printing Office.

U.S. Commission on Industrial Relations. *Final Report*, 5. Washington, D.C.: Government Printing Office, 1915.

Van Nuys, Frank. *Americanizing the West: Race, Immigrants, and Citizenship, 1890–1930*. Lawrence: University Press of Kansas, 2002.

Vaughn, Stephen. *Democracy, Nationalism, and the Committee on Public Information*. Chapel Hill: University of North Carolina Press, 1980.

Vaught, David. *Cultivating California: Growers, Specialty Crops and Labor Crops, and Labor, 1875–1920*. Baltimore: Johns Hopkins University Press, 1999.

Wacker, R. Fred. "Assimilation and Cultural Pluralism in American Social Thought." In *Assimilation, Acculturation, and Social Mobility*. Edited by George E. Pozzetta. New York: Garland, 1991.

Walkowitz, Daniel J. *Working with Class: Social Workers and the Politics of Middle-Class Identity*. Chapel Hill: University of North Carolina Press, 1999.

Weiss, Marc A. *The Rise of the Community Builders: The American Real Estate Industry and Urban Land Planning*. New York: Columbia University Press, 1987.

Wesser, Robert F. *Charles Evans Hughes: Politics and Reform in New York, 1905–1910.* Ithaca, N.Y.: Cornell University Press, 1967.

Whipple, Caroline A. *Americanization in Industry. Bulletin,* no. 693, September 1, 1919. Albany: University of the State of New York, 1919.

White, F. H. "The Growth and Future of State Boards and Commissions." In *Points of View: Readings on American State Government.* Chap. 5, *The State Administration.* Edited by Paul S. Reinsch. Boston: Ginn and Company, 1909.

Who Was Who in America: A Companion Volume to Who's Who in America. Biographies of the Non-Living with Dates of Deaths, appended. Vol. 1, 1897–1942. Chicago: A. N. Marquis, 1942.

Wood, Diane Claire. "Immigrant Mothers, Female Reformers, and Women Teachers: The California Home Teacher Act of 1915." Ph.D. diss., Stanford University, 1996.

Wood, Molly M. "Mapping a National Campaign Strategy: Partisan Women in the Presidential Election of 1916." Chap. 8 in *We Have Come to Stay: American Women and Political Parties, 1880–1960.* Edited by Melanie Gustafson, Kristie Miller, and Elisabeth I. Perry. Albuquerque: University of New Mexico, 1990.

Wood, Samuel Edgerton. "The California State Commission of Immigration and Housing: A Study of Administrative Organization and the Growth of Function." Ph.D. diss., UC–Berkeley, 1942.

Woods, Robert A., ed. *Americans in Process: North and West Ends by Residents and Associates of the South End House.* Boston: Houghton, Mifflin, 1902.

Woods, Robert A., and Albert J. Kennedy, eds. *Handbook of Settlements.* New York: Arno Press and *New York Times,* 1970.

Woo-Sam, Anne Marie. "Domesticating the Immigrant: California's Commission of Immigration and Housing and the Domestic Immigration Policy Movement, 1919–1945." Ph.D. diss., University of California–Berkeley, 1999.

Wyman, Mark. *Round-trip to America: The Immigrants Return to Europe, 1880–1930.* Ithaca, N.Y.: Cornell University Press, 1993.

Yellowitz, Irwin. *Labor and the Progressive Movement in New York State, 1897–1916.* Ithaca, N.Y.: Cornell University Press, 1965.

Yeo, Eileen Janes. "The Social Survey in Social Perspective, 1830–1930." In *The Social Survey in Historical Perspective, 1880–1940.* Edited by Martin Bulmer, Kevin Bales, and Kathryn Kish Sklar. Cambridge: Cambridge University Press, 1991.

Zeidel, Robert F. *Immigrants, Progressives, and Exclusion Politics: The Dillingham Commission, 1900–1927.* DeKalb: Northern Illinois University Press, 2004.

Zolberg, Aristide R. *A Nation by Design: Immigration Policy in the Fashioning of America.* New York: Russell Sage Foundation, and Cambridge, Mass.: Harvard University Press, 2006.

INDEX

Abbott, Edith, 15, 111, 116
Abbott, Grace, 22, 105, 106, 171; 1912 Progressive Party convention, 38; background, 111–12; director of Massachusetts Immigration Commission of 1913, 6; executive secretary of Illinois Immigrants Commission, 108–21; ideas about Americanization, 112–17; leader of national Americanization movement, 15
Addams, Jane, 22, 37, 105, 106, 108, 111, 116
African Americans, 11, 12, 45, 70, 109
Agriculture: California, 47–48; New York, 30
American Indians, 12, 45
American Legion, 10, 132, 163
Americanization: in California, 39–53, 66–83, 117; and class relations, 10–11, 169–70, 172–73; and coercion, 3, 133, 135, 165; diversity of leadership, 15, 107; during World War I, 84–102; and eugenics, 15, 54–59, 63, 149–53; federal program of, 86, 87, 90, 96, 123; in Illinois, 105–21; in Massachusetts, 5, 84, 89–90, 95–96, 99–102, 110–11, 117; of the native-born, 17; in New York, 4, 20–37, 59–64, 117; other meanings of the term, 2; as public policy, 3–4, 18–19, 166–72; racial components of, 11–12, 88, 167; relationship to progressivism, 6–7, 19, 21, 40, 169; role of social environment, 14; role of state, 18, 25, 32–33; as social welfare, 17. *See also* assimilation; educational Americanization; environmental Americanization
American Protective League, 86
Asian Americans, 11–12; denial of citizenship, 14, 45–46, 136, 167; segregation of, 70

Assimilation: Anglo-conformist model, 11, 101, 168; definition of, 2; "melting pot" or mutual, 11, 17, 44–46, 56, 58, 100–01, 112–113, 136, 138; role of social environment, 14; role of state, 18, 25, 44–45
Auerbach, Samuel, 62

Balch, Emily Greene, 37, 111
Baughman, Ruby, 78, 134
Bell, George L., 40, 52, 67, 92, 161
Bent, Mrs. H. K. W., 79
Berke, Mr., 110
Berkman, Mrs., 110
Better America Federation (BAF), 148–49
Bogardus, Emory S., 12
Bourne, Randolph, 13, 113
Breckinridge, Sophonisba, 15, 105, 106, 108

California Association of Americanization Teachers, 135
California Board of Health, 48, 49
California Bureau of Labor Statistics, 47, 48
California: demographics, 4–5
California Commission of Immigration and Housing (CCIH), 5, 39, 61, 109, 119, 120, 147, 170; activities during World War I, 89–91, 97–99; budget 1913–1915, 40; budget 1917–1919, 87; budget 1919–1921, 110–11; complaints resolution, 41, 52; community organization program, 97–99; education program, 73–83; espionage of IWW, 52, 91–93; housing program, 66–72; ideas of Americanization, 44–46; inclusion of non-whites in programming, 45–46; labor camp sanitation program, 48–51; membership, 40; on immigration restriction, 40–41, 160–161; powers, 41; social research, 48.

See also educational Americanization, in California
California Council of Defense, 87, 91
California Division of Housing, 161–62
California Federation of Labor (CFL), 40, 43, 93
California Federation of Women's Clubs (CFWC), 42, 76, 80–81
California Home Teacher Act of 1915, 73–83, 109, 119
California Industrial Accident Commission, 39
California Industrial Welfare Commission, 39–40, 70
California Labor Camp Sanitation Act of 1913, 48, 49
Caminetti, Anthony, 91, 92
Catholics, as leaders of the Americanization movement, 12, 15, 100,
Chase, Amanda Matthews, 77–83
Chambers, John S., 156
Chapman, Charles S., 156–57
Cheney, Nelson W., 157
Chicago Americanization Council, 120
Chicago Women's Club, 109
Chmielski, Henry H., 100, 101
Citizenship: African Americans and, 12–13; Asian Americans and, 45–46, 136, 167; "bad citizenship" 23–34; education, 64, 78, 114, 126, 135–36, 139; progressive concerns of, 9; relationship to race, 13–14; and whiteness, 12
Clark, Marian K., 15, 38; as chief investigator of NYBII, 54; and eugenics, 54–59, 94, 149–51, 157, 158, 171
Collier, John, 135
Committee for Immigrants in America, 38, 63
Committee on Public Information (CPI), 85, 88, 89
Conservatives: and assimilation, 14–15; and citizenship, 9–10; in California, 148–49, 155–57, 162–63, 172; in Illinois, 120; in New York, 152; rejection of mutual assimilation, 11, 17–18, 102, 168; Republicans, 62, 63, 145
Cooley, Helen Wooster (Mrs. Harlan Ward Cooley), 109
Coolidge, Calvin, 159

Cornford, Daniel A., 165
Cotillo, Salvatore A., 157
Council of Jewish Women, 106, 107

D'Allesandro, Domenic, 147
Daughters of the American Revolution, 10, 77, 102, 128, 132, 163
Davis, Abel, 109
Davenport, Charles B., 57
Democrats: in California, 40; in New York, 21, 63, 157
Dix, John A., 35
Doten, Carroll W., 100, 101
Drachsler, Julius, 13
Dreier, Margaret, 22
Dreier, Mary E., 22, 159
Dunne, Edward F., 108
Durst, Jonathan, 46
Durst, Ralph, 46
Dusseffy, Mrs., 110

Edson, Katherine Philips, 70
Educational Americanization: during World War I, 96, 102; home teaching, 73–83, 119, 131, 132, 169–70; factory classes, 94, 129–30; in California, 73–83, 128, 134–37, 140–41; in Illinois, 118–19; in Massachusetts 95–96, 126–28, 129–30, 132, 134, 137–40, 143; in New York, 63–64, 94–95, 124–26, 129, 131, 133–34, 141–43
Ellis Island immigration station, 4, 20, 57, 60, 150, 159
English language instruction. *See* educational Americanization
Environmental Americanization: banking regulation, 33–35; California Housing Institute of 1917, 71–72; California Housing Institute of 1922–1923, 155; dock monitoring, 28, 59–60, 153–54, 170–71; employment agency inspection, 30–31, 60–61; housing reform, 66–72; labor camp inspection in New York, 31–32, 60–61; labor camp inspection in California, 48–51; lodging house licensing, 29, 32–33; transportation regulation, 59–60; during World War I, 96, 102
Eugenics: and Americanization, 13, 14–15, 54–59; and immigration policy 145, 149–51, 171

Finegold, Kenneth, 105
Fornof, John F., 109
Freund, Ernst, 107, 108

Gaiczunas, Dr., 110
Galassi, Pasquale, 100, 101
Gerstle, Gary, 12, 165, 167
Gibson, Hugh, 42, 74
Gibson, Mary Simons (Mrs. Frank Gibson), 40, 119, 134, 135; background, 42; and home teaching 73–83; resignation from CCIH, 156
Goldberger, Henry H., 95, 134
González, Gilbert, 165
Glynn, Martin H., 62
Greenwich settlement (New York), 25
Gurney, Mrs. Herbert, 154, 159

Hanna, Edward Joseph (archbishop of San Francisco), 15, 16, 40, 141, 156, 157, 161; background, 43
Harding, Charles F., 109
Harding, Warren G., 152
Harriman, Mrs. A.E., 57
Haynes, John Randolph, 149
Henry Street settlement (New York City), 22, 25
Herlihy, Charles M., 128
Hickey, Edward V., 95
Hill, Robert T., 95, 134
Hoboken, N.J., 26, 60
Hollis, George S., 156
Howe, Frederic C., 57, 151
Hughes, Charles Evans, 4, 21, 23, 152
Hull-House settlement (Chicago), 22, 37, 105, 106, 109, 112, 116, 120
Hyatt, Edward, 78, 81

Illinois, demographics of, 6
Illinois Department of Labor, 110
Illinois Department of Registration and Education, 109, 110
Illinois Immigrants Commission (IIC), 6, 105–21; budget 1919–1921, 110
Immigrant groups: British, 101, Canadians, 160, Chinese, 69, Cubans, 45, Germans, 13, 94, 101; Greeks, 45; Indians ("Hindoos"), 45; Irish, 101; Italians, 13, 45, 150; Japanese, 45, 77, Jews, 10, 13, 150; Lithuanians, 45; Mexicans, 45, 77, 90–91, 160–161, 163; Poles, 45; Puerto Ricans, 45; Spanish, 45; Syrians, 45
Immigrants' Protective League, 38, 105, 106–8, 111, 117, 118, 120
Immigration restriction, 10, 15, 19, 144, 153, 159–60; CCIH neutrality on, 40, 155; 161; MBI support for, 101, 154–55
Industrial Workers of the World (IWW), 39, 42, 48, 51–52, 84, 91–93, 147
Inter-Municipal Committee on Research, 21

Jersey City, N.J., 26, 60
Jews: leaders of Americanization movement, 12, 15, 22, 42, 107
Johnson, Hiram W., 38, 39, 41, 47, 73, 87, 155

Kallen, Horace, 13, 113
Karpf, Maurice J., 110
Kelley, Florence, 116
Kellor, Frances A., 110, 112, 152, 157, 158, 164, 171; background, 22; career after NYBII, 38, 54–59; chief investigator of the New York Bureau of Industries and Immigration, 21–38; definition of Americanization, 23–25; founder of Committee for Immigrants in America, 38, 42, 63, 65; leader of national Americanization movement, 15; research methodology, 25; view of immigrants, 24; work with African Americans, 12;
Kenyon-Vestel bill of 1919–20, 123
King, Desmond, 165
Krysto, Christina, 81, 148

Lambros, Peter S., 110
Lissak, Rivka, 107
Livermore, Russell B., 157
Loeb, Solomon, 22
Los Angeles State Normal School, 78
Lowden, Frank O., 106, 108, 120
Lubin, David, 41
Lubin, Simon J., 15, 16, 38, 40, 68, 92, 96, 110, 148, 161; background of, 41–42; removal from CCIH, 156
Lusk, Clayton R., 124, 149

Mack, Julian W., 107
Mahoney, John J., 96, 127, 128, 138–140

Marshall, Louis B., 22
Massachusetts Bureau of Immigration (MBI), 84, 89–90, 95, 99–102, 105, 109, 129, 145–47, 163; budget 1917, 100; budget 1919, 111
Massachusetts Committee on Public Safety, 84, 87
Massachusetts Department of Education, 5, 126
Massachusetts Immigration Commission of 1913, 6, 54, 146
Massachusetts demographics, 4–5
Massachusetts Division of Immigration and Americanization (MDIA), 5, 146–47, 153–55, 159–60, 162, 160, 162, 163, 171; budgets 1920–1926, 147
Massachusetts Division of University Extension, 5, 126–28, 129, 132, 134, 137–40, 143, 146
Mayper, Joseph, 15, 38
McBride, James Harvey, 40, 67, 68–69, 157; background, 43
McClymer, John F., 165
Middle class: definition of, 7; values 7–8, 11, 33, 44, 51, 69, 79, 116, 137, 140, 169–71
Migrant labor, in California 47–48, 50–51; in New York, 30
Miller, Nathan L., 124, 152, 157
Moyer, James A., 130

National Americanization (Day) Committee, 38, 111, 123
Mitchel, John Purroy, 87, 94
National Security League, 10, 96, 102, 132
New Jersey, 3, 35
New York, Port of, 20, 27, 59, 60, 153, 158
New York Bureau of Industries and Immigration (NYBII), 4, 20–21, 105, 120, 149, 170; activities 25–37, 59–62; budget 1911, 23; budget 1915, 63; budget 1917, 94; budget 1919, 111; inspiration for other states, 39; in World War I, 84, 89, 93–94; legislation passed 1911, 35; policy goals of, 23; partnerships with other organizations, 25–26, 30; research methodology, 25
New York Charity Organization Society, 25
New York City Licensing Bureau, 28
New York City Police Department, 28

New York City Teachers' Union, 124
New York College settlement (New York City), 22, 25
New York Commission of Immigration of 1908, 21, 34
New York Committee to Investigate Seditious Activities (Lusk Committee), 124, 149
New York Council of Defense, 87, 94
New York Department of Banking, 34
New York Department of Education, 63–64, 94, 95, 96, 124, 125, 149
New York Department of Health, 61, 151–52
New York Department of Labor, 21, 30, 63, 152
New York Division of Aliens, 152, 157–58
New York Division of Vocational and Extension Education, 133
New York Farm Labor Bureau, 25
New York Legal Aid Society, 27
New York Resource Mobilization Bureau Division of Aliens, 90
New York State, demographics of, 4, 30
North American Civic League for Immigrants (NACL), 26, 30, 38, 43
North American Civic League for Immigrants, New York-New Jersey Committee, 26, 38

O'Brien, Miles, 62
O'Connor, John Joseph, 157
Ocheltree, Gilbert B., 156

Palendesch, Mr., 110
Park, Robert, 13
Parker, Carlton, H., 40, 49, 52
Pennsylvania, 3, 35, 54
Perkins, Frances, 159
Pfannestiel, Todd, 149
Pluralism, 3, 13, 113, 138, 166, 169
Power, Mary E., 154
Progressive Party, 37–38
Progressives: Americanizers 14, 17, 167–169; middle class, 6–8; opposition to immigration restriction, 10, 161, 163; political progressives, 9; racial nationalism of, 12; reform methodology, 9, 25, 48, 118; social progressives, 9, 20, 21, 152

Putnam, Jackson, 157

Race: relationship to citizenship, 13–14; theories of, 13
Racial nationalism, 12
Rand School of Social Science, 124, 149
Red Scare of 1919, 105, 106, 117, 145–46, 147, 148–49
Republicans, 62, 63, 145, 149
Rhode Island, 3, 54
Richardson, Ethel, 76, 78, 134–35, 136, 140, 141
Richardson, Friend W., 141, 155
Richardson, Leon, 134
Rosenwald, Julius, 107, 108
Roosevelt, Theodore, 23
Rothwell, Bernard J., 15, 100, 101, 110
Rudovitz, Christian Ansoff, 117

Sayer, Henry D., 94, 152
Schackno, Henry G., 157
Scharrenberg, Paul, 15, 40, 51; background 43–44; opposition to Asian immigration, 43; removal from CCIH, 156
Schiff, Jacob, 22
Schleef, Caroline, 67, 71
Settlement house movement, 18; in New York City, 20, 21. *See also individual settlements*
Shephardson, Francis W., 109, 110
Sheppard-Towner Maternity and Infancy Act of 1921, 82, 132
Sire, Lillian R., 158
Small, Lennington "Len," 120, 121
Smith, Alfred E., 124, 143, 151, 152, 157, 159
Smith-Bankhead bill of 1919, 123
Smith-Hughes National Vocational Education Act of 1917, 123
Smith, Payson, 95, 96, 147
Smith, William C., 95
Sons of the American Revolution, 10
South End House settlement (Boston), 41
Starr, Ellen Gates, 116
Stephens, William D., 72, 87, 91, 155
Stotesbury, Louis W., 87

Tammany Hall, 21
Tichenor, Daniel J., 163
Towne, Charles F., 95, 134

United Charities (Chicago), 117
United States Bureau of Education, 86, 90, 96, 112, 123, 161
United States Bureau of Immigration, 57, 112, 150
United States Bureau of Immigration and Naturalization, 25
United States Bureau of Naturalization, 64, 86, 90, 112, 123, 126, 131
United States Children's Bureau, 79
United States Council of Defense, 87, 96
University of California, 134
University of Chicago, 105, 107, 108, 111, 118

Van Nuys, Frank, 165

Wald, Lillian D., 15, 22, 157, 159
Warburg, Felix, 22
Watchorn, Robert, 57
Weinstock, Harris, 41
Wheatland hop fields riot, 46–47, 48, 109
Whitman, Charles S., 87, 94
Williams, John, 23
Williams, William, 57
Woman's Municipal League (New York), 21, 22
Wilson, Lewis A., 94, 141, 142
Wilson, William B., 92
Wilson, Woodrow, 85, 86, 93
Woerishoffer, Carola, 23
Women's Trade Union League: Chicago, 106; New York, 22
Wood, Will C., 81, 134
Wolcott, Edith Prescott, 100, 101
World War I, 84–102

Yarros, Rachelle Slobodinsky, 110
Young Men's Christian Association (YMCA), 44
Young Women's Christian Association (YWCA), 78, 120

www.ingramcontent.com/pod-product-compliance
Lightning Source LLC
Chambersburg PA
CBHW070940230426
43666CB00011B/2506